RADICAL SURVIVOR

RADICAL SURVIVOR

One Woman's Path Through Life, Love,
and Uncharted Tragedy

Dr. Nancy Saltzman

WoWo Press
Colorado Springs, Colorado

Published by WoWo Press
2910 Bonne Vista Dr., Colorado Springs, CO 80906

Radical Survivor: One Woman's Path Through Life, Love, and Uncharted Tragedy

ISBN: 978-0-615-65819-3
Library of Congress Control Number: 2012944231
Printed in the United States

Front cover photograph © Brad Fowler/Song of Myself
Back cover photograph by Michael Herzog
Book cover and book design by tothepointpublications.com

For Joel, Adam, and Seth

CONTENTS

FOREWORD

WHERE DO YOU START, describing someone who has gone through so much, lost so much, yet has touched so many lives? Someone who seems bigger than all of us?

Nancy Saltzman and her family were, and still are, great family friends of my oldest sister Mary. Having spent many summers at my sister's and at the U.S. Olympic Training Center in Colorado Springs, I got to know many of her friends, Nancy and her family included. Joel always stood out to me, probably because of his good looks. Adam and Seth were my nephews' buddies, with whom they played hockey and tennis and speed skated. You never used one boy's name without the other, it was always Adam and Seth, Adam and Seth. That also helped me remember which of them was older, because Adam's name always came first. I know from talking to my nephews today that their friends' deaths still lie heavy in their hearts. My oldest nephew Scott, Adam's buddy, is now married and had a baby girl last year. I am sure it was hard for Nancy, as she will never have the opportunity to hold a child of Adam's or Seth's. Yet she came to the party to celebrate the birth of Scott's daughter, and was so genuinely happy for him.

Recently an acquaintance of mine, Ashley Buerkett, lost her sister, parents, and two family dogs in a small plane crash. I wished with all my might that there was something I could do for her. Of course I kept thinking of Nancy going through the same thing in 1995. Both lost their entire families in an instant, and in the same way—small plane crashes due to bad weather. However, Nancy was the mom—older, wiser. But does it make a difference? I shared Ashley's story with my sister Mary. She mentioned how Nancy had helped others in similar situations and suggested that I call her. I worried I might be asking too much, but felt I needed to put the two in contact with each other. I talked to Nancy and she generously reached out to Ashley. Ashley responded almost immediately. They have been in contact and maybe someday they will meet. It made me feel good to know I was able to help.

Nancy has faced many losses in her life, including the types of events that are somewhat a given as our loved ones grow older. Her mom got Alzheimer's, her dad died of cancer. We each deal with these losses in our own way. Then there are the events that are not so normal, such as the first major hurdle Nancy had to deal with, breast cancer. She faced it head on. She took it day by day, reached out to others who had been there, done that. Yes she cried, yes she had bad days, but she relied on her inner strength, as well as her family and friends, to get her through. There were times she didn't want to get out of bed, but she kept going, like the ultimate "Energizer bunny." When she was hit with the death of her entire family, she called on the same inner strength and coping tools like never before.

Nancy shows us how life goes on, no matter what. How you never forget, but also how time makes the pain not as acute as the first few days or weeks. She still cries, but smiles often, too, and although the love she has for Joel, Adam, and Seth is still as strong as ever, she has also found she can love again. It takes a strong person to go through a challenge, but to face unbearable loss takes a special kind of "strong"—the kind that Nancy has always had. I've had people compliment me for my strength, character, willpower, and positive attitude, and while I feel I do possess these traits, I also feel I have yet to go through challenges as deep as Nancy's.

I lost my brother to a brain tumor, and for many years his life was not at all what it once was. The last year and a half, especially the last six months, seemed to me unbearable. Yet he got up every day and continued to have a smile on his face. I am not sure I would have had his unbelievable attitude under the same circumstances. However, we really don't know our own strength until we find ourselves in the fight of our lives.

My parents and siblings helped mold me to be that way, and Nancy's story makes clear that part of her strength, her will to survive, and her ability to take things day by day came from her family and her parents. She then built upon that foundation to make her life one of accomplishment and giving back, despite her tragedies.

So thank you, Nancy, for sharing your inner thoughts, as well as sharing Joel, Adam, and Seth with all of us. I know this could not have been an easy undertaking for you—but in your world, few things are. You are an amazing woman, and I feel lucky to have had you touch my life.

Bonnie Blair Cruikshank

Most decorated U.S. female athlete in Winter Olympics history, with five gold medals and one bronze medal—all in speed skating

June, 2012

TO THE READER

THIS MEMOIR IS the story of my life . . . so far. It is not all-inclusive. I learned in my writing classes and from a fabulous editor that not everything I find fascinating is interesting to everyone else. If you are a friend or family member and don't see something you expected in these pages, please believe that it was in a previous draft.

The events I describe are how I remember them.

The letter passages in this book are from actual letters I received before and after the crash. Some have been edited for length; all with names are included with permission of the authors who are still living. I wish I could have included every single one of the thousands of cards, notes, and communications I received because each offered me love, support, and memories. I still have them all.

Adam and Seth both kept journals while they were students at Steele and Broadmoor Elementary Schools. The entries included here are from those journals. My letter to Joel was written eight years after the crash and the one to the boys was written soon after that.

In all letters, notes, and especially the boys' journals, I have included the text as it was written, which accounts for some punctuation and grammatical inconsistencies, as well as misspellings in the boys' journals. Please forgive these for the sake of authenticity.

If you want to know how to write a meaningful condolence note, just borrow the words you see in the letters written to me. They may not take the pain away but they will add some light to a dark day.

PART 1

SEPTEMBER 24, 1995

AS THE SUN peeked through the blackout curtains in our Las Vegas hotel room, I looked over at the boys, sleeping peacefully in their own queen-sized bed. Turning my head, I caught Joel smiling at me. Sixteen years of staring at those impossibly long eyelashes still had not tempered my jealousy of them. He reached out to me. Memories of the previous night, and what we'd gotten away with after the boys fell asleep, were clearly still on his mind. I scooted backwards so we could spoon. We lay that way until I heard Adam whisper to Seth.

"Be quiet, Mom and Dad are still asleep."

Seth, eleven as of the day before, rolled out of bed on his way to the bathroom, holding the stuffed white tiger he'd won at an arcade after seeing the real thing at The Mirage Hotel. He tiptoed by and I winked at him. Reconsidering the urgency of his trip, he climbed into our bed. Adam, almost thirteen, quickly assessed the situation and scrambled in with us. Joel turned suddenly and the tickling started in earnest.

"STOP! STOP!" Adam screamed as his fingers reached unsuccessfully for Joel. Seth and I slid as far away as we could, but before we knew it Adam was on top of us trying to get away from his dad. Yelling and laughing as we poked his ribs, Joel groped blindly for retaliation. Seth and I shrieked and tumbled onto the floor.

"Wasn't that an amazing show last night? How could anyone be that strong?" I gushed, hoping for a momentary distraction. We had seen the Cirque du Soleil show *Mystère* as part of Seth's birthday celebration the night before. The feats had been spellbinding. My change of subject worked. Joel grabbed Adam and they attempted their own version of a Cirque act, with Seth joining in.

"Nice muscles. Maybe you guys should audition," I teased as they rolled onto their backs.

"Who's up for a breakfast buffet?" Joel said breathlessly.

*   *   *

This had been a good idea. Late in August, Joel's friend Homer Osborne had stopped in at Joel's shop, Total Tennis. Homer suggested that they go to Las Vegas to watch the Davis Cup tournament in September.

Homer had a pilot's license. If Joel could get tickets, Homer would rent a plane and fly them to Vegas. Joel couldn't resist an adventure that included tennis, and knew our sons would be up for it as well. As an elementary school principal, I presumed I would be too busy to go, so Joel bought tournament tickets for himself, our sons Adam and Seth, and Homer and his wife Linda.

Then I realized I would miss Seth's eleventh birthday, which was September 23—Saturday of that weekend. I wanted to go with them.

I checked with Homer about joining the trip. He told me the plane had only four seats, and Seth was already going to be sitting on Joel's lap. There was no room for me, so I had booked a seat on a commercial flight to Las Vegas. It was a little convoluted, but everything had worked out. I had enjoyed relaxing by the pool. We'd celebrated Seth turning eleven the night before with dinner and the Cirque show. He would only turn eleven once—I was glad I'd been there.

We got dressed, packed, and delivered our suitcases to the hotel valet. The sun was shining as we walked down the street holding hands. The only people on the sidewalk were families and tennis fanatics like us. The finals between the USA and Sweden would be held at Caesar's Palace after breakfast. We were all feeling a bit rushed: the boys because Joel didn't want to miss any matches; I needed to catch my flight home. It was okay that I was going home a little early—my workweeks often extended beyond Friday. Sundays were for catching up.

"That looks like a good one," Adam announced, pointing across the street to a restaurant with a buffet.

Sitting down to eat, Joel checked with the boys about their homework. They could finish it on the plane ride home, they assured him. I started to think about the school newsletter column I would write on my flight. We'd all be doing our homework high above the Rockies.

"I will keep this hat forever."

Seth was admiring his prized possession from the previous day's matches. By a stroke of luck, we'd seen both Pete Sampras and Andre Agassi after the competition, and they'd autographed the hat.

"It'll be worth a lot of money," he added. My budding tycoon. I smiled and agreed. Adam and Joel were in a deep discussion about the upcoming tennis match.

Joel paid the bill and we walked back out into the September heat. We headed toward Caesar's Palace where the matches would be played. I had a boy on each side of me. I was holding their hands. We arrived at the crosswalk in front of the hotel. I kissed Adam then Seth and said, "I love you" to each of them.

Joel hugged and kissed me. We offhandedly gave each other the I-wish-you-weren't-leaving-but-see-you-soon smile of people who are in love and must separate for a short time. No big deal.

He said, "I love you. Be careful."

I looked straight into his eyes. "I love you. *You* be careful!"

My family continued across the street. I headed back to the hotel, picked up my suitcase, and took a cab to the Las Vegas airport.

* * *

My flight left on time and the trip was uneventful. We flew over the Grand Canyon; I remembered Joel telling me that it was an amazing sight from a small plane. As we flew into Colorado the weather turned bad—it was raining and snowing as we came over the mountains. I imagined that the boys wouldn't fly in this weather but when I arrived home there was a phone message from Joel.

"Hi. It's about three thirty and we're just getting ready to get on the plane to come home. See you tonight around seven. I love you."

Shoshi, our golden retriever, and Squeak, our sheltie-dingo pound puppy, were so happy to see me, I decided to take them to school with me. The three of us weren't the only ones there on a Sunday; my secretary, Lois, was also catching up on work. A little after 7 p.m. I called home to check my messages. There were none. I turned to Lois and made a curious remark.

"My mother told me that it is much harder to lose a child than it is a spouse. You can always replace your spouse but you can never replace a child."

My mother was wrong. You cannot replace a spouse or a child.

* * *

Lois left around 7:30 and I continued to do some work. I kept checking my phone messages. At 8 p.m. I remember that first twinge of concern, an ever-so-slight uptick in my heart rate, a flip-flop in the stomach, quickly overruled by my rational brain. I went through all the possibilities. They could have gotten almost home, run into the storm, and decided to turn back. They wouldn't have been able to contact me until they landed somewhere. The storm could have knocked out power wherever they landed, so there might not be phone service (this was the pre-cell phone era). At 9, I could not stay focused on my work and decided it was time to go home.

Although it seemed impossible that Joel wouldn't have called when they got back, I clung to the idea that perhaps they had gotten busy once home and forgotten to check in. As the dogs and I turned onto our street, though, my stomach flip-flopped again. Dark house. My brain went into overdrive conjuring increasingly implausible scenarios. Perhaps they were inside with the lights off, waiting to surprise me. I pulled into the garage and opened the door into the house. No Joel. No Adam. No Seth. No surprise. The dogs gave me a "So, where is everybody?" look, and I took a deep breath. Before, my worry had been all in my head, and I could somehow keep finding (albeit unlikely) explanations. The dogs' puzzlement was now something outside of my own imagination, third party confirmation of something possibly amiss, and I could feel my muscles tense. I checked the answering machine. Still nothing. I turned on the TV and fed my companions. I read my e-mail. I heard rain on the roof and smelled the damp air. It was now close to 10 p.m.

The phone rang. Finally! My words were poised like marbles, ready to tumble out: "Where are you? Why didn't you call? Don't ever do that to me again—I was getting worried!"

But the voice that spoke was not Joel's. "Hi Nancy, it's Dick Neeley. Say, you haven't heard from Homer, have you?" Dick was a good friend of Homer's.

"No, but I'll let you know if I do." I hung up. More outside evidence that Things Were Not Right.

Several minutes passed. I played with the dogs.

The phone rang again. *THIS will be Joel.* I was sure of it.

"Hello. Is this Nancy Saltzman?"

"Yes."

"This is Roger McDonald from the Custer County [Colorado] Sheriff's Office. I am calling from emergency services. We've got two planes down—one in Wyoming and one in Colorado. We believe that one of them may be your husband's plane." I was suddenly very sick to my stomach. My heart started hammering.

"Do you know something? Do you know what's happened?"

"No, we can't locate the planes yet. The weather is so bad that we have to find the planes using coordinates, and we have to wait until midnight for the satellite to pass to get the second coordinate."

What? Satellites? Coordinates? What the hell are you talking about?

He paused. "Are you religious?"

"No, not really," I said. "Why?"

"Because you need to have somebody with you."

Someplace in my head I screamed, "Tell me, just tell me, please!" but I heard myself repeat, "Do you know something?" in a remarkably calm voice.

A strangely inappropriate composure had sidled up next to my anxiety.

He assured me that he did not know any more than what he had told me. He added that he would call as soon as he knew more. We hung up.

I called my best friend, Donna Sheldon, and woke her up. Usually she turned off the ringer, but not this night.

Again, I heard myself saying with an eerie detachment, "Can you come over to my house? The plane Joel and the boys are on is missing. They don't think I should be alone."

Donna told me later that she turned to her husband Gary and said, "This can't be good." She was at my front door within ten minutes. She hugged me, and we walked upstairs into the TV room. I remember turning the sound down on the TV. Donna sat down in a chair and I sat on the couch. We talked matter-of-factly. We discussed where the plane might be; wondered if they had landed in a remote area, and couldn't call. If they were hurt, we would drive to wherever they were to pick them up. We talked about whether I should call my parents and Joel's to let them know the situation, which I did.

We did not talk about the possibility of my family being dead somewhere on a remote hillside.

But a slow, fierce terror was gnawing at the corners of my mind, as I maintained the equilibrium that shielded me from thinking the unthinkable.

*   *   *

A little after midnight the phone rang. I was in the bathroom. Donna answered and spoke with the caller.

I came out of the bathroom and took the phone from Donna.

"Hello?"

"I'm sorry." Pause. "They found the plane. There were no survivors."

I heard the words and tried to absorb them.

"They were the most beautiful boys," I said to this stranger who had uttered such incomprehensible words.

"I'm sure they were, ma'am. I'm sure they were. I'm very sorry."

For a brief moment, I flashed back on the Cirque performers and their extraordinary abilities. I wished they were here with me now, and could somehow, with brute force, hold together my disintegrating heart. My words came back to me.

How could anyone be that strong?

In my own way, I was about to find out.

I collapsed where I was, on the ceramic tiled steps outside of the laundry room. The terror sprang from where it had been lurking deep inside, devoured whatever control remained, and consumed me.

I sobbed.

CHAPTER 1

HOW TO BUILD A SURVIVOR

THEY WERE THE MOST beautiful boys.

Even as I heard the man on the phone say they had died, I had to imagine them as alive. I couldn't think about them any other way.

I wonder now what my mother might have said, had all of her family—my dad and all of us kids—perished in an accident. I don't think it would have been, "They were beautiful." Perhaps, "They were all so smart." Smart was big in my family. Smart, accomplished, and self-sufficient.

* * *

My mother, Dorothy Jeanne Cohen, was the eldest of two children. She and her brother grew up in apartments in New York City. Mom distinguished herself academically early on. When she was eight years old she received a scholarship to attend Camp Woodmere in upstate New York, where she would return for many summers, later as a camp counselor. Her time at Woodmere would be instrumental in shaping her most prominent traits—confidence, self-possession, industriousness—and she would later attempt to replicate these experiences for her children by making summer camp a major part of our lives as well.

Graduating from high school at age sixteen, my mother attended Hunter College in New York City, receiving a bachelor's degree in psychology. She was awarded a fellowship to pursue her master's degree, also in psychology, at Johns Hopkins University, where she met my father.

After they married and were raising us in the cozy lap of the Midwest, we would take infrequent but memorable trips to New York to visit Mom's family. We didn't look forward to the long car ride, but we loved the city. My grandparents lived in a high-rise apartment building that had an elevator, an elevator operator, *and* a doorman. We took frequent rides in the elevator and asked endless questions.

"Why is the door like a cage?"

"Can it go up and down without an elevator man?"

"How fast does it go?"

"Could it crash?"

On these trips, we would also visit Aunt Beatrice, my great aunt. "Aunt Beatrice cannot hear. She is deaf," my mother told us. I was fascinated when I heard her speak. She sounded different from anyone I knew. Aunt Beatrice's deafness had a significant impact on my mother, which would later influence an important part of her work.

*   *   *

My father grew up in Lawrence, Massachusetts, north of Boston. Dad's parents, Jewish emigrants from Russia, became naturalized citizens in 1939 and 1940. Grandpa Harry and Grandma Fanny lived in what we now call a duplex. They made their living renting the upstairs home to people they didn't know. That fascinated me.

How could people they didn't know live in their house?

My brothers and sister and I loved visiting our Massachusetts grandparents because we could ride bikes around the block, sleep on the couch (they didn't have enough beds for all of us), and eat something called blintzes.

Like Mom, my father was an able, quick learner and graduated from the University of Massachusetts. Also like my mother, he was awarded a fellowship for further studies in psychology at Johns Hopkins.

Dad had three siblings; one died as a child. It wasn't until the end of my dad's life that I heard the whole story of his brother's death, and learned the profound burden Dad had carried.

At six years old, my father was sent outside to get his older brother, Leonard.

"I saw him and called his name. He looked up, saw me, and started across the street. A car hit him as he came to meet me."

*   *   *

March 18, 1996

Dear Nancy,

Since the horrific event that occurred in September, I have been trying, off and on, to conjure up a procedure that I could pass on to you to help you reduce the pain and suffering of your loss. I have not been successful in this venture. I continue to weep, myself, when I pass by one or another of the several photos of your "boys" that we have on display in our home. I guess that all of us will just have to be satisfied with the slow progress we are making in our long healing process.

I love you very much; I think of you often, and I still wish that I could help ease your sorrow.

Love and xxx's
Dad

*   *   *

Mom completed her master's degree and Dad his Ph.D. in June of 1948. They married on June 6 and moved to Bloomington, Indiana, two weeks later, where Dad had accepted an assistant professor position in the Department of Psychology at Indiana University (IU).

As book-smart as they were, Mom and Dad had no idea where Bloomington was. Nor did Mom's parents; my grandmother once sent a letter to them addressed "Bloomingdale's, Illinois." Somehow, the letter found its way to us.

Growing up in Bloomington was in many ways as apple pie as American childhoods get (though my mom was never, shall we say, an "enthusiastic" cook). Like my father, I had three siblings: my older sister, Linda, and two younger brothers, Rob and Andy. We were always in our backyard, or out in the neighborhood, riding our bikes everywhere—around Bloomington, to the IU campus student union, to the public pool, to the houses of our friends.

My mother and father were loving, involved parents. But there were high expectations of us—subtly expressed but keenly felt.

My older sister obliged, with an auspicious plunge into the English language. Mom claimed she was changing Linda's diaper when my sister looked up and said her first word: "light." I don't know if the story is true, but I heard it enough times to make me a believer; you could hear the pride in Mom's voice when she told it. Linda's love of words led to accelerated classes and straight A's. She acted in plays, spent her free time reading, and was always well organized. When each of us started seventh grade, my parents gave us an allowance of $25 per month. From that, we paid for our lunches, clothes, shoes, records, and anything else we needed or desired. My sister kept a running list, to the penny, of everything she spent. I never kept track of anything, though I miraculously managed to stay within budget.

Besides being smart and organized, Linda developed a lovely set of curves right before my envious, prepubescent eyes. Like all little sisters, I borrowed her bras and stuffed them with socks to get a sneak peak at what might be in store, or in bra, for me. We shared a room until I was thirteen, when Linda announced that she refused to "live with a slob" anymore. My mother gave up her study and turned it into a bedroom for me. I didn't get any tidier, but at least Linda couldn't complain.

My brother Rob came along two and a half years after me. He was "Robbie" into his twenties, and I still sometimes call him that. The gods of intellect blessed Rob as well, and he graduated from Harvard Law School, rising to my parents' abiding aspirations. Rob and I were always, and continue to be, extremely close.

When Andy was born in 1958, Linda, Rob, and I woke up to find our babysitter in the living room. A note explained we were about to be joined by a new baby brother. I was seven, and remember the arrival as quite a surprise—apparently, the pregnancy had been unexpected for my parents as well. My mother, not planning on another child, had gone to the doctor about feeling sick. He thought she might have a uterine tumor. Just before her surgery to remove the tumor, they discovered she was several months pregnant. Today, Andy is a six-foot, five-inch, two-hundred-twenty-pound orthopedic surgeon. Not bad for a "tumor."

While all of us bore a family resemblance (though I was the shortest at five feet, four inches), I was the one "not like the others." I wasn't a bad student, but the coveted straight A's that came easily to my siblings eluded me. I liked doing well, but didn't need to be the best—people and relationships were more important to me than performance. I was messy with my space, but neat in appearance. My curly hair was a constant annoyance to me. And my boyish body refused to "bloom" until my late teens.

I was also happy, fun loving, thoughtful, and hardworking—the daughter June Cleaver would have loved to have.

*   *   *

But there were ways in which we weren't exactly the Cleaver household.

We were Jewish, of course, which I don't believe the Cleavers were. But that played a relatively small role in our day-to-day lives.

More notably, it was Dad who woke us, fixed our breakfasts, and got us off to school. He would rise, quickly shower, and dress his six-foot frame in a pressed shirt, bow tie, slacks, and sport jacket, frequently mixing plaids and stripes. His wavy black hair would be slicked back with good-smelling hair tonic. Then he would tend to us.

It would be his voice, hollering up the stairs from the kitchen of our classic split-level, "Nancy, are you getting dressed?" I would yell back, "Yes, I'm getting dressed." Five minutes later he would call to me again and I would drag myself out of bed and check that the big pink rollers had done their job straightening my hair overnight. My sister and brothers would already be in the kitchen eating. Every day, Dad made us eggs and toast. He cooked the eggs just the way we liked them, and we each had an individual order. Mine was fried, over hard.

My mother's morning job was getting herself ready for work. I loved seeing her come down the stairs when she was finished dressing. She wore expensive suits that she bought on sale at Talbot's or other upscale women's stores. Her high heels matched her outfits. She wore clip-on earrings and big necklaces. Her dark brown hair was kept short and styled easily a little below her ears. She always wore Chanel No. 5.

Mom was late for everything, always doing "one last thing." I don't really blame her, but it may not be coincidence that I, too, am always doing "one last thing."

* * *

Accomplishment marked both of my parents' professional lives.

In the middle of my dad's career he was chosen to be the chair of the Department of Psychology at IU. He held the position longer than any previous chair, and successfully led the department through a great deal of change and growth.

In 1958, he took a one-year sabbatical from IU to work at Harvard with the well-known psychologist B.F. Skinner. We lived outside Boston in a house near the ocean. The year was an impressive feather in my father's cap, but my most vivid memory was Robbie falling down the stairs and knocking out one of his front teeth.

Another sabbatical year was spent at the University of Washington, with all of us in tow once again. That was my sixth grade year, and my teacher, Mr. Mack, was the person who first made me want to be an educator. I felt smart in his class, and we stayed in touch for many years—into my thirties.

My father enjoyed his work and the people in the psychology department at IU. We stopped by his office often, just to check in—or to borrow his car. Thanks to a regimen of swimming, golf, and tennis, he had a toned physique, and that combined with his height and distinctive fashion choices (bow ties, plaids, and stripes) made him easy to spot. Whenever he saw one of us, he would burst into a wide grin. If we ran into one of his colleagues, we were often regaled with stories, then told how much they liked working with him. In turn, he loved to brag about his children's successes and always had something special to say about each of us.

Mom used her advanced psychology degree in a number of jobs. When we were very young she and a group of faculty wives started a cooperative nursery school. She also worked as a high school counselor. When she was required to get a special license for the position, she quit—knowing she was amply qualified for the job, she refused to "waste time taking irrelevant classes." It was unfortunate for both her and the school; she loved working with high school students. Later in her career, she was the psychologist for the Indiana University Speech and Hearing Clinic. There, her relationship with my great aunt Beatrice inspired her to help start a preschool at IU for children with hearing disabilities. It was later named the Dorothy J. Saltzman Preschool.

*   *   *

January 25, 1996

Dearest Nancy,

As I sit here looking at the little school photos of the boys, I still think of you daily and can't believe it's been four months since the crash.

You've been so wonderful all along to everyone around you and to all of us who wish we could help in some magical way to ease the pain. These months must have been harder for you than I can possibly imagine, and I only hope the months ahead become a little easier.

You really are an amazing woman and I'm very proud of you.

Here's to the future.

Much love,
Mom

*   *   *

You might presume that having psychologists as parents made our household a "touchy-feely" hotbed. But even though their work dealt with feelings and behavior, my parents were really intellectuals at heart. I think they were more comfortable fostering a passion for inquiry and critical thought in us than making our home Emotion Central.

In fact, I have one memory regarding my parents' chosen vocation that was distinctly *un*emotional, and left a deep impression on me. At one point, Mom was in charge of student testing in our school district. When she received a new test she had to practice its administration. Her children were her guinea pigs. Linda always did well on tests. Rob and Andy also always got very high scores. I hated it. I did well but not as well as my siblings. When I took a test, I would watch my mother's face. Her neutral expression always screamed disappointment to me. What I didn't know was that she was required to show no reaction to our answers.

When I was in my thirties I finally asked my mother, point blank: "Am I the dumbest in our family?"

She answered perfunctorily, "You were all in the superior range of intelligence, although Andy was smarter than everyone else."

That didn't answer my question. Or maybe it did, obtusely. But the truth is, I did have an innate desire to do well, and perhaps feeling like the "dumbest" fueled my own expectations of myself. As siblings, though, we were never competitive—in fact, we've been each other's biggest cheerleaders through the years.

*   *   *

When we became teenagers, our allowances weren't enough to buy what we wanted, and we all got part-time jobs. Linda started working at a cheese shop in the mall. I babysat for twenty-five cents an hour, foreshadowing my long career with elementary-age kids. When I could drive, I took a job selling doughnuts near the IU campus. I also taught ice-skating at the local rink. I cleaned out rat and monkey cages in the psychology lab for my dad. I worked in my high school bookstore. I wasn't popular, but my bookstore position made me known to all, and friends would come by to chat.

We all went our separate ways during the day but we ate dinner together every night. Dinner was usually a casserole my mother had made and frozen on Sunday, then reheated that day. "I am a terrible cook," was her excuse. The truth was, she resented the time it took to cook. It wasn't intellectually stimulating for her. To make up for "lost time," she watched the nightly news on TV in the kitchen or listened to classical music on the radio.

But food was not the focus of our dinners, anyway. Conversation was the main course. We kids sat on an orange, fake-leather corner bench around a rectangular table. My parents sat in chairs opposite us. Linda, Rob, and I were expected to come to dinner ready to discuss what we had learned in school, or current events. Linda was always well prepared. Rob could talk his way around any situation. I was constantly unprepared, and therefore, constantly worried. I would bring a copy of *National Geographic for Kids* to the table. I hid it where I could see it in case it was my turn to share.

There were plenty of nights when my mother pointed out that one of my friends would be better able to participate in the discussion.

"Judy Nakhnikian or Sarah Pizzo would know the answer to that question."

I had to agree with her, though I said nothing.

* * *

October 4, 1995

Dear Nancy,

We were stunned and deeply saddened by the news about Joel, Adam and Seth. Although I only met them once—at your mother's retirement party—I feel like we have known all of you forever, through your parents' eyes, and your mother's camera.

We have watched all the Saltzman kids and grandchildren grow and succeed and triumph over great adversity. When we heard the sad news, we got out our favorite pictures of you and Joel and Adam and Seth to hold them a little longer in our hearts and to mourn them. And to remind ourselves how precious love and family is.

I know from your parents that you are a remarkable woman—that you have repeatedly shown great courage and a zest for life that has brought you much love and happiness. I hope that your wonderful attitude and the love of your family and friends will sustain you during this sad time.

With love,
Carol Anderson

(Friend and colleague of my mother)

* * *

Every night after dinner during our elementary and junior high years, we waited to hear a car horn. We would gulp down the last bites of food, grab our swim gear, and bolt out the door to catch the carpool to swim practice.

Swimming was another Saltzman family tradition. Both my parents swam, and we kids learned early and competed. Rob and I were reluctant participants, finding many creative ways to hide during practice so we wouldn't have to freeze in the middle of winter. We snuck under the bleachers, hid in the locker room, and periodically "forgot" our swimsuits. Most of the coaches never noticed. I do have good memories of two coaches. They were on the highly regarded IU swim team, and both went on to very successful swimming careers. Mike Troy broke the 200-meter butterfly world record five consecutive times and earned two Olympic gold medals. Chet Jastremski was the first man to break one minute in the 100-yard breaststroke, set nine world records and won twelve AAU titles. Rob, Linda, and I quit swimming competitively by the time we reached junior high, but I did swim on Colorado College's women's swim team for two years.

Andy, on the other hand, was a terrific swimmer. At age four, he became the youngest person to swim across Bloomington's Bryan Park Pool. He made All-American on the Princeton swim team. In 1981, Andy swam in the Maccabiah Games in Israel. He smashed Mark Spitz's record in the 100-meter freestyle and won the gold medal with a time of 52:23, compared to Spitz's record of 52:90. He won three gold medals and one bronze in all at the games.

More expectations satisfied.

*　*　*

Just like my mother, at age eight Linda started going to Camp Woodmere in upstate New York. She flew to New York City by herself, and my grandparents picked her up at the airport. She joined the other campers on a train and spent eight weeks away from home each year. In her late teens, she became a camp counselor.

When I was fifteen and Robbie was thirteen, we were also sent off to camp. My mother found Camp Pok-o-Moonshine and Camp MacCready in the Adirondack Mountains and negotiated a "two-for-the-price-of-one" deal. The girl's camp was brand new and Mom assured me it would be a great adventure. Robbie would be a camper. I would be a counselor-in-training.

Like Linda, Rob and I flew on a propeller plane to New York City from Indianapolis. My grandparents picked us up and took us to the train where we met all the other campers. We spent eight weeks at camp. I enjoyed working with the six- to eight-year-olds, and also caught the horse-riding bug. Our teachers were extremely talented horsewomen. They taught me how to ride and jump, and I even won some trophies. I taught little kids how to swim and ride. I hiked and slept in tents in the rain with my young charges. When camp ended, our parents drove east to pick up Rob and me. We visited friends and family on the East coast before going back to school.

Rob and I went to Camp Pok-o-Moonshine and Camp MacCready every summer for five years. I became a full-fledged counselor when I was seventeen and got paid $125.

I enjoyed "growing up" at camp. I held hands with Jeff Scott at a movie. I had my first kiss lying on the football field looking at the stars with Gary Kwok. I thought I fell in love with another counselor but he ignored me the whole summer until the last week of camp when it was too late do anything about it.

Though I didn't find true love there, my passion for working with children was reinforced.

*   *   *

In retrospect, it's clear that my parents instilled in all of us a drive to do our best, and to make good use of the gifts we had been given, by either nature or circumstance. A well-informed, active, and resourceful mind was highly valued. Strength was something to be cultivated, and we learned that it came in many forms. Were we less effusive in showing our feelings for each other than some families? Probably. Was there a subtle message of stoicism and making the best of things? I would say yes. But from their unique child-rearing recipe, I and my brothers and sister emerged with the pragmatism, fortitude, self-possession, stamina, and ability to give and accept love that are the hallmarks of survivors. And for that, I will be forever grateful.

CHAPTER 2

GO WEST, YOUNG WOMAN

DESPITE MY SLIGHT inferiority complex about my academic prowess, I always knew I would go to a college with high academic standards. Everyone we knew in Bloomington had gone, was going, or would go to college. My parents told us we could attend college wherever we wanted if we were admitted, though many years later I learned that they'd had to borrow money to make it possible.

Linda did extremely well in high school and had high SAT scores. She chose to go to Brown University in Providence, Rhode Island.

When I started looking at schools, I decided I wanted to go to a small liberal arts college where I could get a teaching degree. I read about Colorado College in Colorado Springs, and learned that students took one class at a time, or a block, for three and a half weeks. I could also take all classes pass–fail instead of for grades. I liked the way they thought.

Most important, thanks to the high and dry climate, my hair would be straight, not curly or frizzy. Straight hair *and* a quality education? That clinched the deal. I applied and was accepted.

I wasn't able to visit the campus, but our family had driven through Colorado in 1963 on our way to Dad's year at the University of Washington. Based on those memories, and a good feeling about this unconventional school, I found myself at the Indianapolis Airport in August, 1970, bound for Colorado Springs. My parents and brothers saw me off, after a farewell dinner at Shapiro's Delicatessen, my dad's favorite place.

We landed in my new home. On the cab ride from the airport to campus, I spotted Pikes Peak, the granite monolith that defines Colorado Springs' western horizon, out the window. My hair relaxed and so did I. I knew I had made a good choice.

*   *   *

My first roommate at Colorado College (CC) was from Aspen. She liked male college students and drugs. She had sex with men in our dorm room. Apparently she also liked an audience, as I was often there as well, lying in my bed a few feet away, behind two dressers I'd put up as a barricade. She left college after a month. I was not devastated—this left me with my own room in which I, too, could have sex with male college students if I wanted. I wanted, but I had neither experience (I was still a virgin), nor a boyfriend.

I did, however, have classes I liked, and made good friends quickly. I got a job working in the psychology lab cleaning the rat cages. Rat cages *again*.

I loved the dry climate and being in Colorado. I parted my hair down the middle and wore it long and straight. No more sleeping in rollers.

My first block class was a psychology course. The professor was engaging, bright, and had a great sense of humor. The block plan was perfect for my learning style. I was in class all morning, then had time to do my homework and eat lunch and dinner with friends.

After my psychology block, though, I got stuck with two half-blocks, taking two classes I wasn't wild about—in economics and political science—simultaneously for two blocks. I called home, complained, and cried.

"Sounds like you will learn a lot," my parents wryly observed.

I cried each night doing my economics homework. But with the help of my professor, Dr. Worner, I passed. Dr. Bob Loevy, the political science instructor, became one of my favorite professors at CC. If I hadn't decided on teaching, I might even have majored in political science. Dr. Loevy continues to teach, and I attend his seminars to this day.

*   *   *

My social life was the classic college freshman package: new people, new experiences. Some great, some—like my classes—highly instructional.

I met a guy. No, not that kind of "I met a guy." Tom Turner and I hit it off immediately in a platonic but close-bonding way. We became best friends. I learned to ski. A bunch of us would cram into Tom's vintage green Volvo and head for Vail, where Tom's parents had a condominium. We had no idea then, but Tom and I would remain close friends through the years. Upon hearing the news of my tragedy, he would come to Colorado Springs for a week to support me in the early days of my grief.

There was always a party somewhere. In high school, I wasn't into drinking or drugs (the fear of disappointing my parents loomed large). At college, I realized that I enjoyed parties—just not the social lubrication. I didn't like the taste of alcohol, didn't appreciate the calories, and didn't like feeling out of control. Sometimes people would ask about it, or I'd feel pressured, but usually, others would just get drunk and not even notice that I wasn't partaking. Later, when I was teaching, I was conscious of setting an example, even when I was off duty. And when it was time to go home, no one ever complained about having a sober driver available.

I also hadn't dated in high school, but I was definitely interested in changing that state of affairs. Unfortunately, my first experience with college boys was almost enough to swear me off drink and men.

A nice-looking sophomore boy had asked me out. We didn't know each other well—at all, really—but the date was to consist of spending the night with him in a local hotel, where he worked part-time as the night clerk. He wanted "company." I was pretty sure what access to empty hotel rooms and beds meant for our date, but I asked for clarification, just to be sure.

"Yes," he said, "It means we will have sex."

I liked him, and I was tired of being a virgin, so I agreed to go. When we got to the hotel, though, I had a change of heart. I didn't want to be a virgin and I did want a boyfriend, but it suddenly didn't seem to be in the cards for the two of us. I asked him to please take me back to my dorm. He informed me that he would, but it would mean no more dates.

"I've already lined up another date with a girl who will have sex with me," he said. "If you won't have sex, then we aren't going to go out again."

I considered this ultimatum for about a nanosecond, then asked him again to take me back. He did. And sure enough, he was true to his word on the consequences of my choice.

*   *   *

Happily, my introduction to the nuances of college mating circa 1970 did not reflect the attitudes of all Colorado College men. In November of my freshman year I met Mike Bertsch. Like the hotel clerk, he was a sophomore and had sandy blonde hair. But that's where the similarities ended.

Mike was from North Dakota and on a full scholarship as a hockey player. The attraction was immediate. He asked me to come to his hockey scrimmage and said we'd get something to eat afterwards. I had plans but agreed to meet him after the scrimmage.

"You idiot!" Tom responded when I mentioned the date. "Not watching him play is a huge insult!" I had not received that memo. But apparently it wasn't a deal breaker, because Mike and I began dating steadily.

Mike *was* the "I met a guy" type. I loved that he was smart and kind and thoughtful—not the "dumb goon" hockey player stereotype. He liked me because I was different from most CC coeds. I didn't belong to a sorority. And I knew how to skate! He loved to laugh and try new things. He and Tom became good friends, too.

Dating Mike, I learned a lot about hockey, and I got to know the other "hockey wives." Most of them were older than I was but they were a fun, wild bunch. One actually punched an obnoxious fan of the opposing team at a game. Hockey games were always entertaining on and off the ice.

My time was divided between classes, friends, Mike, hockey, and my part-time job. During the winter holiday break my mother took me to the gynecologist in Bloomington and I got a prescription for birth control pills. My mother talked to me about sex. I asked her what "sixty-nine" was. She told me and I looked at her quizzically.

"Some things feel a lot better than they sound," she replied, as if reading my mind.

*   *   *

Mike and I dated throughout college. I was in love with him—and hockey. I had a room on campus, but was at Mike's most nights. He graduated a year before me, and that summer we stayed in Colorado Springs and got jobs.

I worked with children through the Parks and Recreation Department. Mike played hockey and prepared to try out for an Atlanta Flames farm team. As he got ready to go, I moved into an apartment that I would share with Tom and his girlfriend Priscilla for our senior year.

I took Mike to the airport. I cried for forty-eight hours straight after he left. I didn't know what to do with myself, was scared to be alone, and wasn't sure what my year would be like without Mike.

I didn't have to find out. One week into training camp, Mike decided he didn't want to play professional hockey. It wasn't that he wasn't skilled enough; in fact, he was confident he had a good shot. He just didn't feel that he fit in. He wanted to come back to Colorado Springs.

Mike moved in with Tom, Priscilla, and me, and I began my senior year. I had class for one block, then I student-taught second grade for the rest of the semester. Second semester, I would take classes abroad in Paris and Rome.

I loved student teaching. The second graders and I bonded immediately. My cooperating teacher let me take over very early in my placement and I was in my element. I couldn't wait to become a teacher.

Mike also student taught in the fall of 1973. As the time for my semester abroad drew closer, I got cold feet. I didn't want to leave Mike. When I called my parents to tell them I was staying in Colorado Springs, they said, "You're doing *what?*" They tried to talk me into going to Europe, but allowed me to make the decision to stay in Colorado.

* * *

Dear Nancy,

I know I'm late in writing you. I've composed the letter in my head many times a day.

The news of Joel, Seth, and Adam's death has shaken me to my roots. The amount of sadness and hurt I feel is overwhelming and yet, I know, can't begin to touch your loss and pain.

In talking with Mike, he mentioned what an incredibly strong person you are and I know you will need every last ounce to survive this incomprehensible blow. I wish we lived closer so we could see you more often and sit and cry and laugh and be with you.

Please know that my family's thoughts are with you. It is not often that I pray but in your case I have made an exception.

Please call if the mood moves you; we are sending positive thoughts your way all the time.

Love,
Tom

(Tom Turner, my best friend at Colorado College)

CHAPTER 3

LAUNCH SEQUENCE

I GRADUATED IN JUNE of 1974. My parents and Andy came out for the celebration. They stayed just long enough to meet my friends, go out for dinner at The Margarita at Pine Creek, and see the Garden of the Gods, a park and natural rock formation west of town.

Mike and I moved into an apartment together on Weber Street. This was my third apartment on Weber and my dad started calling me "The Weber Street Kid." My parents liked Mike but talked to me about our significant differences in upbringing, religion, and goals. I argued with them because they clearly didn't understand that we were in love and that was all that mattered.

Mike substitute taught in the spring. After graduating, I got a job for the summer teaching pre-kindergarten. But as a new school year approached, I had no offers for full-time teaching. Mike had a job lined up teaching at St. Mary's, a private Catholic high school, and was also coaching hockey.

One week before school was scheduled to start in August, I heard from a CC friend. She had just gotten a teaching job in the Widefield School District south of Colorado Springs, and they were looking for a sixth-grade teacher. I contacted the principal, Mr. Millar, and set up an interview.

My mother would have been proud—I put on my best suit (polyester, of course) and sensible heels (unfortunately, I had no Chanel No. 5), and marched into his office. He stood up to shake my hand. He was at least six foot five. I could have fit four of my hands into one of his. I thanked him for the interview and answered his questions with the enthusiasm of the naïve. When he asked me how I felt about teaching sixth grade I told him, "Great! I have always enjoyed working with kids of all ages!"

Actually, I had rarely worked with kids of any age older than eight. Even when I was a camp counselor, I was always with younger children. I was terrified. I looked closer to eighteen than twenty-two. He offered me the position. I took it. I wasn't sure how one could simultaneously feel lucky and paralyzed with fear, but I did.

I would teach social studies. The curriculum was "the world." It didn't seem to matter that my experience with the world had been limited to "the U.S.," mostly Colorado and Indiana at that.

* * *

One day during the second or third week of school, I was sitting at my desk at the end of the day. One of my students came up to the desk and we chatted. After a few minutes, he asked me if he could give me a shoulder rub. My shoulders were tight and it had been a long day. Besides, he was twelve. (Did I mention how naïve I was for a twenty-two-year-old?)

"Sure," I said. As his small hands moved over my shoulders, he spoke into my ear.

"Can I give you a hickey?"

There were no more shoulder rubs that year.

Another student wasn't engaged in school so I decided to make a home visit. This was unheard-of at the time, and the veteran teachers told me I was crazy. The student's mother was in prison and he lived with his grand-mother. When I got there, two Doberman pinschers greeted me in the yard. The boy stuck his head out from the front porch.

"Watch out! Them dogs will bite you!"

"Well, hold them! I'm coming in."

I talked to his grandmother, and she saw that he had a teacher who cared about him. That weekend he accompanied Mike and me to a Colora-do College hockey game. We had a good time, and after that, the student's schoolwork took a decided turn for the better.

After my lessons in wrangling eleven- and twelve-year-olds, that first year of teaching was one of the best of my career. We might not have cov-ered all the sixth grade content, but my homeroom students and I bonded as a class. We laughed, played, sang, read stories, and learned together. I assumed that all the kids could learn and did everything I could to make that happen.

I carpooled with other teachers and made friends with the staff. They liked to go out for drinks on Friday. I joined them and enjoyed the camaraderie, though the happy hour deals were wasted on me.

*   *   *

Mike and I decided to get married. The date was set for June, after school was out. My parents were not surprised to hear the news, and agreed to pay for the wedding. It would be in Bloomington. Mike and I would spend time with them at Christmas, and I would go to Bloomington during spring break to finalize plans.

Though I was Jewish and Mike was Catholic, we innocently assumed we could get married in any church or synagogue in Bloomington. First we met with a priest who wouldn't marry us. Then we met with a rabbi who wouldn't marry us. My mother suggested a Methodist minister who had married my sister and her husband in a small chapel on Indiana University's campus. He agreed to marry us in the IU chapel. Apparently the Methodists were just happy to see people getting married, regardless of their religious affiliations. We set the wedding date.

My father talked to me directly about his concerns regarding Mike. He saw me as a rising star, someone who would go far professionally. He wanted to make sure that Mike would be supportive of my goals. I assured him that Mike was.

I was not one of those women who spend their lifetimes dreaming about their wedding days. This worked out well because although my mom had not spent a lot of time dreaming about my wedding day either, she did have some very specific ideas about invitations, flowers, and the guest list. I let her take over.

My sister had worn Mom's wedding dress for her marriage, and I was happy it fit me, too, with a little alteration. Most of the guests were people I had grown up with, or were my parents' friends. I loved these people and felt like they were my extended family. Mike's parents and siblings, a few of our college friends, and some of the hockey crowd also made the trip to Bloomington.

On a hot, humid day in June of 1975, we read our own vows and pledged eternal love in the small chapel. We partied in a reception hall nearby.

Before we left on our honeymoon, we flew to New Hampshire, where Mike tried out for the Olympic hockey team. He wouldn't find out if he'd made the team for several weeks, so then we were off for five weeks in

Europe. I wanted to go somewhere overseas—maybe to make up for missing my semester abroad my senior year. It wasn't the same, but I thought it might make my parents happy. We stayed in cheap hotels, rode trains everywhere, and took a cruise to the Greek Islands.

When we arrived home, we learned that Mike had not made the team. The news was a blow, and he felt unsure about how to approach the future. He was teaching and working as an assistant coach at Colorado College. I learned I would be teaching two sections of sixth grade social studies, an hour and a half of kindergarten, and three sections of fifth grade social studies come fall—not a great schedule, but I was happy to have a job.

*   *   *

As 1975 wound down, I had some troubling news from home. My dad had been diagnosed with prostate cancer. I was scared for him, but he had a positive attitude, and the doctors felt that he had a very good chance of recovery. I watched him go through treatment and remain optimistic. Aside from the usual calamities of childhood and the teenage years, I hadn't experienced true life-threatening adversity, and seeing the way he approached his illness made a strong impression on me. Ultimately, the cancer went into remission. And, from the man I admired most, I learned an important lesson regarding how to face significant challenges.

*   *   *

By Christmas I was ready for a break. Mike and I drove to Indiana by way of Omaha to see both sets of parents. I enjoyed seeing my family, but perhaps because of the strain on all of us from my father's illness, a different dynamic had developed. My mother's questions felt invasive and critical. My siblings and I couldn't help responding like we were still children. A fight erupted between Linda and Mom over how to bake potatoes. And Mike's less-than-crystal-clear life plans were still under scrutiny.

*   *   *

Mike had always assumed he would play hockey after college, so after realizing that playing professionally was not for him, and not making the Olympic team, he had to rethink everything. He was still teaching, but being an educator wasn't the calling for him that it was for me. I was busy at school, leading parenting workshops, and immersing myself in a job I loved. I wanted him to find a career he could be passionate about. After defending him for so long to my parents, I could now hear their words coming from my mouth. Despite what I had fervently argued, maybe love *wasn't* all that mattered. I was pushing Mike in ways that were actually driving us apart. When I would ask him what he wanted to do with his life, his answer was that he wanted to be the head hockey coach for Colorado College.

"How realistic is it to only want one job?" I challenged.

"Should you give up your dream just because it's not realistic?" he replied.

Knowing what I know now about relationships, I can clearly see how our young ages, my presumptions, and our different paths to finding meaningful lifework conspired against us. I had been lucky enough to land on a profession I loved early in life, and didn't realize it doesn't work that way for everyone. The Saltzman expectations were alive and well and living in the second generation.

My pushing and his search for a career path had taken their toll. We both felt we needed some time apart.

I moved into a friend's basement for six weeks. Then I got an apartment with a professor from CC, who needed a roommate. I acquired a cat named "Love with Reckless Abandon"—"Reckless" for short.

After many discussions and much soul-searching, Mike and I agreed to divorce. I'm happy to add that even without my pushing (or more likely, thanks to the absence thereof) Mike went on to a very distinguished professional life, including his dream job of coaching the Colorado College hockey team. Today he is an executive with USA Hockey, the national governing body for the sport of ice hockey in the U.S.

*　　*　　*

The day after the crash, Mike came by my house. He was by then happily remarried with children of his own. He gave me a giant bear hug. The kindness he had always possessed was a welcome comfort and never more appreciated. Although I was still in shock, our history allowed me to express some of the grief that was only beginning to set in. He had come to know both Adam and Seth through youth hockey programs, and we talked about what special people they were. We spoke as if they were still alive. I thanked him then for his support and friendship, and I thank him now.

*　　*　　*

It was while I was teaching that I realized I wanted to get a master's degree in Special Education. The University of Colorado at Colorado Springs offered courses in the late afternoon and evening, and on weekends. I continued to teach while taking classes and found this branch of education intensely interesting.

In one of my classes, I met another student named Donna Sheldon. She was a kindergarten teacher and was going through a divorce after being married for nine years. She and I stood in the parking lot after each class and talked and laughed. We had a lot in common and started facilitating workshops for the teacher's association. We also started going out to a local bar, Jose Muldoon's, on Wednesday and Friday nights because it was a favorite happy hour spot for Colorado Springs teachers. We became best friends. We hiked, rode bikes, took tennis lessons, and, after helping each other recover from our respective divorces, once again started looking for love.

CHAPTER 4

THE GUY IN THE TENNIS SHOP

JOEL WALTER HERZOG was born October 17, 1953, in Pueblo, Colorado. The first child of Harvey and Sarah Herzog was not yet due, and Harvey, on a buying trip for work in Denver, told the nurse who reached him that she was mistaken, Sarah could not possibly be in labor. The nurse argued with Harvey. Still dubious, Harvey drove to the hospital in Pueblo, where he saw with his own eyes that he was, indeed, a father.

Harvey (born Helmut) Herzog grew up in Vienna, Austria. He was an only child. Harvey's father worked for a large company in Vienna. His mother was from Czechoslovakia, and Harvey spent his summers there with his parents and grandparents. Tennis was a big part of his life.

In 1938, when Harvey was sixteen years old, the Nazis invaded Austria. Harvey's concerned parents were able to get him a visa to England on a children's transport. There, he was placed with a Jewish family, went to school, perfected his English, and worked in his host family's business. In 1940, his parents attempted to join him in England, but were denied a visa to leave the country. To keep Harvey safe, his parents made plans for him to live with relatives in Minnesota. Even as the arrangements were set in motion, his parents were taken into custody and subsequently transported to the Auschwitz concentration camp. He never heard from them again. It was determined that, along with more than one million other Nazi prisoners, they lost their lives at World War II's most notorious camp.

Initially, Harvey and other teenagers from England were denied a visa to the U.S., and taken to the Dominican Republic. All eighteen years and under, they were required to learn a trade. Harvey got practical experience as a cashier and accountant. He lived in the Dominican Republic until 1945 when his uncle was able to obtain a visa for him to come to the U.S. When he moved to Minnesota to be with his relatives, "It was a pleasure to see civilized people again," he said.

Harvey completed college at the University of Minnesota, where he met his wife, Sarah Zion, on a double date. Sarah was not Harvey's date, but this was only a cosmic oversight in Harvey's eyes. They were married soon after graduation in 1952 and moved to Denver for the milder weather and good jobs. Sarah became a correspondent for *Time* magazine. Besides English, she spoke fluent French and Spanish. Later, this bright, talented, but often quiet woman would obtain her master's degree and teach foreign language to middle schoolers. Harvey became an accountant in Pueblo at Colorado Fuel and Iron (CFI). Sarah had to quit her job when she became pregnant, and they moved to Pueblo to be closer to Harvey's job.

*   *   *

In 2003, eight years after the crash, I wrote this love letter to Joel.

Dear Joel,

I miss you with all of my heart. Really, I miss you with my whole being. Even after eight years. When I crawl into bed I still slide over to where you used to be. I can see your muscled back and your cute butt. I reach out to tickle you knowing that you'll turn over to face me. I can hear your voice saying, "Kiss me. The real thing, with tongue."

I breathe you in. Well, you and the unmistakable scent of our bedmates, the dogs. I'm smiling because at this point you would banish them from the bedroom, where they now live with me.

For just a moment I can imagine you really are here with me. I can hear your voice again: "You are so beautiful." I know that scars and all, I do look beautiful to you. "I love you," I whisper in your ear.

Then you attack me. . . .

*   *   *

After Joel was born, four siblings quickly followed: Marge, Lee, Michael, and Tracy. As the oldest, Joel was both hero and tormentor. Strong-willed, he and Harvey often butted heads when Joel didn't agree with his father's rules, or when Joel stood up for his younger siblings. But there was also plenty of love to go around.

The Herzogs lived in a one-level, three-bedroom house, with one bathroom. For most of their childhood, the boys slept together in one bedroom, the girls in another.

Harvey taught all the kids to play tennis at the city park as soon as they could hold racquets. Once Joel had the basics, he started playing with the "Dawn Patrol," a group of Harvey's friends who played before work. Soon Joel had moved beyond Dawn Patrol and started playing in youth tournaments. His brother Lee also became a skilled player.

At the end of each school year, tournament season began. Joel and Lee would compete locally as much as possible, then hitch rides with friends to matches in Colorado Springs and Denver, often spending the night in the bedrooms, or on the floors, of other junior players.

Joel played competitively through high school, and was offered a scholarship to the University of Northern Colorado, where he excelled in tennis, partying, and serial dating. He also did well academically. When he graduated in 1976 with a degree in business, he took a job as an assistant tennis professional at the Colorado Springs Racquet Club (CSRC). It was like coming home for him; he had played many tournaments at the CSRC growing up. He also strung racquets and worked at Le Bounce, a local tennis shop.

While tennis was his passion, Joel was also a businessman. As a boy, he'd had a paper route, and recruited Marge and Lee to help. Later he gave tennis lessons. In college he had a steady stream of income stringing racquets, and was able to purchase a home soon after he graduated.

*　*　*

It was June of 1979. I was walking in downtown Colorado Springs thinking about my life. I had been single for over a year. A master's degree was on my resume and I had just finished my fifth year teaching elementary school.

I was looking forward to a move to Charlottesville, Virginia, in two months; I had been accepted as a doctoral student at the University of Virginia (UVA). I would also be working as a graduate assistant at the Learning Disabilities Research Institute. Glancing up at Pikes Peak, I noticed there was still snow clinging to the top. Was there a more beautiful place in the world to live? I didn't think so. I would miss the mountains, but was excited to become Dr. Saltzman.

I took a turn from Tejon Street onto Boulder Avenue, headed for Le Bounce, a local tennis shop. I had been taking tennis lessons and was thinking about buying a new racquet. Maybe it would improve my game. At least a new outfit might help.

I looked through the storefront window, just before entering. There was a young man standing at a T-shaped machine. His palms were pressed together with a fibrous strand, weaving up and down, going side to side. He was stringing a racquet. I could see him very clearly, from head to toe.

Tanned. Muscular biceps. Good hands. Gorgeous face. Tight abs under his tee shirt. Nice butt. Powerful calves. About my height.

All of this went through my brain simultaneously. Angels did not sing, but my body did: blood rushed to my face, my heart pounded, butterflies flitted. I looked away. Instead of going into the store, I kept walking. Maybe I was running—who can remember anything when you've unexpectedly come face to face with the man of your fantasies?

I rushed home and called Donna. Her dad was one of the best tennis players in town.

"Hey. I think I might have fallen in love today. Do you know anything about the guy who works at Le Bounce on Boulder and Tejon?" As I'd hoped, Donna said she would call her dad and ask. Minutes later, the phone rang.

"His name is Joel Herzog. My dad plays tennis with him. He says he's a great guy."

*   *   *

. . . I wish I had been with you on the plane. If either boy had survived, I never would have let them leave home again. Ever.

I wish you had survived, even if you were seriously hurt. You might not have wanted to survive, if you were permanently injured and couldn't play tennis. I wouldn't care, I would want you back no matter what shape you were in.

I have had the next wish many times since the crash. I wish there really was a Superman. I would ask him to reverse the orbit of the earth, just like he did for Lois Lane, when she died in a car crash. He would spin us back to the time of the crash and stop the plane from flying into Colorado. . . .

*   *   *

Donna and I set about figuring a way I could meet Joel. It seemed the best plan was to run into him in a bar. This seemed much superior to simply walking into the shop and introducing myself. That would be way too sensible and mature.

We had an idea.

The next day I went to a city tennis tournament, and sat next to Don, an acquaintance who knew the players around town. It's hard to sound casual when you're asking for information on the man you've fallen in love with at first sight, but I tried my best.

"Hey Don, what do you know about Joel Herzog?"

He paused, thinking. "He's a great guy."

The same words Donna's dad used.

"He and his brother can beat anyone in town. He's opening his own tennis store."

Puh-leeze. What do I care that he's opening a tennis store? Obviously, my question was, does he have a girlfriend? Sheesh.

"Don. Can you do me a favor? Can you set me up with him? My best friend and I go to Jose Muldoon's every Friday night. Can you get him there this Friday?"

Don looked at me, inscrutable.

Has he done this for other women before? How many girlfriends does Joel have?

The crowd cheered an ace.

"I'll try," Don said.

Though I hadn't heard anything from Don, Friday afternoon Donna and I checked with each other five or six times to discuss what we would wear that night. It was a warm day but not too hot. Jeans? Shorts? We finally decided that jeans and summer tops would work. We reminded each other of our favorite adage.

"If you feel good about yourself, don't look in the mirror."

Although I only lived five blocks from the bar, I drove. My little blue Datsun B210 purred into a parking spot. Donna got out of her Honda and I nervously hugged her tiny frame. At five feet tall and not even one hundred pounds, she was even smaller than I was. Forgetting our promise about mirrors, we stopped in front of a picture window and checked ourselves out.

"You look great."

"*You* look great."

We walked in, waved at people we knew, and made a couple of laps around the bar. She ordered a beer and took a drink; I ordered a beer to carry around with me.

* * *

An hour earlier, Joel had flopped onto his couch. He and Lee had just lost a tournament doubles match to a team they should have blown off the court—in fact, *had* blown off the court dozens of times previously. What had happened? Whatever it was, he was in no mood for analysis. Maybe just a low-key evening at home to get ready for tomorrow's matches.

Then Don had showed up.

"C'mon, you need to get your mind off the match," Don had lobbied. "Let's go get a beer at Jose Muldoon's."

"Nah. I'm not really up for it. Think I'll just stay close to home tonight."

"Right. And beat yourself up for losing? Nope, we're going out. Grab your stuff."

Lee pushed for going out. Joel gave Don the evil eye, but reluctantly agreed.

I will always be thankful to Don and Fate for pulling him off that couch.

* * *

The bar was semicrowded. I looked across the room and saw Don. Next to him was Joel . . . and a second Joel. He had a twin? This guy was full of surprises, and I hadn't even met him. Time to remedy that.

I walked up to Joel Number One, whom I believed to be the real Joel. He was about my height. He was also wearing a tee shirt that said, "Tijuana Pussy Posse." Above the words was a caricature of a man in a sombrero holding a cat by the tail.

Hmm. I believe I will overlook his taste in menswear for the moment.

Joel's jeans were ripped down the side, revealing a muscular thigh.

"Hi, I'm Nancy."

"I'm Joel."

Joel's doppelganger said, "Hi. I'm Lee, his brother."

Joel looked at me and said, "What do you do?"

"Great line Joel, great line," Lee deadpanned. We all laughed.

I told them that I had been teaching for five years and was getting ready to move to Charlottesville, Virginia, to start a Ph.D. program. Joel thought about that. Then he said, "Do you want to come over to my house? I'm having a party."

Wow. Good timing.

I found Donna and told her about the party at Joel's house. She was deep in conversation with a tall, good-looking guy. I hugged her. She whispered, "He's a teacher!"

"You look hot," she added.

"*You* look hot," I repeated.

"Have fun!"

* * *

. . . I remember our last dinner together. Seth got out of his chair and came to sit on my lap. It was his birthday and he asked me if he could fly home with me. I asked you what you thought. You said, "Hey, these guys came with me to watch the tennis and they are going to stay with me. It's a guy thing." I laughed and agreed that he should stay. It was such a good decision at the time, only unbearably terrible in hindsight. I marvel at the small things that later carry significance. . . .

* * *

Joel drove a yellow Datsun 280z that made a distinctive throaty roar as he pulled out.

I didn't want to lose him, so I stayed close on his tail. I listened to a James Taylor cassette, singing along.

Shower the people you love with love . . .

It was a good sign, I thought.

I pulled into the driveway of a small brick house with a clean front porch. Joel walked back to my car to meet me. He put his arm around me as we walked in silence into the house. I might have been holding my breath. I hadn't been this attracted to someone in a long time.

The carpeted living room was furnished in "Early College Days": brown plaid couch, matching loveseat. I could see dishes on the kitchen counter, but the house was surprisingly clean for a male in his mid-twenties who hadn't been expecting company. Oh, right, the party.

As it turned out, the party had been rather spur-of-the-moment and only one guest had been invited: me.

Joel told me he had bought the house himself and had a roommate who was a pro at the Broadmoor Tennis Club. I got a quick tour of the two bedrooms upstairs. His room barely held the king-sized waterbed that nearly touched every wall. It was covered with a huge comforter featuring an orange, yellow, and brown sunrise. The theme continued onto the wall, where a painted sun was rising over a mountain.

Back in the living room we sat on the couch and kissed, tentatively. I sheepishly told him about seeing him at Le Bounce and accepted responsibility for dragging Don in on what now seemed like a highly embarrassing plan to meet him. He didn't seem put off by my capacity for subterfuge.

We talked about our families. I was surprised to learn of his Jewish background and moved by his grandparents' story; we decided the chances of one Jewish person randomly meeting another in Colorado Springs were about the same odds as winning the lottery. He told me of his dream to open his own tennis shop and I told him about going to the University of

Virginia. I felt completely at ease, and was overcome by wanting him to know everything about me, and vice versa.

Instead, we walked out to his front porch. We reached for each other's hands and his warmth traveled through my body. There were those butterflies again. I wanted to go back into his house and curl up next to his body; we would fit together perfectly I was sure. I wanted to hold him all night. But we walked down the steps to my car. As I opened my car door he turned me around. So close that I could feel his breath on my face, he started to kiss me, slow and soft. My heart jumped as his tongue touched my lips. I kissed him back and this time the embrace was long and sweet.

Maybe he was going to invite me back into the house. Maybe I should just take his hand and lead him back into his bedroom.

He smiled. "It's late and I have a tennis match tomorrow. My brother and I are playing in the morning at the Broadmoor. Would you like to watch?" I wasn't going to make the same mistake I'd made with Mike and hockey.

"I'd love to!"

"Pick you up at 8:30."

We exchanged one last kiss before I got into my car. We weren't going back inside, but at least I was going to see him again.

He watched me back my car into the street. I saw his hand waving good-bye. James Taylor was still singing.

I looked at his ripped jeans and his obnoxious tee shirt, and waved back. He was so wonderful to look at, not to mention a good listener with a great sense of humor.

It took me a while to fall asleep.

Was he as attracted to me as I was to him? It seemed like it.

Was he at home wondering why he didn't ask me to spend the night? I certainly was.

Would he remember the directions to my apartment and actually show up in the morning?

And—ever practical—*what should I wear?*

*   *   *

... When I saw the pictures of the crash I thought of your most recent physical. The doctor told you two weeks before the crash that you were in terrific shape. "Very few forty-one-year-olds are as fit as you." Strutting around the house that night you called yourself a stud. I had to agree. There was no fat on your body, only muscle. I wondered why you didn't just walk away after the plane crashed—you were so strong. ...

*   *   *

At 8:30 a.m. sharp I heard the 280z's low roar outside. I looked out my window and caught the muscular hop from his car. Those thighs again! I greeted him with a kiss and a hug.

"I'm so happy to see you," I said.

"You look beautiful." I honestly think he was checking me out for the first time—sober and in the daylight. The short jeans skirt and sleeveless top seemed to pass muster. It was the first of thousands of times I would hear him say those words to me. They never got old.

He opened his car door for me and I slid into the deep bucket seat.

"I wasn't sure you'd show up."

"I wasn't sure you'd still want to go."

We laughed and the tension broke.

Driving to the Broadmoor, Joel told me how much tennis meant to him and about his history playing with his brother. I learned about the tennis scholarship, and that they both taught tennis. He mentioned that I would be meeting his father, mother, and youngest sister. They were driving up from Pueblo to watch the match.

Okay. First date, meeting the family. I wonder if he even remembers my name?

We pulled into the parking lot. As I got out of the car I saw Donna and her dad, who was also playing in the tournament. A big smile spread across her face when she saw the two of us.

Joel joined Lee on the court to warm up. Joel hit a ball and looked at me. Lee yelled at him, "Pay attention!" Joel hit a ball again and looked at me. Lee yelled again.

I had never seen such fast tennis in my life. It was as if the brothers were psychic. Short but quick, they knew exactly where a ball would land, and one of them would reach it before it even hit the ground. If a ball went over their heads, one would yell "mine" and a winner would rocket across the net, obliterating the chance for any return. Joel was a crowd pleaser. His definition of a good shot was "the shot that brings the crowd to its feet."

My heart swelled with pride every time the Herzogs won a point. Joel and Lee beat their opponents in two straight sets.

In the stands, Donna and I had a chance to talk. I told her about my visit to Joel's house and the "party."

"Did you spend the night?"

I shook my head no.

"Maybe tonight . . . "

Donna was excited to tell me about Gary, the band teacher she had talked with the night before. It had been quite a night for both of us. There were definitely stars in our eyes, but we would still have been stunned to know that we had both met our future spouses on the same night.

Following the celebration and trophy ceremony, Joel asked me to join his family at Mr. Steak. I was introduced to his mother, father, and one of his sisters, Tracy. Everyone was looking up at me . . . literally. They were all shorter than I was! Joel's father, Harvey, pulled out a chair for me, then sat next to me. He looked like Joel and Lee but was thinner, darker, and slightly balding.

The quiz began in a clear Austrian accent.

"What do you do? Where are you from? How old are you? How did you meet Joel? You're very pretty."

Harvey was funny, extroverted, and full of compliments. His wife, Sarah, sat next to him and listened. Joel was on my other side, deconstructing every point of the match with Lee. He obviously felt I could hold my own with his parents.

Sarah and I exchanged a little small talk. I told her I was a teacher and that I was getting ready to go to the University of Virginia to work on my Ph.D.

"I am also a teacher," she shared. We talked briefly about education, and then I turned the tables on them.

"Is Joel the oldest? Where did he learn to play tennis? How long have Joel and Lee played together? When did he graduate from the University of Northern Colorado?" Many months later I learned that Harvey had figured out I was two years older than Joel. When I asked him when Joel graduated from college, he subtracted a couple of years and said, "1974," so we would seem the same age.

During the Q & A phase of the luncheon, Joel held my hand. He touched my thigh. He kept talking with his brother, sister, and mother while Harvey talked to me. Lee and Joel were teasing each other about the match they'd lost the previous day. It all reminded me of lunches with my family: talking, eating, laughing, questions, discussion, and love. I didn't want it to end, and when it did I wasn't sure what our plans were for the rest of the day. Or night.

*   *   *

 . . . I will always wonder what you were doing when the plane hit. Did you know what was happening? Were you holding Seth? Was Adam asking you if everything would be okay? Could you see anything? Did Homer warn you? Did you think of me? Were you making jokes? I think you might have been telling a funny story to keep the mood light. After the crash, people would tell me jokes *as a way for us to remember you. I still can't remember a joke to save my life. I need you here to tell me one of your ridiculous tales full of sexual innuendo. I still laugh a lot but not as much as when you were here chasing me around trying to tickle me. . . .*

*   *   *

We walked out of Mr. Steak and the Herzogs hugged each other. They waved goodbye and began their drive back to Pueblo, about fifty minutes away. Joel and I got into his 280z.

"It was fun to meet your family."

"Hey, thanks for doing that! Was my dad behaving himself?"

"Oh yes. We played twenty questions, but I got to ask a few of my own. Your dad worships you, by the way."

Joel paused. "Well, I *am* the oldest son."

"I'm number two out of four—and of course my mom's favorite."

Joel said he would take me home. He needed to shower and get caught up on some racquet-stringing at Le Bounce.

At a stoplight he turned to me. "Would you like to get together after I get off work tonight?"

*   *   *

. . . Joel, I've read Seth's journal, which miraculously survived the crash, over and over. One of my favorite passages is his simple view of us:

> *"I'd like you to meet my family. First there is my Dad. He goes to work at 9:00 in the morning and comes home at 6:00 at night. He works at a tennis store and sells shoes, racquets, strings and balls. My Mom is a principal at Broadmoor Elementary. My Mom used to teach 5th and 6th grade at another school. My brother is in seventh grade. He is 12 years old. He plays hockey, tennis and soccer. My dogs are one and four. The one that is one is a Sheltie and part Dingo. The one that is four is a Golden Retriever."*

I loved being in this family.

Love always,
Nancy

*   *   *

It was after 7 p.m. when I heard the increasingly familiar rumble of the 280z again. I gave Joel a quick tour of my apartment and introduced him to my roommate and Reckless the cat. We said goodnight to roommate and cat, and drove to Joel's house. We held hands on the way up the front porch and when we walked into the living room, Lee was sitting on one of the couches. Joel and I sat down across from Lee. The brothers began discussing the tennis match. I leaned against Joel while listening to their banter. After about ten minutes their conversation stopped. I looked at Lee.

"I've been waiting all day to get your brother alone, and if it's okay with you, I am now going to take him into his bedroom."

Both Lee and Joel burst out laughing.

"I like her, Joel," Lee weighed in as he got up to leave.

Joel and I made our way to the waterbed and the sunrises.

CHAPTER 5

EDUCATION AS A CAREER, LOVE AS A TEACHER

"IF YOU LOVED ME you would stay in Colorado."

"I do love you, but I can't stay in Colorado."

Thirty-one days before, we'd spent our first night together in the sunrise bedroom. Except for work, we had been joined at the hip, literally and figuratively, ever since. Now we had to face reality. I had already resigned from my teaching job, and was two weeks away from driving my car, a U-Haul, and everything I owned across the country to begin the doctoral program that awaited me at the University of Virginia. Only three doctoral students had been admitted in 1979; I was one of them. Equally important, I had landed a plum assistantship at the Learning Disabilities Research Institute (LDRI), working with some of the top people in the country in my field. I simply could not turn it all down, though I would be in Charlottesville, Virginia, for at least three years.

I was five feet, four inches of churning, contradictory emotions. I had fallen head over heels in love with Joel, and the feeling was clearly mutual—the last thing I wanted to do was leave him. I also looked forward to achieving my goal of becoming a university professor—I couldn't pass up this opportunity. Joel was working at Le Bounce and in the process of opening his own tennis shop, Total Tennis. He would be the only employee. He couldn't leave Colorado Springs and I couldn't stay.

The negotiations began.

I put my hand on his leg. "I would be happy to distract you on the trip to Virginia if you would drive me there." He smirked, but only slightly.

"I will also pay for your airfare back to Colorado."

I probably had him with my first offer, but the ticket home sealed the deal.

*   *   *

The petite hauling trailer I rented fit easily behind my Datsun B210. My clothes filled it to the top. Although I had promised my roommate that I would take Reckless with me if I ever moved, she agreed to adopt him.

An unfortunate coincidence was that my brother, Rob, was just moving *to* Colorado Springs, to work for a law firm. At the same time I was getting ready to leave Colorado, he was making plans to arrive. It wasn't great timing.

It was, however, a great time to have a party. Rob had just taken the Colorado bar exam. My teacher friends came by to say goodbye to me. We celebrated all the changes. Joel and I clung to each other.

*   *   *

Joel drove most of the way to Charlottesville. I took the wheel only when he got tired. He could sleep sitting up with the seat reclined a bit. I tried to lie down by putting my head on a pillow on his lap. I would look at Joel driving, my heart would beat faster, and I would feel awash in happiness. I tried not to think about the saying goodbye part. Instead I thought about why I was going to UVA.

I want to be a professor and teach at a university.

I want to learn more about teaching and study with the best educators in the country.

I want to be Dr. Saltzman like my sister and my dad.

I made the choice to do this. I set it all in motion. It is what I want.

I can't make a decision based on a man at this point in my life.

We listened to cassette tapes of James Taylor and the Eagles. If we could get any reception, we listened to the radio. We stopped at rest areas, made out in the car, made love in hotels, and ate at fast food restaurants.

I remember how humid it was when we stopped in Bloomington so Joel could meet my mother and father. As we drove into town, I showed him where I had lived and gone to school. The IU campus was mostly deserted so we drove by the psychology building and the Speech and Hearing Clinic. True to form, my hair was frizzy and curly by the time we reached my parents' home.

The front yard was lush with trees and bushes. I rolled my window down as we pulled up and savored the smell of freshly cut grass. It was late in the afternoon and a mosquito buzzed by my head. We parked on the street and I honked the horn.

My mom and dad came out on the front stoop. I ran to them and gave them big hugs. Joel greeted my dad with a handshake. There was a polite hug from my mother for Joel. The men brought in our suitcases.

I followed everyone downstairs to Andy and Rob's old bedroom. My mom pointed to the twin beds.

"There are clean sheets on the beds. You can push them together if you wish." She smiled at me and walked out. Joel and I burst into laughter. He grabbed me and observed, "The apple doesn't fall far from the tree."

We went back upstairs where we made chitchat, then sat down. My mom's interrogation began almost immediately.

"So, where did you go to college?"

"What was your major?"

"What have you been doing since college?"

"Can you make a living running a tennis shop?"

Joel handled the questions with ease. Then there were questions for me.

"Do you know what classes you'll have?"

"What will you be doing for your assistantship?"

"When will you two see each other again?"

I was also able to answer my questions easily—except the one about Joel and me. We didn't know for sure and said so. Then, feeling as though we had passed our first test, we went downstairs to push the twin beds together.

*   *   *

We left early the next morning after a breakfast of eggs and toast cooked by my dad, just like the old days. We arrived in Charlottesville on August 5 in the middle of the day. It was ninety degrees and over ninety percent humidity. My mind was becoming increasingly overrun with questions—and doubts. The emotions continued to churn.

What am I doing?

I lived in Colorado Springs for nine years. Why, WHY, did I have to meet this man four weeks before moving away?

"Look, tennis courts!" Joel reported as we drove into town and through the campus. He had never been to Virginia, but noticed a very important fact about the place immediately. People at UVA played tennis. I had only been to Charlottesville when I rented my apartment several months earlier and was happy to have Joel point out things about my new home.

We pulled up outside the apartment building, met the landlord, and got a key. My place was on the second floor of an old house at the end of Fraternity Row. We were soaked by the time we got the car and U-Haul unpacked, but Joel maintained a positive perspective.

"It's a lot easier to carry things up a flight of stairs when you aren't at six thousand feet like in Colorado. I bet it'll be great to play tennis here."

It was a good sign that he was already thinking about future visits. He had to leave the next day to go back to work. I would take him to the airport in Charlottesville and then start my work as a graduate assistant at the Learning Disabilities Research Institute.

We decided to eat at a little pub near my apartment. We held hands as we walked there. "When do you think we'll see each other again?" I tried to ask casually.

"I'll have to wait and see how things go with the business."

We made a commitment to write every day. I would not be able to get a phone for at least two weeks and long distance calls were expensive. Neither of us had much money and what we had was going into our respective dreams. It was a frustrating position—to each be excited about doing what we wanted, but to not be together.

As we climbed the stairs to my apartment after dinner, we suddenly realized what awaited us: no air conditioning, a twin bed, and many cockroaches. Happy to be together, we ignored the discomforts and fell sound asleep.

*   *   *

The drive to the airport the next morning was way too short. I fought back tears with varying degrees of success. I walked with Joel to his gate. When they called his flight and we had to say goodbye, the dam burst, and I couldn't stop crying. He kissed me passionately through the waterworks and said, "I love you." I watched him walk outside to the small plane that he boarded. I waited until the plane taxied out onto the runway. I sat in my car and cried for a while longer.

What have I done?

How will I survive here all by myself?

How could I have forgotten how bad my hair would look in Virginia?

*   *   *

I started classes and my work at the LDRI, and met all the doctoral students in special education. Dr. John Lloyd, the professor I would be working with that year, introduced me to Norma Cameron, a second year doctoral student in special education. I liked her immediately. She was funny and described each doctoral student to me in detail. We talked about our boyfriends and past teaching experiences. There were only three in my group but twelve of us all together. It was an interesting, colorful, competitive bunch—bright, outgoing, and friendly. Several of us met periodically at the pub where Joel and I had our dinner on my first night in Charlottesville. I stayed busy with classes, my assistantship, and, of course, writing letters to Joel.

On the home front, my landlord replaced my twin bed with one that was queen-sized. All that remained of the roaches was the faint odor of the chemicals that had killed them. Joel and I spoke on the phone almost daily. Our first month apart, my phone bill was $400. His was at least as much.

I started running two miles every day, when I could. I turned Joel's letters into incentives, only allowing myself to read them after I had finished my run each day. Of course, the exercise was quickly canceled out by the chocolate chip cookies I would bake as a reward for completing my homework.

However, both the running and the cookies would continue as important elements in my life. I ran (or I should say, jogged) for more than twenty years until an injury sidelined me. And Seth and I had a special tradition of making chocolate chip cookies together; he would perch on the counter and talk to me as I sifted and stirred. After the crash, when I was especially sad, I would make a batch of cookies and pretend Seth was sitting on the counter, regaling me with his adventures of the day. Only my school staff benefited, though—I could never bear to eat them.

*   *   *

By October, Joel and I were missing each other terribly. He found someone to watch the store for a week and flew to Virginia. It was the first time he had left the store since it opened. Seeing him when he walked down the steps from the plane, I fell in love all over again. We hugged, held hands, and kissed. I took him to the LDRI and introduced him to everyone.

Then reality hit. I had to go to class, work, and do homework. I was gone all day and he had nothing to do except hang out at the tennis courts. He was bored and worried about the store. It was great to see him, but I was not very successful at balancing my life when Joel was in Charlottesville. When I dropped him off at the airport we were both sad but relieved. He needed to be in Colorado and I needed to be in Virginia.

Thanksgiving came quickly. I spent it in New Jersey with Andy, who by then was going to school at Princeton. I also managed to ignore the fact that the most important paper of the semester was due the following Monday. When I got home late Saturday, I started typing and worked on it for twenty-four hours straight. I turned it in Monday morning feeling confident I'd done a good job. I would have to defend this paper in February before a committee of professors who would decide if I could remain in the doctoral program at UVA. Until that decision, all doctoral students were probationary.

I went to my seminar that week but did not get my paper back. Other students did. My level of concern rose. I asked my professor about the paper; he told me to check my mailbox. I found my paper with a big, fat, red F at the top. I had never received anything less than a B. In any grade. At any school. I could barely read the comments through my tears. I had not proofread my paper and there were so many errors that the professor had written, "This paper is unreadable in its present form due to typos and errors."

I took the paper to Norma's apartment. She took one look at it and said, "Put it under your bed and don't look at it again." It was ideal advice. That's exactly what I did until I had to rewrite the paper. I was allowed to resubmit it and defend it in February. I passed my preliminary oral exams. The professor who had given me the F said, "You have a lot of poise." To this day, I hate proofreading.

* * *

Jan. 14, 1980

Dear Nancy,

I was delighted to receive your letter and learn how well you did on your courses at UVA. I'd say I was proud of you but it might embarrass you. I'll say it anyway. I'm proud of you! I'm tempted to send a $1 bill for every A, just like the old times. But I've gotten too cheap in my old age. Besides, I know there'd be a lot more of them coming and I don't want to set (or reinstate) such a costly process.

Keep up the good work.

Love ya,
Daddio

* * *

Despite the hardships of a long-distance relationship and the rigors of my program, I was very happy at UVA. My typo-ridden paper notwithstanding, I learned I could compete at the doctoral level. I was challenged and stimulated. Lesson design and the mysteries of human development came alive. I realized I could play a leadership role in other places besides the classroom. I discovered a new perspective on students with behavioral issues, along with strategies to improve my relationships with parents. Dr. Lloyd included me as a co-author, along with Dr. James Kauffman, in an article published in *Learning Disability Quarterly*. By the time I finished my first year at UVA in May, I was very committed to getting my Ph.D.

Dr. Lloyd had given me approval to complete a required internship at the University of Colorado, Colorado Springs (UCCS) over the summer. But he seemed to read between the lines, cautioning, "No one leaves the University of Virginia doctoral program once admitted." I assured him that I would return in August.

Arriving in Colorado Springs, I moved into Joel's living room, kitchen, and sunrise bedroom.

My internship at UCCS was with a summer school program for elementary-aged, learning-disabled students. I was the administrator in charge, and we had the whole school to ourselves. There was a five-to-one student-teacher ratio, and the instructional techniques we used were the ones I had learned at UVA. Besides classroom time, we took the kids to the zoo and local tourist spots so they could write about their adventures. The students made greater academic gains than expected, the student teachers grew as professionals, and the staff coalesced as colleagues and friends. I could see the impact I had made as the administrator, and it was heady stuff.

Summer was Joel's favorite time of year. Total Tennis was always busy. He played in tournaments and we had parties at the house. We met each other's friends.

By the middle of the summer I realized that Dr. Lloyd's suspicions had been well founded: once in Colorado, reconnected and recommitted to Joel, I didn't want to return to Virginia. I met with the chair of the special education department at the University of Denver (DU). They would admit me to their Ph.D. program.

There were many considerations.

Would Dr. Lloyd give me a year's leave to see if things worked out with Joel?

Would DU be as challenging and stimulating as UVA?

Would Judy Stahlman (another graduate student with whom I had signed a lease in Virginia) forgive me if I walked out on her?

Dr. Lloyd did indeed give me a year's leave, and wished me luck. Judy wasn't surprised to hear I wasn't coming back. I hope she forgave me.

*   *   *

Joel and I drove to Virginia to pick up my books and belongings. When we got back to Colorado I found out that I had received an assistant-ship working for the Bureau of Educational Research (BER) at DU.

At UVA my main area of study had been special education, with a secondary focus on early childhood education. I had seen myself becoming a professor and teaching at the college level, like my father had. But over my summer internship, and during my time at DU, I realized how much I enjoyed holding administrative roles in school settings. I changed my focus to educational leadership, and took classes in the School of Business, minoring in public administration. Although I hadn't been there long, and I did miss my colleagues in Virginia, I already felt at home at DU.

*   *   *

I was feeling great about all the changes I had made—but ironically, Joel and I were not in sync. At dinner, early in the semester, he said that we needed to talk.

"I'm feeling claustrophobic."

"What do you mean?" I responded.

"When your sister was here I started feeling claustrophobic."

Anxiety welled up in my chest. Linda had visited late in the summer, and I knew she had taken up a lot of my time. But I didn't think I should be held accountable for feelings Joel had when she visited.

"Well, what can we do about it?"

Joel said, "I think you may need to move out."

I took a deep breath. Although it made sense for me to live in Denver because of the long commute, I had not expected this turn of events.

"I left a great program at the University of Virginia to be with you, after swearing that I would never again make a decision based on a man."

We sat looking at each other.

"Do you still want to be with me?"

He assured me that he did.

"Okay. I'll look for a place to live and move at the end of September."

I hoped that Joel was telling the truth about just needing some space. I knew that this was his first serious relationship and wanted to respect how he was feeling. I didn't want to force the relationship and have it end. I was perplexed and scared, but he held all the cards.

I found a room to rent in a house north of DU's campus. I convinced myself that it would be okay for October and November. My classes would be finished in December and hopefully I could move back to Joel's house. It would give us some time to figure things out.

I stayed in Denver Monday through Friday and came to Colorado Springs on the weekends. I spent many days with Donna (who was now exclusively seeing Gary, the man she had met the night I met Joel) because Joel was working, playing tennis, or spending time with his single friends. I moved my things back into Joel's house before I went to Indiana for Christmas.

But when I returned, Joel had not changed his mind about our living arrangement.

"I love you. But I'm not ready to get married."

Who said anything about getting married?

For my part, though, I was in love and wanted to be with him. He said he wanted to have the freedom to see other people in addition to dating each other. I didn't want to be with anyone else.

I was devastated, but I agreed to the arrangement. I wasn't ready to tell him goodbye.

I found an efficiency apartment in Denver, one block from campus, and moved in the first week in January. I called him and sent him letters and cards. I taught a class through DU in La Junta, Colorado, every other weekend. To get to La Junta, I had to drive through Colorado Springs. I would spend Friday night with Joel, then drive south to teach class. I was frustrated with the arrangement, but didn't put pressure on Joel.

By February I had reluctantly started going out on dates in Denver. My heart wasn't in it. Joel and I talked on the phone and saw each other every other weekend, but there didn't seem to be much hope for our future together.

*   *   *

September 27, 1995

Dear Nancy,

Since reading the news of the death of your husband and two sons, my thoughts have frequently been with you. Having two sons of my own, I can only imagine the shock, sadness and pain you must be feeling. My purpose in writing is to let you know you are not alone in your suffering.

The hurt you feel should eventually, with time, subside, but never completely go away. This is as it should be when a person has experienced the loss of something very precious and irreplaceable.

I remember you as a bright, caring school administrator; someone who is good for young people. May your career help you through this difficult time.

Dick

(Dr. Richard Koeppe, superintendent of a school district I worked with as a graduate student at DU)

CHAPTER 6

MARRIAGE AND OTHER
TRADITIONS

IT WAS MARCH and I was living in Denver full-time. I hadn't heard from Joel for a week because Lee had talked him into playing in some tournaments in Mexico. He half-heartedly argued that he didn't want to be away from the shop, but March was usually cold and wet; a slow month for sales. Mexico sounded warm and sunny and the brothers would have a good time playing together. There was also talk about testing their skills in international competition.

Most of my time in Denver was spent working and studying, but when a good friend from Colorado College, Rob Wheeler, invited me to a Linda Ronstadt concert in Boulder, he didn't have to ask twice. I drove to Boulder, had a great time at the concert, and drove back to Denver afterwards. I got to my apartment at 2 a.m.

Weird. That yellow 280z parked in front of my building looks just like Joel's. Of course it's not. He's in Mexico.

I pulled up behind the little sports car.

The car door opened, and Joel got out.

"What are you doing here? Is everything okay?"

"I missed you and wanted to come back to see you." It was a little awkward because of the hour. He looked concerned—about where I was, or more specifically, who I'd been with.

"I was in Boulder with Rob Wheeler at a Linda Ronstadt concert."

The wary look was replaced with a big smile. He leaned forward to kiss me and I kissed him back. We held each other in the street and kissed again.

"I did a lot of thinking while I was in Mexico. I have a question to ask you."

He paused.

"Will you marry me?"

Another pause.

"Why?"

"What do you mean 'Why?'"

"Well, you asked me to live with you, then you asked me to move out. I'm just not sure what's going on."

"Fine, I won't ask you again."

"NO! I mean, I'm sorry! Of course I'll marry you. Will you please ask me again?"

Silence. I waited, not patiently. He said, "Let's go inside."

I kept my mouth closed as he got his things out of the car. We walked silently into my apartment. We sat down and looked at each other.

I apologized again. "I'm just confused, I guess. Why the sudden change of heart, especially with how things have been going?"

"I had time to think when I was in Mexico. I realized I don't want to travel around and play tennis. I kept thinking about you . . . us . . . and how much I love you. I want to be with you and start a family." He paused again. "Maybe you don't feel the same way."

"Of course I do! I love you and I want a family, too! I really am sorry about how I answered your question . . . will you please ask me again?"

"Nancy, will you marry me?"

"Yes!"

*   *   *

We called our family and friends. August 22, 1981, was set aside on calendars. I tried to talk Joel into having a small wedding because I had been married before but he would have none of it.

"Well, it's my first wedding and I want a big one."

There wasn't a lot of money (and I figured one wedding was enough for my parents to pay for), but Joel was able to trade goods and services with other small businesses. That was how we secured a photographer, a florist, and a wedding cake.

We made an appointment to see the rabbi at Temple Shalom. As we walked into the sanctuary, Joel squeezed my hand.

"This is perfect."

We met the rabbi and he explained what we needed to get married at the temple. We talked about ourselves and described our ideal ceremony.

Then he said that we would need to carry the chuppah from the back of the temple to the front during the ceremony. A chuppah is a canopy under which a Jewish couple stands during their wedding. It consists of a cloth or sheet stretched over four poles. We didn't mind the chuppah, but having to carry it to the front of the temple while dressed in our wedding finery, in front of all our guests, was not part of any Jewish tradition we knew of. We politely asked if there was perhaps an alternative. The rabbi was adamant. Eventually, we realized our attempts at changing his mind were futile, and gave in.

I was still feeling uncomfortable about all of the "big wedding" trappings, especially buying a wedding dress and having bridesmaids. So when Joel's friend, Barbara Simon, offered me her wedding dress, I was happy for it to be my "something borrowed." It was beautiful and fit perfectly; my mother helped me find a veil.

Joel contacted some Pueblo friends who played in a band. We booked them for the wedding.

My year at the BER at DU ended and I was offered a position as assistant director of special education for the Pikes Peak Board of Cooperative Education Services (BOCES). Luckily I received permission to start work, get married, go on a honeymoon, and come back to work.

As I planned for my marriage to Joel, I reflected on my first wedding. Mike and I had been in love, the real deal, "forever" as we'd said. Now here I was, about to promise the same to another man. Would this one "take?" Or would we find ourselves slowly veering down divergent paths—worse still, on parallel paths that gave the impression of proximity but rarely intersected? I'd seen marriages sputter out, including my own. Were Mike and I just too young, too naïve? Not vigilant enough at heading off the myriad ways love can wane?

I only knew that I loved Joel with a fierceness and totality that eclipsed any doubts I might have about wading into these waters once again.

*   *   *

The day of the wedding dawned clear and warm. It had been a fun week. Lee and Joel had played in the Colorado State Open tennis tournament and our families had cheered them on. They'd done well, but had both lost in the late rounds. Donna's parents held a lovely party for us. Now we were all at a pre-wedding luncheon, eating and toasting. Joel made his usual toast.

"My top to your top, my bottom to your bottom, my middle to your middle, here's hoping you get a little."

In Jewish tradition, the wedding starts after sundown, so we arrived at Temple Shalom in the late afternoon and met the rabbi for last minute instructions. He asked to see our rings. I showed him Joel's, a simple gold band that had been my grandfather's and fit Joel perfectly. Joel gave him my ring.

"You can't use this ring. It has stones in it."

Joel asked him for more explanation.

"The ring has to be an unbroken circle."

We once again pleaded our case, but knew it was a lost cause from our chuppah experience. Gary "Bubba" Snyder, a good friend of Joel's and our Jewish witness, was standing nearby. His wife Tina had a solid gold band, which she was happy to temporarily donate to the cause. I wanted my own ring, but I wanted to get married to Joel more.

Before leaving to get dressed, we saw the chuppah at the back of the temple. We looked at each other and giggled. As soon as the rabbi was in his office, we scurried into action and carried the chuppah to the front of the sanctuary. He could marry us with someone else's ring, but there was no way we were going to schlep a chuppah through the temple during our ceremony.

* * *

It was time to get married.

I could hear people entering the temple and peeked out of the dressing room. About three hundred people had been invited and it seemed most of them were now sitting a few feet from me. The chuppah was still up front. Gary, Donna's boyfriend, was playing his trumpet with a brass quartet. I saw Joel, standing with his brothers and the rabbi on the vestibule, and was overcome by how much I loved him.

Our siblings and Joel's parents walked down the aisle. My bridesmaid Tracy and maid of honor Donna followed. The quartet played Pachelbel's Canon in D, my cue. My mother took one hand; my father took the other. I looked up and saw Joel and made my way to his side.

The rabbi welcomed everyone and led a traditional wedding ceremony. At the end Joel stomped on the glass, we kissed, and everyone yelled "Mazel tov!" We were then escorted to the rabbi's office where, according to Jewish tradition, we were to consummate the marriage. This was one tradition we were happy to uphold.

More celebration ensued. Kosher food was served. The band started. We were hoisted and carried on chairs as family and friends danced around us, honoring another Jewish tradition. Joel persuaded the band to play an extra hour. Finally, our friends walked us out to Joel's 280z, which was adorned with "Just Married" in shaving cream and cans tied to the back bumper. Our first night as a married couple was spent in a hotel near the airport. The next morning we left for a week in Cancun, Mexico.

The best party of our lives had ended, but the best part of our lives was just beginning.

*   *   *

Nancy and Joel, on the occasion of your wedding—

About two weeks ago, I sprained my back. As it turned out, it wasn't serious, but it was painful and for several days I had trouble standing up straight and walking. One of the things I thought about was how disappointed I would be if I didn't recover in time so that I could walk down the aisle with Nancy and Dottie on August 22.

So I am very pleased to be taking an active part in this beautiful and important ceremony, to have walked down the aisle with Nancy and Dottie, and to have been able to come to Colorado and meet Joel's family and so many of Nancy and Joel's friends.

I would like to address a few words to Joel.

Joel, I speak to you as a happily married man, a man who has been married to a wonderful woman for more than 33 years. I would like to point out to you something that you may not have noticed: that Nancy and Dottie are very much alike in lots of ways. Let me list a few. A: They're both attractive, B: They're both bright, C: They're both considerate, D: Both dependable, E: Energetic, F: Forthright, G: Generous, H: Helpful, I: Industrious, J: Joyful, K: Kind, L: Loving . . . and so on.

What I am saying, Joel, is that because Nancy is so much like Dottie, you, like me, are a fortunate man. To coin a phrase, like mother, like daughter.

Congratulations, Joel. Speaking as the head of the Saltzman clan, I joyfully welcome you to the family and wish you the best.

Mazel tov!

(Note from my dad)

CHAPTER 7

ONE PLUS ONE EQUALS THREE

WE WANTED A FAMILY.

I was twenty-nine; Joel, twenty-seven. We were busy—I worked in fifteen school districts and Joel had his hands full at the shop—but we started trying right after we got married. It took only four months. We were ecstatic; so were our parents. This would be the first grandchild on both sides of the family. The baby was due September 28.

Even though I wasn't hungry for anything other than peanut butter, I loved being pregnant. When we heard the baby's heartbeat for the first time, it brought tears to our eyes. The heart rate indicated to the doctor that it was probably a girl, but in those days we had to wait until the birth to find out for sure. We called the baby Herzoglette and Yogurtla—don't ask me where we came up with the latter. Joel hoped for a left-hander because it would be an advantage on the tennis court.

We bought books of baby names. We liked Danielle or Dani for a girl. At first we liked Benjamin for a boy, but as we got closer to the delivery date we fell in love with the name Adam. William had been my grandfather's name and we thought Adam William Herzog had a nice ring to it.

The summer before the baby was born I would go to the Colorado Springs Racquet Club. I lay in the sun, watched Joel play tennis, and stood in the swimming pool. I was hot and big, and standing in the water felt wonderful.

In August, the Herzogs asked us to join them on their annual trip to the Aspen Musical Festival. Besides attending concerts, Joel played tennis and I took naps and read. We talked about what kind of parents we wanted to be. We laughed as his parents shared stories about raising five kids in a three-bedroom house with one bathroom. At night Joel put his hand on my stomach and felt the baby move and kick.

As the summer came to an end, I met with my advisor to talk about my dissertation and finishing my degree.

"When you got married, I was concerned that you might not finish your doctorate. Now that you're pregnant, I can pretty much say that you'll never finish," he predicted.

"I will finish," I predicted right back. I knew I would, even if it took me the maximum seven years the university allowed.

*   *   *

It was midnight. I'd started having contractions a few hours earlier. They were now five minutes apart, and I put on my maternity clothes for the last time.

Joel turned me towards him, and looked me in the eyes. He held me for a brief moment. We were excited and scared.

The 280z was flirting with the speed limit all the way to the hospital. My contractions were getting closer together by the minute, or at least that's how they felt. Once at the hospital, the nurse said I was eight centimeters dilated—only two from the promised land of ten centimeters and being able to push! The doctor arrived and Joel and I started the breathing techniques we'd learned in our class. Techniques that would help with the pain. Techniques that, much to my surprise, made absolutely no difference. It now felt like someone was repeatedly sticking a knife in my belly, then pulling it out, but my labor was too far along for me to have pain medications.

Finally, the magic ten centimeters.

My delivery nurse was a former midwife from Germany, and I was thrilled to hear she'd done this many times before.

"NANCY! POOSH!"

I pooshed.

"ZOOPER POOSHING, NANCY! ZOOPER POOSHING!"

I managed a tortured giggle between contractions.

At 3:37 a.m. on October 5, 1982, seven-pound, fourteen-ounce Adam William Herzog was born. The first thing he heard was,

"IT'S A BOY! IT'S A BOY! IT'S A BOY! IT'S A BOY!"

That was Joel.

I said, "So I guess you wanted a boy."

*   *   *

Dorothy Cohen and Irv Saltzman, my parents, married in June 1948.

My sister Linda, age four, and me, two.

Mom and Dad with me, Linda, and my brother Robbie, at our house outside Boston, 1956.

Siblings: Robbie, Andy, me, and Linda in our split-level home in Bloomington, Indiana, 1961.

Seventh grade (before braces), 1963.

The roller method of hair straightening, before high school graduation in 1970.

Senior yearbook picture. Looking forward to attending Colorado College.

Celebrating my twenty-first birthday with my parents and Rob in Colorado Springs, 1973.

With my college sweetheart, Mike Bertsch.

Donna Sheldon, Joel Herzog, and me, summer of 1979.

After packing the trailer we drove to Virginia, August 1979.

A classic Joel tennis pose, in a Total Tennis tee shirt and his ever-present shorts.

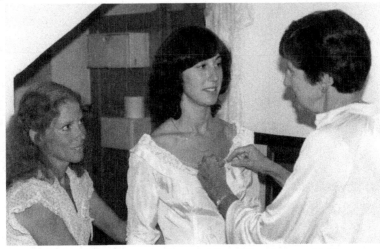

Last minute adjustments to my borrowed wedding dress, with Donna and Mom, August 22, 1981.

Mazel tov! Next to Temple Shalom's famous chuppah.

Happy and pregnant just before Adam was born, October 1982.

Adam William Herzog showing off his big brown eyes at six months.

Bath time for Adam in Bloomington, March 1983.

One of my favorite pictures of Adam, in our backyard, fall of 1983.

Eleven-year-old Adam.

Adam at one of our favorite spots in Aspen, August 1995.

Joel trying to keep up with Adam in the annual Ruth Washburn Cooperative Nursery School Foot Race.

"Look Ma! No hands!" Joel and Adam's balancing act in my parents' living room.

Good place for a nap—Adam on Joel's back.

My three favorite men in the world in 1983: my dad, Adam, and Joel.

Joel and Adam at the Cheyenne Mountain Zoo.

Seth gets a ride on his dad's back.

Proud Uncle Rob holding Seth for the first time.

Birthday number three for Seth.

Seth on the sundeck.

Seth with a friend.

Welcome baby Seth! September 1984.

Team candle blowing—Seth's birthday, 1987.

Adam, Uncle Lee, Seth, and Joel—future doubles teams.

Seth and Adam conserving bath water.

"Let's go to the hop!" at Broadmoor Elementary, spring 1991.

Right after my first chemo treatment, summer 1992. Note James Taylor tee shirt—we had just seen him live.

Seth helping match my shoe choice with my wig.

Family solidarity in dealing with my hair loss, August 1992.

Spring break in Mexico, 1993. Hair growing back, morale rebounding.

The Saltzman tribe at my parents' fortieth wedding anniversary in Bloomington. Front row: Seth, Adam, Mom, Dad, Linda. Back row: me, Joel, Andy with daughter Rachel, Andy's wife Mary, Rob, and Rob's partner Ed.

The Herzogs in Pueblo, Colorado. Front row: me pregnant with Adam, Joel's mother Sarah, his brother Michael, sister Marge, and dad Harvey. Back row: Joel, his sister Tracy, and brother Lee.

My favorite family photo, Tucson, 1995.

Back to School Night at Broadmoor Elementary, September 1995. Joel sitting at Seth's desk with Seth's self-made portrait and shirt on the back of the chair. The last photo I have of Joel.

Note that came with flowers from Joel during our first
holiday together.

Some of the things I remember about Adam . . .

— *How much I enjoyed making his afghan when you were pregnant*
— *Calling himself "Addie" when Seth was just an infant*
— *How he loved being called "Buddy" by his dad*
— *Standing in Joel's hand, being lifted into the air*
— *Running around without any pants on*
— *Sitting between the shoe boxes at Total Tennis*
— *Warning me, "Don't look, Aunt Lin!" when we were watching* Robin Hood *and a gory part was coming up*
— *Knowing all the words to* Home Alone

(From a letter my sister Linda wrote to me for my forty-fifth birthday)

*   *   *

When Adam was born he was a little jaundiced, a fairly common occurrence in Colorado because of the altitude, but we were assured that after a few days at home he would be fine. He was also hungry, and I was able to put my little breasts to use. Actually, they weren't so little any more. Adam caught on to the drill right away.

Grandparents arrived. Harvey and Sarah came to visit from Pueblo. Grandma Dot and Grandpa Irv flew in from Indiana. I loved showing off The Most Beautiful Baby Ever Born.

I also hated the thought of any discomfort every befalling TMBBEB. But two days after his delivery, we were back at the hospital to make sure he was no longer jaundiced. Grandma Dot and I chatted in the waiting room about what we would do for lunch. When we were called into the examination room, it suddenly became clear: the nurse was going to stick Adam in the heel with a razor blade to draw blood. I felt sick to my stomach. I held him while he screamed at the top of his lungs. My mother held me. Adam cried. I cried. My mother did not cry, but had her hands full with the two of us. Happily, the test for jaundice was negative. I nursed Adam for a little while so we could both calm down.

*   *   *

Adam had his own room right across from ours. My parents had given us a crib, and through the generosity of friends, we had diapers, toys, clothes, washcloths, mobiles—everything a baby could need or want. A friend had painted a rainbow on the back wall of Adam's room to match the rainbow on his crib. The room smelled like baby, diapers, and talcum powder.

Harvey and Sarah had to get back to Pueblo, but my parents stayed and helped, which was much appreciated. They stocked our refrigerator with food for breakfast, lunch, and dinner. They held Adam when he cried, or when I was getting ready to nurse him. My mother and I gave him baths. Joel, Adam, and my dad watched sports in the living room; I loved seeing the three of them doing "guy stuff." My mother urged me to take naps when I could, and she cooked her famous casseroles.

Along with being incredibly helpful, Grandma Dot had some specific ideas about how to raise a baby. She had raised four children of her own, after all. She thought that Adam should be on a set schedule for eating, napping, and bedtime. If he was supposed to be taking a nap and woke up, her opinion was to let him cry and learn to comfort himself. He should be in his crib for the amount of time designated for his nap. She discouraged me from nursing him between set feeding times.

Joel had not raised four children, but he also had some pretty specific ideas about how to care for Adam. My opinions fell somewhere in between the two of them, but Joel was my coparent, and I respected his instincts. We listened respectfully to my mother's suggestions, but I nursed Adam whenever he cried. We picked him up when he was finished with whatever *he* considered to be the appropriate length of time for a nap. This did not stop my parents from making suggestions, and it did not stop us from following our instincts.

It made me a little crazy, but it didn't bother Joel in the least.

*   *   *

October 18, 1990

Once I lost when I was playing football in my yard. I was very mad, but my friend said it is only a game. Then I thought about it and said your right. And we played another game of football. And I won. [sic]

(*From Adam's second grade journal*)

*   *   *

About a week after Adam was born, we had a ceremony in our living room called a Brit Milah. A Brit Milah is a Jewish circumcision performed on eight-day-old male infants by a mohel, a person who is trained in this Jewish ceremony. The rabbi who had married us was also a mohel and agreed to perform the ceremony. I had never been to a Brit Milah, let alone hosted one. Donna's parents, Howard and Dorothy Sheldon, had agreed to be Adam's godparents, and were required to be present at the ceremony. Also in attendance were all the Jews we knew and some friends, including Donna and Gary, Bubba and his wife Tina, Joel's brother Lee, and the two sets of grandparents.

The rabbi arrived and my eyes immediately shot to the small table he was carrying. I saw the straps that apparently would hold Adam's tiny arms and legs down while his foreskin was liberated from his penis. Just like at the hospital check for jaundice, reality hit me in a cold rush of panic. I took Joel into the bedroom. What were we thinking, having surgery done on our newborn, by someone who was not a medical professional, in a distinctly non-medical facility?

"This is barbaric. I don't want to do it."

Joel seemed torn. I think he was having similar twinges, but was prepared to trust Adam's manhood to the rabbi and a god-awful strap table.

"It's too late to change our minds. I want him circumcised and we can't go back to the hospital. I know he'll be okay."

I started to cry. He held me. We talked. I knew that this had been going on for thousands of years, with millions of babies, but those babies were not TMBBEB. Finally, he won me over. He waited patiently until I stopped crying.

We emerged from the bedroom and I took Adam from my mother. The rabbi soaked the end of a napkin in red wine and gave it to Adam to suck. Everyone got in a circle around the rabbi and Adam. While Adam was wine tasting, we took off his diaper. He stopped sucking and started crying. I turned away and buried my head in Joel's neck while the deed was done. Adam's cries went to a new pitch. He was quickly released from the table and handed to me. I took him into our bedroom. Joel put on Adam's diaper and I nursed him until we were both able to stop crying. The ordeal was over, though I now had a "celebration" to oversee. That evening Joel and I swore that if we had another male child we would have him circumcised at the hospital.

*   *   *

I took six weeks off work to be with Adam. Joel was busy at Total Tennis so Adam and I brought him lunch and kept him company. We had a backpack and a front snuggie pack that Joel could wear when he was working. He could string racquets with Adam on his back, and we set up a playpen in the back of the store for naps. I left the two of them alone each day to run errands. Joel wanted to see what it would be like for him to take care of Adam when I went back to work.

In the evenings, we loved hanging out with our tiny human entertainment center. Joel would lie on the couch with Adam on top of him. Sometimes they'd both take naps. We tried giving Adam formula but he threw it up immediately, demonstrating his projectile vomiting technique. We were impressed by how far such a small person could propel something from his stomach, but unfortunately his reaction meant that I had to pump my milk when I wasn't going to be around for a feeding.

I tried a manual pump but it took hours to get one bottle of milk. I rented an electric pump and sat on the floor in the bathroom, feeling distinctly bovine. There was a comical rhythm to it that I embellished for Joel's sake.

"MOO." Swish. Laughter.

"MOO." Swish. Laughter . . .

*   *   *

Dear Nancy,

As I can't find adequate words of sorrow maybe a positive memory would make the best condolence. In that regard, I did not know either Joel or Seth very well but do feel qualified to say a few words about Adam, who was part of my season as a Little League coach. He impressed me, not only with his obvious talent but also with the way he handled himself with the other boys and me. I never knew him to "dog" it; he always did his best. He always had something positive to say. Even when one of his teammates had just booted one, it was, "Good try." Finally, he treated me with respect, even though in a lot of ways he knew more about baseball (not to mention playing better) than I. In sum, a JOY.

I remember you taking time to talk with me about the kids. Now take time for yourself. Know that we are all pulling for you (even from great distances) and that you and your men are in our prayers. Also know that Robert said you would be back, because "she loves kids." May God be with you.

Mark Gregory

(One of Adam's Little League coaches; Mark's son Robert was one of my students)

*   *   *

Thanksgiving came just as my maternity leave was ending. My brother Rob now lived in Los Angeles and had moved in with a friend from law school, Ed Pierce. We invited them and the Herzogs for the holiday, and Ed—an extraordinary cook—promised to make Thanksgiving dinner in honor of Adam, even though Adam could neither appreciate nor partake in the feast. No matter, we stuffed ourselves on Adam's behalf, and took a long walk afterward.

About two weeks after the Thanksgiving visit, Rob called me.

"I have something to tell you," he began. I was pretty sure what it was going to be. Joel and I had discussed the probability of Rob being gay many times. When we visited him and Ed in California he always "gave up" his bed and slept with Ed so Joel and I could have the master bedroom. We couldn't figure out how to ask him without seeming intrusive, and had just left it to him to tell us if and when he wanted.

"It's something that I talked to Andy about this week," Rob continued. "Andy said that he thought I was acting kind of strange. I told him that it might be because I was not being open about who I am. I told him, and I want to share it with you guys. I'm gay. I love Ed and Ed loves me."

Without missing a beat I said, "Rob, I'm so glad you're telling me this. I love Ed, too, and of course I understand why he would love you."

I hung up the phone and told Joel. Like me, he was pleased Rob had found someone who made him deeply happy. Everyone should be so lucky.

* * *

Before having Adam I had convinced my boss to let me job share and work three days a week. On my work days, Joel took Adam to the store with him. Friends and shoppers stopped by to see and hold Joel's new "partner." I loved hearing about Adam's adventures. Joel had a long list of people who came in to feed and diaper Adam each day—it was still a tennis shop, but Adam was now the main attraction.

That holiday season was especially busy for Joel and the store. He kept Total Tennis open late the week before Christmas and finally closed at 6 p.m. on Christmas Eve. We had celebrated Hanukkah with Joel's parents in Pueblo, and on Christmas Day we flew to Indiana. Linda and Andy were there to meet Adam. Rob had to stay in California for work. The family dynamics that had made recent past visits tense gave way to everyone's excitement and fascination with Adam. He *was* endlessly captivating, if I did say so myself.

Joel had not celebrated Christmas growing up. Although Jewish, we always had. Every year, my parents loaded us in the station wagon after Thanksgiving and drove us to a tree lot outside of town. After the obligatory arguments over the best tree, my mother always made the final selection.

I don't know when I realized that Christmas was also a religious holiday. When I was five or six, my mother overheard a friend ask me if I was Jewish. I said, "I'm either Jewish or not Jewish. I can never remember." I must have figured out at some point that I was Jewish but not religious. I guess you could call us holiday opportunists—we celebrated gift giving at Christmas and sometimes lit candles for Hanukkah. Any excuse for a celebration. Raising our own family, Joel and I gave Adam and Seth a similar upbringing, though Joel was a little more traditional. While we didn't "practice" a religion, we identified ourselves as Jewish. When Seth was five or six he saw the tree that Joel had in his store window. He told Joel he had a question.

"Dad? Are we Christmas or are we Jewish?"

"We are Jewish."

"Why do you have a tree in the store?"

"Because other people celebrate Christmas. They buy presents in my store."

"Oh."

This seemed to satisfy him.

* * *

Joel may have consented to a tree in his store a few years later, but that first holiday with Adam in Bloomington, he could not get over the tree in my parents' house. A Jewish family celebrating Christmas made absolutely no sense to him. I loved getting presents, and any occasion that called for it was okay by me. Joel also knew how much I enjoyed being with my family, and kindly only shared his misgivings with me.

Our second night in Bloomington my mother and I were baking cookies and watching *White Christmas* on TV. We were talking about Adam and how great it was to be a parent. My mom stopped and looked at me.

"Do you think Rob will ever get married and have children?"

I paused and simply said, "No."

"Do you know something I don't know?"

I wasn't sure how to answer. Clearly, Rob had not talked to my parents. I didn't know where he stood on them knowing. But I also didn't want to lie.

I told her what Rob had said to me. She calmly answered, "I've thought he was gay since high school."

Later, when I called Rob to tell him about the conversation, he chuckled, "Well, I wish she would have told me that back in high school!" He made plans to visit my parents in January so he could talk to them in person.

CHAPTER 8

OF BABIES AND MARATHONS

WE LOVED BEING parents. So much so that we decided to go for it again. Coincidentally, I got pregnant the exact time of year as I had with Adam (probably New Year's Eve). Once again, I was a happy pregnant lady. Once again, the doctor told us the heartbeat indicated it was a girl. And once again, we chose Danielle as a name. For some reason, we were sure this one was going to be a girl, and we didn't even seriously consider boy names.

I had the summer off to get ready and to finish writing my proposal for my Ph.D. It was approved at the end of the summer, right before I went back to work in August. Joel starting taking Adam to work with him again.

On September 23, the baby's due date, I woke up at 5:50 a.m. with contractions. A crystal clear thought went through my mind

How could I have forgotten how much this hurts?

By 7 a.m. the contractions were five minutes apart. We had arranged to have Adam stay with friends, and after dropping him off, we headed for the hospital. If the pain of the contractions was any indication, my labor was progressing quickly.

At the hospital, I was hooked up to a monitor to measure the intensity of the contractions. I felt the surge of pain coming on. This would be a major one, I could tell. Joel and the nurse watched the monitor. I moaned.

"That was not a contraction," Joel announced.

"You're in false labor," the nurse added, as if Joel was the doctor, and she was confirming his assessment.

In exceedingly colorful terms, I begged to differ with them.

The nurse told us to go home and come back when I was really in labor. I wanted to tell her to go home and come back when she was really a nurse. But since it was two against one, we left, picked up Adam, and went to the Daylight Donut shop. I ate a Daylight special; Adam smeared chocolate all over his face.

I got into bed at home and tried to relax. The contractions backed off a bit. At 11:30 a.m., they were getting closer together again. Five minutes apart.

"We need to go to the hospital," Joel said.

Ha! I wasn't falling for that humiliating trick again.

"No way. They were five minutes apart before, and you and that nurse told me it was false labor."

At 12:45, the contractions had progressed to considerably less than five minutes apart, and Joel said in his sternest voice, "We are going to the hospital. Now." I decided he might be right, and was looking forward to proving to the nurse that I was, in fact, in labor.

We didn't want to bother our friends who had watched Adam earlier, so Joel called his brother Lee to see if he could help out. He was playing tennis, but that was no problem. We drove by the courts and handed Adam off to Uncle Lee. With every contraction, I could feel Joel push harder on the gas pedal, which made me want to push right along with him. But I knew better. We arrived at the hospital a little after 1 p.m.

Forty-five minutes later, little Danielle arrived. Except that Danielle was a boy. (Our doctor was wonderful, but he obviously had no business predicting baby gender based on heart rate.) Joel and I looked at each other with blank stares. The delivery nurse said, "What do you think of the name Seth?" And just like that, Adam William Herzog had a doubles partner: Seth Michael Herzog. The Other Most Beautiful Baby Ever Born.

* * *

Mom
Nice, woman
Sharing, talking, kissing
A very great person
Principal

Happy Mother's Day, Mom!
Love,
Seth

(Mother's Day card to me, made by Seth)

* * *

I took six weeks off again and went back to work after Thanksgiving break. Joel took both boys to the store on the days I worked. Unlike his urp-inclined brother, Seth had no problem with formula and took a bottle easily. No more "MOO," swish, laughter.

I loved that Joel took the boys to the store with him. Some days I would arrive after work, and it would be utter pandemonium: customers waiting for racquets, Seth in the playpen crying, Adam opening boxes of shoes. None of it seemed to bother Joel. No matter what happened during the day, he reveled in having the boys with him. I frequently told him that I had no idea how he was able to manage everything—he just looked at me like I was crazy. I felt like the luckiest mother in the world, and never worried about the boys when I was at work. They were with Joel, the best babysitter—and father—ever.

We were now a busy family of four, but my determination to achieve my dream of being Dr. Saltzman had not diminished; in fact, if anything I was more committed than ever to finishing this marathon.

All I had to do was collect my data, finish writing my dissertation, and complete my defense for my Ph.D. A walk in the park.

* * *

Okay, not quite a walk in the park. Maybe more like a climb up Pikes Peak.

Every day was packed. I was either at my job or immersed in my dissertation. Joel was at the store Monday through Saturday, and had the boys Tuesday, Wednesday, and Thursday. He tried to play tennis on Sunday mornings and maybe once a week during the day or in the evening. I was collecting data for my dissertation, which meant Mondays and Fridays were spent shuttling between school districts, with Seth and Adam in tow. I always tried to work a stop at a playground into the day, but while the boys played, my mind buzzed.

Adam got a pretend motorcycle that he named "Ah-me," or at least that's what it sounded like, since he couldn't spell. He would push himself around the neighborhood on the sidewalk, while Joel and I trailed behind with Seth in the stroller or on our backs. After their nightly baths, Joel would read to Adam and I nursed Seth. After the boys were down, we would watch a little TV together, or Joel would read and fall asleep. I listened to my research tapes, recorded data, or did some writing. I usually passed out about 1 a.m.

By the end of the school year, Adam was almost three and Seth was nine months old. I was able to spend more time with the boys again. I also finished writing my dissertation. When I completed a chapter I would send it to my father to read and give me feedback. I asked for his help with proofreading—this was one "paper" I couldn't afford to get an F on. Dad would call me on Sundays and go through each paragraph with me.

Finally, on July 24, 1985—five years, eleven months, and twelve days after I had arrived on the University of Virginia campus to begin my doctoral program—Joel and the boys drove me to the University of Denver for my two-hour oral defense of my dissertation. Since it had been a joint effort to get this far, I figured they deserved to be there for the home stretch.

Defending a doctoral dissertation usually involves the candidate sitting before a jury of senior academics who have read the dissertation. The candidate then answers questions from the jury about the dissertation, which can include explaining research presented, conclusions reached, and other aspects of the dissertation that determine its viability.

As I sat in the DU conference room, being peppered with questions about my research, I could see out the window. Joel and Adam were running up and down the big hills. Seth was perched on Joel's shoulders. They were all screaming with laughter. Adam would run up, then roll down. It was a striking contrast: the intense intellectual focus of the proceedings in the conference room, versus the carefree joy of the scene out the window. I realized how vital both of them were to my life. My mind, here, thoroughly engaged in the calling I felt so passionately; my heart outside with the family I loved completely.

When the grilling was over, I was asked to wait in the hallway while the committee discussed my defense. I stuck my head out the door and waved to Joel. I mouthed, "I'm almost done. I'll find out in a few minutes." I closed the door and waited. The advisor who had four years earlier predicted I wouldn't finish my doctoral program came out of the room. He took my hand and shook it.

"Congratulations, Dr. Saltzman."

He gave me a hug. I went back into the conference room and thanked my committee for awarding me a Ph.D. Then I headed outside to thank the three men who had helped me cross the finish line.

* * *

Dear Nance . . .

I wanted to write to tell you how great I think you are to be doing what you're doing. When I'm honest with myself, I'm forced to admit that one of the main reasons I never finished my doctoral degree was that I was just plain too insecure and scared to lay myself on the line the way you are. It sure as hell is a hard thing to do.

All of which is just my way of saying good luck, keep your chin up, try to relax, and I'm sure you'll do a super job. You are terrific, and anyone who doesn't recognize that is an idiot! (And I, of course, am a completely impartial observer!) One thing I really am sure of is that we need bright, sensible, caring, sane, good-natured people like you in education.

Love,
Mom

CHAPTER 9

BOYS MEET WORLD

HAPPILY DONE WITH school, I was able to go back to work full-time. Although it worked having the boys at the store while they were babies, and Joel knew he would miss them, once they got older we needed a caregiver who could give them undivided attention.

Over the next several years, we were lucky to find wonderful women who loved Adam and Seth and were loved and appreciated in return. They would take the boys to the zoo or parks, read to them, play with them, and keep them happy and safe. Well, mostly safe.

One young woman we hired lived in a rural town east of Colorado Springs. She hit it off with the boys, and seemed like a good fit. She owned a truck and would come to the house when Joel left for work. I would relieve her when I got home after a day in the schools.

She had worked for us for about six weeks when Joel, the kids, and I were driving on a major local highway. Adam suddenly chirped up, excited.

"This is the curve we went around when I almost fell out of the babysitter's truck."

Trying to not jump to conclusions, I asked for clarification.

"I was sitting in the truck when the door opened. I almost fell out but the babysitter caught me." He was very proud of himself—and her.

We were also impressed with her quick reflexes—less so with her supervisory skills. Other care arrangements for the boys were quickly made.

* * *

Dear Nancy,

The smile of Seth. The understanding, smiling face of Adam when we were pulling Seth's leg about something. Seth's great laugh! Adam's ability to listen and comprehend with a maturity above his years. Oh, what wonderful kids. They had a compassion for people they surely learned from their father! (And, of course, Mom!)

We all miss the great people they were destined to become.

Sincerely,
Brian Reed

(The boys' P.E. teacher)

*   *   *

Joel decided to move his store downtown. It would be more convenient for customers who wanted same-day racquet stringing and also closer to the Country Club of Colorado and the Broadmoor Tennis Club. I was ready to make a professional change, too. I wanted to work in one place instead of fourteen school districts.

Sam Merrill, the principal at Horizon Middle School, hired me to be his assistant. He said he liked me because I had spaghetti sauce on my blouse when I interviewed (Sam is Italian).

Dynamic, funny, smart, and committed to providing a great environment in which students could learn, Sam was a terrific mentor. He taught me how to have fun and be an effective and strong leader at the same time. After Sam had worked with me for two years, he encouraged me to apply for jobs in a larger district, where I'd have a better chance to become a principal.

Timberview Middle School (TMS) was going to open in January of 1988. I was offered the position of assistant principal. Until the opening, I would be in charge of TMS students in trailers behind another middle school. We would use the other school's gym, cafeteria, and bathrooms but other than that, we were on our own. I had seventh and eighth graders. Bill Shell, who would be Timberview's principal, had sixth graders at a nearby high school. I loved going to work; the kids and staff made me laugh every day. It was a great semester but we were all very happy when we moved into our own building in January.

*   *   *

Life with a houseful of men was fun because Joel made it that way. He bounced out of bed every morning, ready to get the boys up by tickling them, diapering them when they were young, helping them dress when they got older. He fed them breakfast while I got ready for work—exactly as my dad had done when I was growing up. Seth always helped me pick out my shoes for the day. It was a funny, small tradition that we both enjoyed. The only day the boys and I were on our own for breakfast was Saturday, because Joel went in to work early. We would show up at the store around lunchtime with burgers and fries. Joel would stop whatever he was doing and act as if he hadn't seen us in days.

Early in our lives as parents I had a glimpse of Joel as the father of athletes. Adam and Seth's nursery school held a fundraiser. One of the main events was a running race, held at Acacia Park in downtown Colorado Springs. The race was on a sidewalk, from the corner of one block straight to the opposite end.

The three-year-olds, including Adam, lined up at the starting line. Adam had a race number tightly pinned to his chest. He had practiced his "starts" with Joel before the race. Joel held Seth in his arms as he walked halfway down the block to watch the race. At "GO!" the kids took off. Adam put his head down and charged. He led from beginning to end. I hustled down the sideline with all the other parents to the finish line. Adam out-ran all the competitors, and Joel out-yelled all the parents. If there had been buttons on Joel's tee shirt they would have been popping off right and left.

From the race in Acacia Park, Adam never looked back. He was a natural athlete who excelled at every sport he tried. Seth also became a good athlete, but was more interested in having fun and entertaining his friends with his mastery of farting and giggling.

Joel signed the boys up for soccer and t-ball as soon as they were old enough. They had been playing tennis from the time they could hold a junior racquet. They took swimming lessons when they were infants, and Adam had mastered all four strokes by the time he was six. Seth convinced me that I could teach him to swim so he never took formal lessons. He was happy messing around in the water and doing the crawl. T-ball gave way to Little League for both boys.

Skiing was another sport in their repertoire. Joel had skied with his family growing up and could handle any terrain. I had learned how in college but was barely more than a beginner.

We enrolled both boys in ski lessons at the Broadmoor ski area when they were five and seven. They had class twice a week after school during the winter months. On Sundays, Joel would take them to Broadmoor, situate their mini skis between his, then fly down the slope with them. I waited at the bottom of the hill, listening to their peals of laughter all the way down.

On the last day of lessons at Broadmoor, Joel took a final run with the boys. It had gotten icy at the top and Seth fell. Joel took one look at Seth's leg twisted sideways in his boot and knew it wasn't good. Seth was brought down the mountain in a toboggan and Joel carried him to his Jeep.

I was supposed to have been at the lessons to watch but was still at school. Joel had driven the carpool that day, so was responsible for Adam, Seth, and a neighbor boy. At the hospital, Joel called me. I think if he could have strangled me through the phone he would have. Not only was he dealing with Seth, who was in terrible pain, he'd also had to take the neighbor home before heading to the hospital.

"You were supposed to be there."

"I know, I'm sorry."

"Yes I know you're sorry, but you were supposed to be there."

I rushed to the hospital and arrived just as Joel was going into the emergency room with Seth. Adam and I waited outside and could hear Seth crying.

He had broken his tibia and fibula, both bones below the knee. They needed to be reset, but because he'd eaten recently, they couldn't give him general anesthesia. Adam and I could hear him scream as the doctor set his bones, with only local anesthetic to dampen the pain. Honestly, I was relieved it was Joel behind the curtain with Seth, not me.

Seth came home from the hospital with a cast that went all the way up to his groin. He would have to wear it for several weeks and couldn't walk or go to school. He was too small for crutches, so Joel was carrying him everywhere. We got him a wheelchair. He hung out with his dad at Total Tennis. After four weeks he got a walking cast, but it was quite an ordeal.

Even after that experience, he chose to ski again the next winter, this time staying with me on the beginner slopes until he could keep up with his father and brother.

*   *   *

Some of the things I remember about Seth . . .

— *How much I enjoyed visiting him right after he was born*
— *His broken leg, and pushing him in the wheelchair*
— *How incredible he was at hockey, despite being small*
— *Holding and dancing with him to the song about peanut butter*
— *Him shoveling sand in the big inner tube at Cape Cod, oblivious to everyone and everything*
— *WoWo, his stuffed dog*
— *The time he went up on stage as a volunteer when we took him to the symphony*
— *Walking him to school and being introduced to his whole class*

(From my sister Linda's letter for my forty-fifth birthday)

* * *

Although I wasn't much of a skier, I was a good ice skater. I had taught skating in high school. When Adam and Seth discovered photos of me at Colorado College playing hockey, they decided we should all try skating.

Our first spin on the ice, Joel clung to the side of the rink for dear life and pulled himself along. I spent most of my time worrying about another trip to the ER, but I also enjoyed being better at a sport than he was. The boys started out using their dad's technique, but were soon skating circles around Joel. He pointed out that Adam and Seth were a little closer to the ground, so falling was not as big an issue.

The boys liked skating and were encouraged by a good friend of Joel's, Mary Polaski. Mary's sister is Bonnie Blair Cruikshank, the five-time Olympic gold medalist in speed skating. Mary worked with speed skaters and allowed Adam and Seth to join them on Sundays. Mary's sons, Scott and Nic, were close to Adam and Seth in age and the boys became fast friends. As Adam got better at skating we thought he might have fun playing hockey in a junior recreational league. He was up for it.

Adam's first hockey coach was Doug Dragoo, the dad of one of Adam's friends at school. Mr. Dragoo was very patient with the boys and knew a lot about teaching hockey. Adam was a quick learner who loved the equipment and going fast. Once he got the hang of it he was fun to watch. He even scored a goal occasionally. Seth looked forward to being old enough to play.

We laughed a lot during those early hockey days because watching kids play was like watching a group of ants chasing a grain of sugar. There was no distinction between offensive and defensive players; the boys just followed the puck in a pack.

Once Seth started playing, our lives became more hectic. Practices were typically twice a week for each boy, sometimes back-to-back. Each had a game on weekends. The rinks were all over the city. Many evenings we met for dinner between practices, at Wendy's, McDonald's, or Taco Bell.

Joel and I enjoyed hockey and the people we met. When I was late getting to the rink from school, Joel usually forgave me because he was having such a good time watching the players and socializing. He had his own harem of hockey moms whom he kept entertained with his jokes and banter. It was all in good fun, and I loved his gift of gregariousness. No matter how boring the practice, Joel could always light up the room—or the bleachers.

As the boys got older, the sports became more competitive. There were tryouts for teams. During the school year the boys would have school, homework, hockey practice, and a game each weekend. Summer meant hockey camps, more hockey practice, and games. It also meant tennis practice and eventually tennis tournaments for the boys and for Joel. I was head cheerleader.

Our lives were full, but we thought it would be great to have a third child—maybe even a girl. Getting pregnant with the boys had been easy, but the third time was not the charm. It turned out that I had endometriosis, which made it hard for me to conceive. So, during Christmas vacation of 1989, I had surgery to correct the problem. Despite the operation and our "best efforts," I still didn't get pregnant. We decided that we were very lucky to have the amazing children we did, and chose to count our blessings.

*   *   *

Dearest Nancy,

Our hearts and thoughts are with you. Hope and faith exist. Know that friends such as us will keep them for you. Your grief must be overwhelming, but know our love and support is unending. The dark days do not last forever.

Adam's sauntering walk, coming around the corner at school, is fresh in my mind. Always looking like the cat who swallowed the canary. Always in the middle, surrounded and admired by his great friends.

Seth, in his too-big shirt with that very contagious smile, is there, too. His buddies yelling, "Seth! Seth! Over here! Pass!" And off he goes, the star of each field. Seth-er-oo-nee forever.

And there is sweet Joel, always zooming around in his old red Jeep, waving to me over the steering wheel. Forever posed against the school fence, waiting for his boys and you.

Nancy, your lifetime of kindness and always trying to "do the right thing" has touched hundreds of people and we are all here for you, anytime.

We love you!
Elizabeth and Doug Dragoo, and family

(Doug was Adam's first hockey coach)

CHAPTER 10

FIRST THEY TAKE YOUR RADIO

ON THE LAST DAY of school at Timberview Middle School in 1990, I was honored to give the graduation speech for our eighth graders. Their families attended and I shared pictures of the Timberview staff from when they were in eighth grade. It was a fun and festive celebration. After the ceremony, some of the staff went out for drinks to celebrate a successful year. I remember sitting with my friends, nursing an iced tea, and thinking what a great life I had: a wonderful family, fun people to work with, a job that had a real impact on the lives of adolescents, and an approaching summer vacation. Couldn't ask for much more. Reaching under my arm, I absently scratched a minor itch.

My fingers landed on a lump.

Almost instantaneously, there was an even larger lump in my throat.

The one under my arm reminded me of a marble but was more malleable. I didn't say a word to anyone, finished my drink, and drove straight home.

The world around me was reassuringly normal. The kids were playing in the back yard; the babysitter left when I arrived. School was over for the year, everyone was happy. It was probably nothing—after all, I felt fine. Still, when Joel arrived home from the tennis shop, I enlisted a non-professional second opinion.

"I need you to do a thorough breast exam." A wry little smile played on his lips.

"Actually, I'm worried about this lump under my arm," I said, a bit exasperated.

"It can't be anything, you're too young." I was thirty-eight.

"I want to have a doctor check it out right away."

I had a regular ob/gyn, but I wasn't sure how quickly I could get in to see him. Joel had a friend who was a gynecologist. He called and made arrangements for me to see the doctor the next day.

*   *   *

Although I was worried, the lump *wasn't* in my breast. I told Joel I was fine going alone. I had a lot of end-of-year work to do at school, so I would be distracted until my appointment in the afternoon.

I sat anxiously in the waiting room and filled out forms. Several pregnant women were doing the same.

I wish I was pregnant instead of here with a lump.

I wondered what I had done to cause the marble in my armpit. I'd always made fun of my breasts for being small.

Did I get this lump because I was ashamed of them? Like when I put on my sister's bra and stuffed it with socks and pranced around the bedroom? I used to look in the mirror trying on different shirts to see which offered the most cleavage. I went to school with Kleenex-stuffed bras. All those contortions in gym class so no one would see. Maybe this was payback from the body gods because I wasn't happy with the breasts I'd been given.

The doctor asked me how Joel was doing. He told me to stand up without the gown. It occurred to me that I might see him again socially and felt a little embarrassed, but he was very professional. Also, my worry seemed to outweigh any potential awkwardness. He felt the lump.

"Nancy. I don't know what the hell that is. Do you know any surgeons?"

No, no, no. That's not your line. Your line is, "Oh, that? I've seen thousands of them. Just a cyst. Happens all the time. Besides, it's not even in your breast. No, nothing to worry about here."

I shook my head no.

"I'm going to call a surgeon and set up an appointment for you as soon as possible. Why don't you get dressed, and I'll explain my thinking."

Your "thinking"? All you did was feel it—how can there be "thinking" to explain already?

We met in his office. He sat behind a big desk with informational pamphlets about women and their bodies. A small model of a woman's uterus "sat" to his left. He checked my records.

"It's good that you had a mammogram done earlier this year, and it was normal. I still don't know what to tell you about that lump. A surgeon will be more familiar with this kind of thing. I have arranged for you to see one today at 3 p.m."

Today? 3 p.m.? That's an hour from now.

As much as I wanted answers quickly, I also didn't want to be the dire case that doctors cleared their schedules to see immediately.

I asked the Big Question.

"Do you think it's cancer?"

"I don't know. Cancer usually has a different feel."

A different feel! He said cancer had a different feel. Yes!

A thimbleful of relief tempered my growing panic. I asked to use the phone in the office to call Joel. When he answered, I started crying.

"He doesn't know what my lump is, and I'm going to see a surgeon now."

"I love you, babe. I know it will be all right."

I needed someone to yell at.

"All right?! How can it be all right?!"

"Your breasts are too perfect to have anything wrong with them." I could smile at that—he was being deliberately lighthearted, and his blind optimism buoyed me.

"I'll talk to you after I see the surgeon. I love you."

I drove to the surgeon's office and went through much the same process as before. He sent me to the hospital for another mammogram.

Afterward, I drove south on Highway 25, deep in thought.

Don't jump to conclusions. Yes, this looks bad, but we don't know for sure, so why go there? On the other hand, if I prepare for the worst I'll be ready and it won't hit so hard. Could I really have cancer? I do eat junk food sometimes, but I'm only thirty-eight. That's young. Shouldn't a person be able to get away with junk food now and then when they're thirty-eight? It can't be cancer.

I walked in the door and hugged the boys. When Joel came home, the boys were playing and I was cooking. He walked straight to me and gave me a long hug. Almost immediately the phone rang. I recognized the surgeon's voice.

"Mrs. Saltzman, I have reviewed your mammogram and I think you have breast cancer. You are most likely going to need a mastectomy or bilateral mastectomies but you can have reconstruction. I would like you to schedule surgery as soon as possible."

Bam! I hadn't seen the two-by-four that hit me, but its impact sent me reeling. I tried to continue the conversation that seemed no more meaningful to the person on the other end than a reminder call for teeth cleaning.

"Let's get you scheduled as soon as possible. I hope you've been flossing."

"Okay. Ummm ... can my husband and I come in and meet with you? I have some questions ... and I think I'd like my husband to be with me ... he may have some questions as well."

"I can answer any questions you have at the time of the surgery; there is no need to meet beforehand."

Whap! That one came from the other side, not as hard, but still a blow.

"Well ... I would like to meet with you before the surgery."

He paused.

"Mrs. Saltzman, I don't need to meet with you but I will tell you one thing." He paused. "If you go in looking like a girl, you'll come out looking like a girl."

I was terrified and livid in equal measures.

*   *   *

Through the shop, Joel also knew a few surgeons, one of whom he was sure would have a better bedside manner. He called Terry O'Rourke that night and scheduled an appointment.

A good-looking, fit, and friendly man, Dr. O'Rourke found Joel and me sitting in the examination room holding hands. In stark contrast to the phone call from the previous surgeon, his warm personality and smile put us both at ease. We looked at the results of the two mammograms. My breast tissue had changed in the six months since my baseline mammogram. He thought that the lump under my arm was an infected sweat gland. Joel joked, "How could that be? You never exercise!" The three of us laughed.

The lump would need to be biopsied, along with tissue from my breast. Dr. O'Rourke said that the odds were in my favor. He was pretty sure that it was not cancer because 85 percent of biopsies of the breast are benign. Surgery was scheduled and we felt like we had been given a reprieve.

A week later, the biopsy took place in the hospital. I was taken into an examination room with a big machine and a cold examination table. A stocky young male hospital technician stood on my left side while my small and very cold right breast was released from the gown.

"I will be compressing your breast. It won't hurt because breast tissue does not have any feeling." He placed my breast into the machine.

"OW! That hurts. I think my breast tissue has feeling."

"Well, it shouldn't."

"Mine does."

"I need to compress this to make sure I mark the tissue correctly. I will stick a needle into the area that I can see on the mammogram while I am compressing your breast. I will leave the needle in your breast. When you go into surgery the doctor will be able to see the area that I have marked and he will remove the tissue."

After the initial thirty-second needle plunge into my breast, it turned out that the technician was partially correct about the pain. The numbing of my mind and body from fear did lessen the "discomfort." It didn't do much for my functionality, however. I had a sense I might pass out, but I couldn't fall down. My body could go nowhere while my breast was held hostage by the smashing machine.

"Let me check that. I'm not sure I got it in the right place."

He took another stab. Literally.

"That hurts."

"Hmmm. It isn't supposed to."

"Yes. So you said."

Finally, on the third stab, he was satisfied with the placement, apparently. I wasn't looking.

"The nurse from surgery will come get you when they're ready for you. You can wait here."

I was alone, sitting on a table in an examining room, waiting to have surgery. I thought about two previous times I had been in the hospital—both happy occasions. Maybe this would end in a positive way—not like bringing children home from the hospital, but with a cancer-free diagnosis. I would regale friends and family with the tales of my experience. I would appreciate my life even more than I already did. If I did have breast cancer, maybe I would be able to get a new set of breasts that were bigger than the originals. I was nervous and scared, but I was trying to put a positive spin on what my mother was calling an "adventure."

"Miss Saltzman?" The door opened and a nurse appeared.

"We'll be going into surgery now."

We entered the operating room. Three people were adjusting machines that were beeping and pinging. The nurses looked at me and signaled that I should lie down. I smiled; they smiled. I lay back and looked up into a bright light. I heard the doctor's voice as he came into the room.

"Good morning, Nancy!"

Joel had given Dr. O'Rourke's sons tennis lessons and he was very fond of Joel. I hoped he liked me a little, too. His presence helped me relax.

"We are going to be getting things going here in just a minute. The anesthesiologist will be coming in to talk to you. I'll be right back; I'm going to go scrub up."

The anesthesiologist came into the room. He took hold of my left arm and said, "You will feel a little stick and a burn as I put the IV into your arm. You will taste something metallic, then feel sleepy."

Suddenly, I was more relaxed than I'd been since before discovering the lump.

* * *

I was waking up. Joel was there.

"Dr. O'Rourke said he got a good sample of tissue. He thinks everything is benign." I looked at Joel and tried to remember if benign was good or bad.

No sooner had he spoken than Dr. O'Rourke joined us.

"I think everything will be fine. We need to do a frozen section, so we'll have more results in about twenty-four hours. I will call you tomorrow."

Joel helped me get dressed, wheeled me out, and loaded me in the car. He drove the mile to our house from the hospital. I was a little groggy and walked up the stairway to our bedroom. I looked at all the eight-by-ten pictures of our family that lined the walls.

"What cute kids we have," I said. Then I crawled into bed and fell fast asleep.

I woke to the sound of Adam and Seth coming up the stairs, shushing each other.

"Are you still sleeping?" I heard one of them say as they poked their heads into the bedroom.

"I'm awake." They crawled onto the bed with me.

* * *

I had to stay home from work the next day. I was sore from the surgery, but buying into Dr. O'Rourke's optimistic assessment. I had called my parents after the surgery to give them the hopeful news. A huge bouquet of balloons offering "Congratulations!" was being delivered just as the phone rang.

"Hi. This is Dr. O'Rourke. How are you feeling?"

I told him I was a little sore but doing fine.

"I have something I need to share with you. I'm sorry to tell you that the frozen section that took twenty-four hours to analyze showed that you had some cancerous cells in your breast."

The "Congratulations!" balloons bobbed gently next to me.

At least I didn't feel like I'd been hit by a piece of dimensional lumber again. Dr. O'Rourke's bad news delivery style was exponentially more sympathetic than the first surgeon's. But it was still bad news.

Crap.

* * *

I made appointments with an oncologist and a radiation oncologist. We learned what "carcinoma in situ" and "lobular carcinoma" meant. I went to the library to look at pictures of women who had undergone mastectomies. I couldn't understand how a surgeon could just remove your breast. I imagined a hole the size of my breast in my chest and wondered if they used something like a paper cutter to remove it. The pictures helped. I hoped I wouldn't need a mastectomy.

I wanted to talk to someone who had survived breast cancer. Joel had a friend whose wife had recently completed treatment, so he connected us. She told me about her experience after her diagnosis. She was upbeat, had worked during most of her treatment, and was doing well. It helped to hear her story.

There was some difference of opinion about the best course of treatment for my case. They had not gotten "clean margins" on my biopsy, a euphemism for not removing all the cancer. So no matter what treatment I chose, I would need more surgery to try to get all the cancerous tissue. If I kept my breast and had a lumpectomy, I would need to have radiation therapy. The radiation oncologist believed he could prevent a recurrence of cancer using this treatment, but the odds were not as good as removing the entire breast. The surgical oncologist recommended a mastectomy— more radical, but a better chance of getting all the cancer. There was the option of following up the mastectomy with a relatively new breast cancer drug, tamoxifen, which was showing good results. And, there were some suspicious lumps in my left breast, so I needed to have a biopsy of those lumps during the next surgery. It was all stressful and confusing, with no guarantees. And it was my decision to make. I needed time to figure out what to do. Dr. O'Rourke assured me that a few weeks would not affect the outcome.

I sent my medical records to a family friend, Dr. Tony Pizzo, in Bloomington. His daughter Sarah had been one of my classmates. Her brother was also a doctor, and father and son both reviewed my case. They recommended a mastectomy. As hard as it was to consider the more radical route,

I knew the Pizzos were giving me the same advice they would give their own mothers, sisters, or wives. I talked it over with Joel. He also encouraged me to go with the more conservative decision of a mastectomy, agreeing that we needed to ensure the best odds possible. We chose to not follow up with the tamoxifen, however, because I was still hoping to get pregnant and the drug was not compatible with pregnancy.

I scheduled the surgery for the end of July. I didn't want to miss my twentieth high school reunion in June. Joel, Adam, Seth and I went to Bloomington, and I had a good time. It was nice to be with my parents, to have some time to unwind after the school year, and to talk to my mom about the cancer. She was supportive and pragmatic, as always. I also spoke to one of my mom's friends who was a cancer survivor. Talking to her made me feel hopeful.

*   *   *

Returning to Colorado Springs from Indiana, we discovered that someone had broken into my car and stolen my radio. That night, the boys were still talking about it. I decided it was time to let them know about my surgery.

"Hey guys. I have something to tell you. I have these bad cells in my breast and I am going to have some surgery so they can take them away. They'll have to take my breast off." There was a pause and they both looked at me. Then Adam realized the full extent of the injustice.

"Mom. That is amazing. First they take your radio, then they take your breast!"

Indeed.

Seth, with the classic train of thought of a six-year-old boy, asked, "But what do they do with all the breasts they take off?"

I told him they put them all in a room for men to come look at.

*   *   *

The night before my mastectomy, Joel and I lay in bed. I knew my right breast was history, but they would also biopsy my left one while I was in surgery. If they found cancer, they would remove that one, too. My breasts might be small, but they were mine and they were real, and the fact that I could wake up without either of them swept over me in a tide of sadness. I rolled over on top of Joel and started crying.

"So after the surgery, I might have no breasts. Are you still going to love me? Will you still want me?"

Joel looked at me and rolled me onto my back. He pointed at my right breast and said, "They can cut that off." He pointed at my left breast and said, "They can cut that off." He pointed in between my legs and said, "But they had better not cut that off." Despite my anxiety, I burst out laughing.

The next day my right breast was removed. My left breast was cancer-free. I still had one of my own, and that made me very happy.

After I got home from the hospital, Joel and the boys were at my beck and call. It hurt to move around, and I loved having food brought to me in bed. But I also wanted to get back to our normal routine as soon as possible, so Seth and Adam would know I was going to be okay.

My biggest challenge was figuring out what to wear to disguise my newly lopsided bust. Having small breasts turned out to be an advantage in that department; the discrepancy wasn't overly obvious. A volunteer from "Reach to Recovery" from the American Cancer Society came over and showed me how to pin a fake breast, made of fiberfill, into a camisole.

The things you learn with only one breast.

When I put on a blowzy shirt, I felt almost normal.

*   *   *

Dear Nancy,

I've thought a lot about you this past week. It's too bad that sometimes it takes scary news to make us stop and think.

I don't know if I've ever told you that I think of you as one of the wonderful people in the world. I admire you, your attitudes, your success, your husband and children, and on and on. It struck me as I thought about you this week that it shouldn't take news like this for me to tell you what I think.

At any rate, we all send our love and best wishes. Let me know if there is anything I can do to help you whip this thing.

Talk to you soon.

Love,
Andy, Mary, Rachel, Michael, Anna

(My brother Andy and his family, after my cancer diagnosis)

CHAPTER 11

LIFE IN THE
SALTZMAN/HERZOG LANE

SETH STARTED SCHOOL at Steele Elementary with Adam that fall. Adam took his responsibility as a big brother seriously and made sure he found Seth after school each day.

We had a new day care situation. Susie Chambless, a friend and mother of two boys, lived near the school. Adam, Seth, and several other children walked to Susie's house after school. The boys loved going there because Susie had a huge yard and lots to do.

* * *

October 5, 1995

Nance,

I know that you know how loved you and your family are. The loss of Joel and your boys is being felt by many.

One of my fondest memories occurred when I was taking care of the boys after school when they were at Steele Elementary. We had four ducklings. The male was extremely protective of his girls. As they all got older, Mr. Peepers would chase anyone who would come into the yard. My boys weren't bothered by him, but sweet little Seth, with his well-loved, stuffed dog WoWo, was terrified. It got to the point where Seth really didn't want to come to my house anymore because of this duck.

Without any regrets, I found a home for the ducks up in Lake George. I truly wanted Seth to feel safe and comfortable in my home.

I will miss your boys and their beautiful smiles.

All my love,
Susie

(Susie Chambless, Adam and Seth's caregiver)

*   *   *

Joel and I lived in the "Old North End" of Colorado Springs and loved it, because the streets were flat, there were lots of children, and it was wonderfully eclectic. On one side of us was a family of fundamentalist Christians. On the opposite side lived "Squid"—a twelve-year-old boy who became buddies with Seth and Adam—and his family. Across the street was my jogging partner, a lesbian whose two daughters became friends with the boys. Next door to her was a stand-up comedian. We were always the test audience for his latest routine. There was a house with two apartments, where we observed a young woman making love on her deck late one evening. Across from the apartment house was a pink stucco house where a retired Air Force officer who worked at the Air Force Academy lived with his partner. I don't think there was a more interesting block in all of Colorado Springs.

*   *   *

I was getting back into work when I learned there was an opening for a principal at Broadmoor Elementary. The principal had resigned the first month of school, and they needed to find someone right away. The job would start at the end of October. I met with my current superintendent to see if I could be released from my contract if I got the position. With the support of my administrative team, I turned in my application.

I was ecstatic when I got called for an interview. I arrived early and walked up and down the halls, imagining what it would be like to be the principal of my own school. I had worked there when I was with BOCES, so was familiar with the school. Still, it looked completely different through the eyes of a potential principal. I met with the staff for an hour, a group of parents for an hour, and then the school board. I really wanted the job, and hoped my enthusiasm had been apparent.

Several days later I was offered the position. I was over the moon. Leaving the great staff and students at Timberview would be hard, but I felt like this was what all the hard work—the master's degree, the Ph.D., the jobs leading up to now—had been in preparation for. I would finally have my own school.

I met with the teachers at Broadmoor and asked what I could do to support them. They suggested parking lot duty before and after school. This entailed standing in the parking lot, welcoming kids to school, greeting parents, and encouraging those in cars to drive safely. The first few weeks of parking lot duty, Joel accompanied me. He knew many of the parents and it was great having his support. Although there were times when I was yelled at, waved off, or ignored, I loved greeting students and parents at the beginning of every day. I think I may have even saved a life or two in the parking lot.

One advantage for employees in my school district was that their children could attend their school, and at the end of my first year as a principal, Joel and I decided that Adam and Seth would love Broadmoor Elementary. I also wanted the boys at school with me. I had already missed much of what they had experienced in school at Steele Elementary. So, in the fall of 1991, Seth started first grade, and Adam third grade, at my school. They already knew some of the kids from hockey and tennis, so the transition was very easy.

I loved being a principal, and I loved Broadmoor. Life was back on track.

*   *   *

The boys were getting older but we still needed babysitters if we went out in the evening. Toby and Matt Tieman, brothers only a few years older than Adam and Seth, were an ideal solution. Joel knew their mom and dad, Linda and Jack Tieman, through tennis. Matt and Toby were always up for doing something athletic, which Adam and Seth loved.

One Saturday Toby was watching the boys and they were all with me at Broadmoor Elementary. The boys got the floor hockey equipment out of the P.E. office and set up the nets. They were involved in a heated game when Seth shot a puck at the goal and missed. The puck sailed through the cafeteria kitchen and shattered a window. Toby announced, "I'm sorry, Seth, but I'm going to have to call the police."

Seth burst into tears. Adam burst into laughter. Toby quickly told Seth he was kidding, and they found me in my office to tell me the story. Seth let me hug him and all three went back to the gym to finish the game.

Stephanie and Michael Sachs also babysat for Adam and Seth. The siblings were the children of one of my teachers, Sue Sachs. Stephanie started babysitting for the boys when she was a sophomore in high school. Each day, Stephanie would pick the boys up from school, take them home, and make them a snack. She supervised the completion of their homework and then took them to hockey practice or tennis matches.

The boys thought of Stephanie as their older sister. No question was off limits with Stephanie, and she was comfortable answering all of their queries. When Stephanie went off to college, her brother, Michael, took over some of the babysitting responsibilities. After Stephanie graduated from college she moved back to Colorado Springs for a time and once again took on the role of big sister and head babysitter.

*   *   *

Dear Dr. Saltzman,

It has taken me awhile before I was able to write this, but I wanted you to know how much I cared about Adam and Seth. After spending so much time with them, it was like they were my little brothers, but at the same time, they also became two of my best friends.

I remember when babysitting after school, we would always do our homework in front of the TV and Seth and I would make macaroni and cheese together. Every once in awhile, I'd let them steer my car around the parking lot after school because they wanted to show off to their friends. And of course, I'll never forget the great talks at McDonald's over french fries.

Other times we were at tennis lessons, baseball games, or hockey practice. I learned all about how to score a tennis game and how to help dress Seth in his hockey equipment, although he said that Joel was better at tying his skates.

I'll never forget skiing with Adam on Broadmoor ski trips, Seth's laugh and his big brown eyes, Adam always knowing how to do everything, how much Seth looked up to him, but also seeing Adam watching out for his little brother.

I remember the three of us in Adam's bed late at night watching TV until Seth fell asleep, because he was too scared to be alone.

I loved Adam and Seth very much. They were wonderful kids and I enjoyed every minute I was able to spend with them.

Love always,
Stephanie

(Stephanie Sachs, Adam and Seth's babysitter)

*   *   *

For Christmas 1991, we decided to go to California. Rob picked us up at the airport Christmas morning, and we went straight to an open house at a friend of Rob and Ed's. One of the hosts greeted us as we came in. He first gave Rob, then Ed, a kiss. I noticed Seth had an intrigued look on his face. The next man who came in was also given a kiss. After our host had greeted a couple more guests similarly, Seth looked at me.

"Is everyone here gay?"

"Pretty much," I replied.

Seth considered this for a moment.

"Oh," he said casually, then moved over to the snack table and started eating.

I had done a lot of thinking about when and how I would tell the boys that Rob was gay. But it was clear that Seth had figured this one out on his own. As with so many things adults get worked up about, it was a non-issue in the innocently wise mind of my youngest son.

*   *   *

Along my daily drive to work, there was a house that had been for sale since I'd started as principal at Broadmoor. It was within walking distance of the school. Although we loved living downtown, it seemed logical to look for a house closer to the school where three of us spent our weekdays. We were also concerned that if enrollment got too high, the boys would have to go to another school. We didn't want that to happen and had started thinking about moving.

We made an appointment to see the house. We loved it. It was a remodeled split-level with five bedrooms, three and a half bathrooms, a dog run, and a huge front yard. It was open, airy, and light. The back yard was a common area full of trees with a stream running through it. The asking price was out of our range, but Joel thought it would be a great investment. We made an offer and were thrilled when it was accepted. Our downtown house sold in one day to a woman Joel had known in Pueblo; she was as thrilled to have our house as we were to have a new home. Now we just needed to wait and see if all of our loans got approved. We wanted to close on both houses during the summer.

*   *   *

Eng 121-003
Sept. 19, 1997

The Death of My Heroes

*On a foggy night in late September of 1995, a private plane carrying
five went down just outside of Westcliffe, Colorado . . . An elementary school
principal and survivor of two breast cancers, the strong-hearted lady received a
phone call instead of a family. Her two sons, ages eleven and twelve, and her
husband . . . had been killed in the plane crash.*

*If you're wondering where I fit in, I was the babysitter. Our relationship
was more than just babysitter to child, though. Our families were very close and
the boys and I were practically surrogate brothers.*

*The boys, Adam and Seth, were beautiful kids. They each had long
eyelashes with big brown eyes. I would take the boys with me everywhere. They
were the most popular kids at my high school basketball games. While Nancy
was going through her breast cancer, I was on-call as a sitter. If she had to go to
the hospital in the night, I would go stay with the boys and make sure they got
off to school. We always told everyone we met that we were brothers. We became
very close and I loved them with all of my heart.*

*As I grew older, Joel became more of a secondary father figure to me.
When I was in high school, he and I would sit outside on the porch and talk. I
remember he would reassure me that all the strict rules my dad had were for my
own good. He would talk to me as a friend and not preach as a parent.*

*As the two-year anniversary comes up this next week . . . I will always
remember the good, laugh at the fun times, cry for the pain . . .*

I love you Adam and Seth!!!

*(Essay by Toby Tieman, one of Adam and Seth's babysitters, for a class
assignment)*

CHAPTER 12

YOU CAN'T HAVE A BAD HAIR DAY WITHOUT ANY HAIR

AFTER MY MASTECTOMY, I had moved on fairly quickly. It had been an ordeal, no argument. And I had a new group of friends who were breast cancer survivors. The surgery had left a horizontal scar on the right side of my chest and I wore a prosthesis in my bra. But for me, cancer was over. I didn't feel any less of a woman, in large part thanks to Joel. He truly loved me just as I was—and our sex life was as robust as ever. My body felt normal, too. I was focused on the future.

So I was caught off guard when, about a week into buying the new house and selling our old one, I noticed a pea-sized lump just below the scar, on my right chest.

Dr. O'Rourke recommended that I have it removed and biopsied. The procedure was performed in the hospital with local anesthesia. Dr. O'Rourke and I chatted about the boys as he numbed my chest. Although the area was covered with a drape, I could see his face as he removed the mass, and it wasn't encouraging. I had a sinking feeling his hunch wasn't going to be wrong this time.

The biopsy results came back, he looked at them, and his expression didn't change.

"I'm sorry to tell you, but the whole lump was a ball of malignant cells."

My heart sank. I asked him to come with me to tell Joel, who was in the waiting room.

"The lump was malignant," I said.

He looked at Dr. O'Rourke, who nodded. Joel reached for me and held me while I cried.

We scheduled an appointment to meet with an oncologist. I went home to call my parents and sleep for a while.

"One more adventure" is how my mother characterized it. I appreciated her perspective, but having already been through one bout, cancer was not an adventure I'd have chosen to repeat. I was scared and so was Joel.

The oncologist, Dr. Sayre, recommended chemotherapy and radiation. He also suggested a hysterectomy. This would decrease the estrogen in my body, which could reduce the chance of the cancer recurring. Another doctor in his office recommended a prophylactic mastectomy on my left breast.

We decided to get a couple of other opinions. A doctor at the University of Colorado Medical Center in Denver also supported the chemotherapy/ radiation route, as did Dr. Pizzo in Bloomington, whom I consulted again. I decided to have the chemotherapy, radiation, and hysterectomy, but chose to keep my left breast intact.

*   *   *

Dear Nancy,

Rob has told me of the ordeal you are facing with the recurrence of cancer. My own experience of illness has made me realize what one assumes everyone would already know: it's frightening and very challenging, physically and emotionally, to be sick.

We really bring all of ourselves to a crisis and you have great strength and maturity to use in this battle. While the chemotherapy and radiation battle the cancer, you have the tremendous battle of making the most of your life during a painful and difficult time. I don't think I understood what "a good attitude" meant until I was sick; I didn't understand the temptation to give up or the exhilaration of surviving with my humor and some joy in life intact. Your family will help you, I know.

Well, good luck. Don't hesitate to complain; remember, getting through this is what counts—not being the perfect patient.

Fondly,
Rand

(Rand Schrader, a close friend of my brother Rob)

*   *   *

I received the news about my cancer the same day I heard that both we and the woman who was buying our house were approved for home loans. The buyer's real estate agent came over to talk to me about the sale. I was sitting on our front porch watching the boys play across the street. She sat down next to me.

"I heard your cancer is back."

I was taken aback that the news had traveled so fast, but I told her it was true.

"Maybe you should rethink moving. How will Joel make the house payment if you die?"

I was stunned that someone I barely knew would say something so personal and presumptuous. I looked her in the eye and stated that the payments would not be a problem for Joel. I think what galled me most was her assumption that I hadn't thought about the possibility I wouldn't survive.

"I know you have cancer, but you probably haven't realized you might die, so I thought I'd point out a possible consequence of that to you."

"Wow. Thanks for reminding me."

No, I had indeed considered the possibility, both the first time through and now. Thought about it a lot, actually. And while I was fully aware that it would leave Joel with a house payment, I was much more worried about another sad circumstance it would create.

I would never have seen James Taylor in concert.

I told Joel that the one thing I wanted to do before I died of breast cancer, if I did die of breast cancer, was to see JT live. I was in luck; he was going to be in Denver that summer. Joel talked to our good friends, Mark and Chris Reischmann, and Mark and Joel were able to find scalped tickets.

Reckless as it probably seemed to the real estate agent, we proceeded with selling one house and purchasing the home of our dreams.

* * *

Before I could start my treatment, I had to have a catheter put in my chest, which would allow me to get chemotherapy and blood tests without painful sticks in my arm several times a month. Joel and I watched a video to learn what would happen and how I might react to the treatment. One of the drugs I would get was Adriamycin, which makes your hair fall out. Many women shave their heads before this happens. I was convinced that because I loved my hair so much, I would be the one person in the world whose hair would not fall out and refused to cut my hair.

Joel took me to my first chemo treatment and Donna stopped by, too. It took most of the day to get the chemicals into my body. The nurse wore two pairs of extra-thick rubber gloves, one on top of the other. This was because her skin would burn if it came in direct contact with the caustic drugs.

Wonderful. And this stuff is being pumped into my bloodstream?

When it was over, I felt spacey. Joel took me home and I crawled into bed. The boys came home and gave me kisses and hugs. I wasn't sick to my stomach—yet. It was good to have the first treatment over, and to know what to expect. One round down, five to go.

By the next day, I was nauseated and throwing up. I made so much noise that Seth and Adam started imitating me. I loved that they were able to see humor in the situation; it added a welcome lightness to the atmosphere at home. After three days, I was feeling better and I still had all my hair. I had succumbed to the nausea, but maybe I really was going to get to keep my hair!

We tried to keep things as normal as possible. I took the boys to school with me so I could finish hiring teachers and complete the end-of-year reports. We had joined the Country Club of Colorado, and Adam and Seth and their babysitter, Matt Tieman, would go to the club to swim, play tennis, and hang out with friends. That gave me some time to work or sleep.

The James Taylor concert in June was everything I could have hoped for. It was a gorgeous night, JT was in good form, and it seemed like he played for hours. The opening chords of each song would ripple through my body with familiarity, and I sang along in pure bliss. People jokingly say, "I can die happy now" when they experience a long-anticipated wish. For me, it wasn't a joke. I didn't want to die, but if I did, at least it wouldn't be with regrets of never having seen James Taylor.

We were on our way with friends to their ranch in Vail when the chemo curse struck. I absentmindedly ran my fingers through my hair, and was suddenly holding a huge clump of dark strands. Boom. Just like that. There was so much when I took a shower the next morning, I was afraid it was going to clog the drain. When we were back in Colorado Springs I relented and got a short cut. At least when it fell out, it was easier to get out of the drain.

I made several trips to the wig store, trying to decide what to buy. Seth accompanied me on one trip while Adam was at hockey practice. I tried on a long blonde number and Seth broke out into gales of laughter. The woman running the shop thought we were making fun of her wigs and asked us not to mess up her displays. I eventually bought two dark brown wigs that looked very much like my own hair. I didn't want the kids at school to know that I was going bald.

* * *

Nancy . . .

> *May your spirit remain strong . . . I will be here for you any time . . . My heart and hands are open . . . You made such a positive difference in my life. May I do anything for you?*

Loving you,
Ann Junk

(One of my Breast Friends)

* * *

When I went back to work in August, I had completed three rounds of chemotherapy and had three to go. I would throw up for three days after each treatment, then feel better. Though the weather was still mild, I also got cold easily, a side effect of the blood thinners I took to keep the catheter from clogging. Spending time in hockey rinks was pretty miserable, so that fall I missed many of the boys' practices and went only to games.

After my fourth treatment, I was sick and tired of being sick and tired. And I wanted to be able to keep working. One day I was talking about this with one of the moms at my school.

"I just need to relax so I can get through the last two treatments," I shared. She said she knew a great therapist who might be able to help and gave me his name.

I met with Dr. John Bermudez and told him my story. He hooked me up to wires and showed me where I was holding all of my stress. Then he taught me how to breathe and relax. I met with him several times and using biofeedback, I was able to learn to calm myself. He also taught me strategies for relaxation at work when dealing with tough situations.

After my third session he casually asked, "How is your relationship with your mother?"

I burst into tears. We spent the next couple of sessions talking about the expectations in my family and some of the pressure I put on myself. He helped me see things in perspective. We also identified the ways my parents had helped me become successful.

I talked to him about the boys. Adam appeared to be doing fine, but Seth seemed much more anxious than usual. Dr. Bermudez offered to talk to them and provide some feedback. Joel worried that having the boys see a counselor might give them the impression there was something wrong with them, but I felt strongly that therapy couldn't hurt. We disagreed, but Joel acquiesced.

I took the boys with me on my next visit. Adam walked right into Dr. Bermudez's office and met with him by himself. I took Seth in with me and he sat on my lap. The doctor asked Seth some questions about himself, then some questions about me. Dr. Bermudez's assessment was that Adam was handling my treatment well and had a realistic sense of what was happening, but that Seth was anxious because I was giving him too much information about my treatment. In Seth's case, less was more.

I asked what I should tell Seth when he asked me if I was going to die. "Tell him that you love him, and that you will always love him."

It was the same thing that one of my friends had told me to say. I started keeping things simpler when I talked to Seth, and watched his anxiety level decrease significantly.

*   *   *

With the skills I learned from Dr. Bermudez, I was able to relax enough to complete my six chemotherapy treatments. The only complication was my white blood cell count—it got so low that after each treatment I needed daily shots of Neupogen for two weeks. This helped boost my immune system and warded off infection. Joel got to play doctor and give me the shots, but it was no fun for either of us. I clearly remember the morning he stuck the needle in my thigh and I yelped. "Sorry, I guess that went in a little crooked," he said sheepishly.

My last chemo treatment was in November. I had made it through six months of hell and felt very proud of myself. However, I still had two phases of treatment to go.

One thing I had learned about getting through this trial by cancer was that it was good to take mini-vacations. Thanksgiving was coming up and we wanted to do something fun for our whole family. Joel talked to our good friends Margie and Phil Soran, who had moved from Colorado Springs to Minnesota, about joining them for the holiday. Joel had known Margie growing up in Pueblo, and they had both gone to University of Northern Colorado. Joel knew Phil through tennis. Joel had gone out on one date with Margie, but it was Phil who was smitten. The way he told it, "I figured if she'd go out with Herz I had a pretty good shot." Phil asked her out, and it was love at first date. They got married soon thereafter. We'd become close friends in Colorado Springs when their first daughter, Alysa, was born about the same time as Adam. Christy came along soon thereafter, as did Seth, and the four kids had also become friends.

When the Sorans had moved they'd extended an open invitation, and were thrilled we wanted to visit. Adam and Seth were excited to see the girls again. It was a wonderfully rejuvenating trip. We were in Minneapolis for one of its biggest snowstorms ever, and we made snowmen and snow forts. When we returned to the Springs, I felt ready for the next battle in my war on cancer.

*   *   *

Nancy,

I think it goes without saying that these types of letters are very hard to write. I am not able to put down all the memories, since there are so many, but I want to attempt to show the depth and influence of the relationship our families have shared.

One of the most clear Joel memories that I have turned out to be one of the defining moments of my life. It was fall quarter of my sophomore year. There was this cute girl I was intrigued with from Pueblo, Margaret Selby. Coming back from the Greeley night life one Friday, I followed Joel and her into Weibking dorm. A lump came into my throat when I noticed he was holding her hand. If Joel Herzog could take her out, Fudd the Stud Soran could surely get a date. The rest is history. I never did get the guts to ask him if he kissed her goodnight.

Our paths would cross again when I got a teaching job in Colorado Springs. Joel had found this beautiful woman to marry, and she was pregnant, too. I have a vivid recollection of the first time we had you over to our house. I can see so clearly Joel and you walking through the door. Things clicked. I saw a totally different Joel Herzog—one much different than the image I had of him at UNC. He was a concerned person—interested in us, interested in being a good husband, interested in being a good dad.

My strongest memories of our families happened at your Rockrimmon and our Flintridge houses. Now the memories include four kids—Seth and Christy in the middle of the fray, trying to keep up with the other two. We discussed Adam marrying Alysa and Seth hooking up with Christy.

Joel was one of the funniest people that I have known. He was my idol. But more often than not we talked about how we were doing with the important things in life—our wives and kids. He often caused me to stop and reprioritize how much effort I was putting towards these areas. I have never known anyone whose wife and kids were more important to him than they were to Joel Herzog. The only time I saw him let down his guard was when he talked about you, Nancy. Your relationship gave him meaning in life. Your excellent relationship with your kids was just an extension of the relationship between you two. He was a role model for me as a husband and even more so as a father.

The deaths of Joel, Adam, and Seth have been a crushing experience for me. I will always feel an empty spot in my heart. I will always remember them. I will always miss them. I loved them.

You are one amazing person. I don't know how you will find the strength to keep going, but I know you will do it.

Love,
Fudd

(Phil "Fudd" Soran, our good friend)

* * *

Round Two was radiation. This required getting pencil-tip-sized tattoos on my chest, which would allow the radiologist to treat the same area each visit. I had no idea that getting even tiny tattoos would hurt so much. I still have respect for anyone who voluntarily chooses to get "inked."

I knew that I would have to schedule my daily appointments around school responsibilities so I asked if I could come early in the morning. I was told that treatments didn't start before 9 a.m. because "that would require someone to come in early to turn on the machines." After school wouldn't work because I always had lots to do at the end of the day. Treatment was not given on weekends because there was "no one to turn on the machines." Apparently this issue with turning on the machines really had the hospital over a barrel. So I would finish my lunch duty, head to the hospital for the few minutes of treatment, then return to school. I made this work for the four weeks of radiation.

Compared to chemo, radiation treatment was much easier for my body to tolerate. Many people have skin problems and pain, but I was one of the lucky ones. As with the chemo, I tired easily, but it wasn't debilitating. I was able to keep working.

The last hurdle was having a hysterectomy. This had been a hard decision for Joel and me. We were still holding out hope that I might get pregnant again. However, Joel was adamant that we do everything possible to thwart a recurrence of the cancer. Sacrificing my one healthy breast seemed like overkill, but the hysterectomy made sense. We also trusted Dr. Sayre and his recommendation; it was obvious he cared immensely about his patients and their survival.

The surgery was scheduled. For the first time since I had been diagnosed, I was going to have to miss four to six weeks of work. I asked one of my teachers who was certified as a principal to fill in for me. We scheduled the surgery for November so that I could take advantage of the holidays around Thanksgiving and Christmas and miss as few workdays as possible.

I wanted Dr. O'Rourke to be my surgeon for the hysterectomy, but he explained that I would be better served by a specialist. He agreed to assist in the surgery.

I asked him for an additional favor.

"While I'm asleep, will you pierce my left ear, with one hole?"

I wanted to have something to look forward to when I woke up. Besides, I was already on my way to rocker chick status with my tattoos—the piercing seemed like a natural progression. It was also something to remind me that I had stared down cancer twice, and come out whole where it counted—in my head and heart. Dr. O'Rourke contacted a friend of his who was a plastic surgeon to do the piercing. I was impressed—I thought maybe he'd just call someone from the mall earring store.

When I woke up after surgery, I had lost a uterus, but gained a beautiful symbol of triumph.

*   *   *

February 18, 1992

Today my mom is finished with radtion. Im very happy. Me, my mom, my dad, my brother are going out to dinner. I forget were. [sic]

(From Seth's first grade journal)

*   *   *

Once my treatment was complete, our lives once again settled. Joel's business was growing. Our evenings and weekends were often spent in hockey rinks. The boys and Joel hit tennis balls whenever they could find time.

At school, I was working with a teacher who was on a plan of improvement. I wanted to support her in making the changes I expected. This included observing her at least once a week and then meeting with her to discuss her progress. Working with teachers was one of the most rewarding parts of my job, but when an educator and I didn't see eye-to-eye on job performance, it was very stressful. I couldn't discuss what I was doing with anyone on my staff. I talked about it with Joel quite a bit; always out of earshot of Adam and Seth. Joel was very supportive, listened attentively, and sometimes offered suggestions.

During one meeting I had with the struggling teacher, she shared, "Do you know how hard this is for me? To meet with you weekly and be under so much pressure to perform?" I looked at her and said, "Do you have any idea what I've been going through myself, during this process?" She knew about my cancer recurrence and struggles to work while going through treatment. Then she said, "People handle things differently." I looked at her and said, "You know what? You're right."

After our meeting, I thought about what she had said. We do indeed all bring our own baggage of backgrounds, hot buttons, fears, and issues to rough times in our lives. For some, physical challenges are more stressful than emotional blows. For others, it's vice versa. The teacher's comment reflected how distressing it was to have been called out and placed under scrutiny, with the pressure of improving in ways she didn't agree with. For her, that kind of stress was as difficult as what I had been through. I was reminded once again to always treat our fellow humans with kindness and to acknowledge that we all are facing trials that are uniquely formidable for each of us.

*   *   *

When the school year ended, my hair had been growing in for seven months. I had worn a wig all year and decided to go au naturale the last week of school. It was still short but looked okay. Monday morning, as I got out of my car in the parking lot, two arriving kindergartners looked at me quizzically.

"Who are you?" said the first one.

"I'm Dr. Saltzman."

"Oh!" said the other one. "Now I recognize your voice!"

At the beginning of my treatment, I knew that I had to meet all the responsibilities of the principalship or take time off. In the end, I had achieved my professional goals for the year, spent a lot of time with a teacher on her program of improvement, and survived chemotherapy, radiation, and a hysterectomy. Like my student, there were times when the only way I'd recognized myself was by my voice. But it was a determined voice. I ended the year knowing that I had accomplished what was required, and more. Even I was impressed. I had tapped into a well of personal strength, and it was incredibly empowering.

CHAPTER 13

BALANCE AND BRANCHING OUT

JOEL AND I were both raised to value education, personal performance, and a strong work ethic. Family was also extremely important, and we carried that belief into our marriage. Although it wasn't always easy to make the trips to see parents and siblings, we set aside the time and were glad we did.

As for religion, we opened presents on Christmas Day in Indiana and lit the Hanukkah candles in Colorado. Joel and I agreed that Adam and Seth would know they were Jewish, but would not attend religious schools or have bar mitzvahs. It may have been confusing to others but it made sense to us.

The biggest challenge Joel and I faced in our marriage was figuring out how to balance everything. I realize this may well be the case for 99 percent of American families, so it's not exactly a unique dilemma. But it doesn't make it any easier when you're doing it in real time—just sitting down to dinner with your family, and the phone rings with a call from a distraught parent.

Joel did the balancing act without complaint. He never seemed frustrated when expected to do several things at once. The boys and I were always his top priority; I knew that he was thinking about me when I was at work, he showed me affection all the time. When we were together he was always touching me, looking at me, telling me he loved me. He was able to make me feel like I was the most important thing in the world, and the boys felt the same way.

I, on the other hand, wasn't nearly as good at setting my priorities. For me, everything was at the top of the list. I would stay late at work, call Joel and tell him I was on my way, then arrive home thirty minutes later, even though we only lived five minutes from school. When I walked in the door, the phone would ring. I would talk to someone regarding work for another half hour. I won't say I was late to hockey practices on purpose, but if I knew Joel was there, I might have been guilty of trying to do one or two last things at work before leaving. All of this drove Joel slightly crazy.

I always had an excuse. "If I don't deal with this now, it will turn into a big problem tomorrow." Or, "If you were a parent calling me about Adam or Seth, you would want to hear back from me right away." He understood that my work was different from his and that many of the things I dealt with were urgent in the minds of parents or teachers. He considered me a world-class wife and mother, and told me so constantly. But he also thought there was room for a small shift in my priorities. I would agree, and then try to re-arrange my time and set boundaries. Invariably, I would fall back into being a principal 24/7. It was hard not to: I received a lot of positive reinforcement by being available to solve problems for teachers, parents, and students.

In truth, though I loved my boys to the ends of the earth, I did not feel that I was as good a mother as I was a school administrator. By contrast, I could see that Joel was an amazing husband, businessman, *and* father. I didn't think my mothering lived up to his fathering. When I would share my feelings with him he would tell me that I was a fantastic mother. If I would just look at Adam and Seth, he said, I would know that I was a good mother.

"They are wonderful, well-adjusted boys and it took both of us to make that happen." I thought about that.

But I love being at school and doing my job as much as I love being a mother.

I felt guilty, watching Joel consistently make the decision to leave the shop to do something with or for the boys. Leaving the shop was hard for him, because his business depended so much on his presence in the store. Even when I had the chance to take off time during my chemotherapy treat-ments, I didn't, because I wanted to be at school. A big part of that was wanting the boys to know that everything was okay. But another part was wanting to convince *myself* that everything was okay—going to work made life feel normal.

Ultimately, while we didn't always see eye-to-eye, and he wasn't afraid to let me know when he was frustrated, Joel never forced the issue. He al-lowed me to find my own balance between family and career. Which, of course, only made me love him more.

* * *

Dear Dr. Salt\zman,

Thank you so very much for all you do on behalf of the children, especially mine. I let them go off to school every day knowing that they'll be educated, loved, and looked after. Believe me, I wouldn't say that to just anyone!

Even though I wouldn't do everything exactly as I see it done, I couldn't be happier. I know you want the best for all children. I admire your abilities as a human being and a principal.

Cynthia Lemesany

(A Broadmoor parent)

*   *   *

When Adam and Seth attended Steele Elementary, Joel walked the kids to school, chatted with their teachers, and helped periodically in the classrooms. He spent the whole day with each boy on their birthdays. At Broadmoor, he helped in their classrooms and played with the kids at recess.

When Seth started first grade with Mrs. Dorhrmann, she asked Joel to read with each student. His job was to have the student read the alphabet out loud, then say the letter sound and a word that started with the sound.

Joel took a student into the hallway. She said, "The letter is A. It says 'a-a' like apple." She went all the way through the alphabet. The next student did exactly the same thing. Then he took Seth in the hallway. Seth did not know his letters or sounds. Joel came straight to my office.

"What is the matter with Seth? He doesn't know the letters of the alphabet."

"Some children take a little longer. Seth will get it, and we can work with him at home. You need to relax."

"I think Seth may have a learning problem."

"He doesn't. He will learn this in his own time."

Adam walked at a little over nine months; Seth at fourteen months. Adam used words early; Seth, late. Seth was going to read when he was ready. That did not stop Joel from going over the alphabet, and the sounds, every night with Seth. It didn't make much difference in Seth's performance, but they enjoyed the time together. And it did make Joel feel better. Eventually, Seth learned to read just fine—in his own time. He was never, however, as intent on good grades as his parents might have wished. Like me, he often goofed off until the last minute when he had to get something done. Once, after I'd been less than thrilled at a D he'd received on a test, he replied, "Hey Mom, that's nothing. I got an F last week!"

*   *   *

Recess was fun for Joel, the boys, and the students in their classes. Joel liked to chase them or toss a ball around. One recess, Joel was playing Nerf football with the kids. Kyle Reischmann, the son of our friends Mark and Chris, joined the game. While the boys weren't looking, Joel rolled the ball in a big puddle, then threw the ball directly at Kyle's chest. Water exploded everywhere. Kyle was covered with mud and water; the boys howled with laughter. It was only when recess was over that they realized Kyle couldn't go back to class looking like a muddy, drowned rat. They all showed up in my office to report that, "Mr. Herzog pegged Kyle with a muddy Nerf ball." As principal, I would typically have called the muddy student's mom or dad to ask for clean clothes, apologize for the incident, and set things right. In this case I made Kyle and Joel call Chris themselves as their consequence. She brought Kyle a clean shirt, gave Joel a hard time, and laughed to herself all the way home.

*   *   *

Dear Nancy,

Joel possessed an insight into matters of the heart that was more impressive than either his extraordinary wit or ability to play tennis. The most valuable lessons I learned from him had nothing to do with forehands or backhands. As an adolescent, I revered the lifestyle of a footloose tennis pro, but it is the standards Joel set as a husband and a father that I value as an adult. On and off the court, he had the remarkable talent of making things seem effortless. Appearances notwithstanding, such talent is the result of a commitment, desire, and devotion that can only be truly appreciated by one's family. I will remember Joel as a man whose integrity, wisdom, and charm were outstanding.

Speaking for Susan and myself, I offer our condolences to you and all the Herzogs.

With love,
Hayes

(Hayes Fraser, longtime friend)

*   *   *

Saying that Joel had friends is like saying the Sahara has sand. He knew people from all over Colorado, and the country, through tennis. And he remembered everyone he met. If you shopped at Total Tennis, Joel memorized everything that was worth knowing about you—i.e., what shoes you liked, what size you wore, and how you liked your racquet strung. His joke- and story-telling skills were legendary. Many of the jokes were for more adult ears and shared only with his guy friends. Other, more goofy ones, he took special joy in telling the boys and me. All Joel had to do was start telling a joke and everyone would dissolve into laughter.

"There was this monk who was looking for a bell-ringer . . . "

But while Joel had many friends, once we were married, he was not constantly "out with the guys." He would try to get a tennis game in once or twice a week, but most of his free time was spent with the boys and me. His brother Lee was his closest friend. I sometimes thought he might benefit from cultivating a few more deep friendships. I knew how much my close friends meant to me.

In 1994, he started playing squash at the Country Club of Colorado. At first it was a challenge; just enough different from tennis to require a new type of coordination and power. Before long, he was quite good. This new racquet and ball sport was fascinating and fun.

Playing squash also introduced him to some new people, and he was invited to join a squash club that was being built near our house. Joel was member number eleven of Guillermo's Squash Club. He was impressed with owner Bill "Guillermo" Palmer's business sense and love of squash. It may have reminded him of his own passion for sport combined with entrepreneurship.

When Guillermo's was completed, Joel was excited to show me the facility and introduce me to his new friends. It was clear that he'd found something special that enhanced his life. Now he had a place to go after work, have a beer, enjoy the camaraderie. He took Adam and Seth to the club, where they also learned to play squash. But most of the time Joel went to Guillermo's by himself to be with his buddies. I watched him work at creating more meaningful friendships, making them a higher priority than he had previously, and I enjoyed seeing the pleasure it brought him.

It was apparent that the members of Guillermo's had formed a special bond with each other, but they also welcomed family members with open arms. This meant a lot to me since Joel thought so much of these people.

To celebrate the opening of the club, the first annual Christmas party was held after a tournament for members. It was a wild celebration. Awards were given, stories told, and I could see how much they all cared about each other. A special step stool had been made for Joel, with his number painted on the step, so he could reach the towel hooks in the shower. No one laughed harder than Joel.

We had friends in the tennis and hockey communities; but this close-knit group of squash players had staked out a special place in Joel's heart, and therefore in mine.

*   *   *

I had been open with the school community about my cancer treatments, and it was widely known that I was a cancer survivor. When I received a request from a nurse at Penrose Hospital to talk to other cancer survivors, I readily agreed. I talked about my experiences going through treatment, and, as any good educator would, I had visual aids to go with my stories: pictures of myself with two breasts, then with one. I kept in mind the philosophy that "people handle things differently" as I put together my presentation. My initial talk was well received and I was asked to speak again.

Two years in a row, I asked the superintendent in my school district to let me give the speech to the teachers at the opening convocation. I surprised some when I pulled my wig off and revealed I was totally bald. The look on their faces was priceless when I took my prosthesis out of my bra, and held it up to see. I had overcome obstacles and wanted them to know that they could, too.

I didn't just talk about breast cancer. My favorite part was describing the humorous and wonderful experiences I'd had as an educator. I saved notes and cards that students had given me over the years, and read these aloud. Using story-telling and personal notes, I conveyed that teachers make a difference in the lives of so many—and do it in spite of significant challenges.

I also spoke at Rotary meetings, middle and elementary school conferences, church potlucks, and women's groups. Adolescents were one of my favorite groups to entertain. The local Girl Scouts and Junior League teamed up to provide a one-day conference for seventh grade girls in the Pikes Peak region. I was asked to be the keynote speaker for their Young Women's Conference. There were 1,000 girls packed into a ballroom at a local hotel for my thirty-minute speech. I showed pictures of what I looked like as an adolescent, talked about how hard it was to go through my teen years, and then shared with them my story of surviving breast cancer. The conference became an annual event and I had the privilege of repeating this keynote for eight years. Eventually, the event was held four times a year, in different locations.

I had high visibility in the community because of my job, my public speaking about cancer, and because Joel was always bragging about me to his customers. This meant that when women he knew found out that they had breast cancer, I was frequently the first person they would call for information or support. I was happy to help, in the same way other survivors had given me hope.

After meeting the first couple of women who had been recently diagnosed with cancer, I realized that meeting other survivors would be a positive experience for all of us. When I received a call, I would contact the other women I had met since my diagnosis. We would get together for lunch at the Dale Street Cafe, a restaurant near Joel's store. A requirement for the "meeting" was that the location have a large restroom, and Dale Street offered spacious facilities in that category. After everyone was introduced, we would order lunch, and eat. Each woman would share her story and explain why she chose her treatment. After eating, we would adjourn to the ladies room, lock the door, and take our shirts off. The new person could see what women looked like with mastectomies, bilateral mastectomies, reconstruction, and/or breast enhancement. We always made sure we had a variety of "looks" to share. I have no idea what the owners of the Dale Street Cafe thought when they heard laughter coming out of the bathroom. We didn't care.

Eventually the group grew so large that we came up with a name, the "Breast Friends." Angie Adams, the longest breast cancer survivor I knew in Colorado Springs, put together a member list with phone numbers and addresses. We began meeting new survivors in people's kitchens or backyards. Twelve members of this group eventually made a calendar of tasteful photos of their breasts and chests, raising money to provide information for women diagnosed with breast cancer.

* * *

Dear Nancy,

Thank you so much for organizing the informative dinner for me. What a group of wonderful, courageous women. I learned a lot, was inspired by such courage and warmth, and I haven't laughed all the way through a meal in a long time!

So . . . my mastectomy is Wednesday the 19th. It should be outpatient surgery.

Thank you again.

(From a young breast cancer patient I introduced to "Breast Friends")

* * *

Adam graduated from sixth grade at Broadmoor Elementary. The occasion was particularly memorable because Joel wore long pants and a long-sleeved shirt. It was the first time most people at school had seen Joel not wearing shorts, and the resulting reaction and jokes were predictable.

We were the proud parents of an almost-thirteen-year-old going into seventh grade. Adam was excited about graduating but was concerned about being at Cheyenne Mountain Junior High. He had heard that seventh graders got stuffed into lockers by bigger students. We reassured him that rumors like this had been circulating through schools since the beginning of schools. We did not tell him that sometimes rumors have basis in truth, and enrolled both boys in a weekend family workshop through a program called Kidpower. There, they learned how to handle threatening situations, using words and their own strength to stay safe.

Joel and I attended Kidpower graduation and were excited to see how much Adam and Seth had learned. They demonstrated what to say when threatened, and how to kick and hit an assailant (okay, an instructor in pads), even when grabbed from behind. Joel and I had tears in our eyes when we saw their strength and dedication to keeping themselves safe.

The summer ended with a visit from Lee Herzog. He was going to school in Los Angeles to become a psychotherapist, supporting himself by teaching tennis. Lee gave the boys some lessons and told Joel that they were turning into great tennis players. Joel and the boys loved having Uncle Lee in Colorado Springs and looked forward to seeing him in California in the upcoming year.

*   *   *

I miss my Uncly [Uncle Lee] because my Uncly useto live by me and we played with him all the time. But he moved and I was really sad. And we visited him lots of times. [sic]

(From Adam's second grade journal)

*   *   *

Adam's anxiety about starting seventh grade quickly evaporated when he discovered he loved it. By the end of the first week, he had made new friends, and realized that the dreaded lockers were too small for him to be stuffed into. He balanced hockey, tennis, and homework much better than I balanced my obligations. He was proud that he and a friend got the dancing started at the end-of-the-first-week-of-school dance. His humble opinion was that they were the best dancers on the floor. Joel and I attended Back to School Night, where we heard with pride, from several teachers, that Adam had already impressed them with his kindness and academic abilities.

Seth had started fifth grade at Broadmoor. He was already busy entertaining his classmates. He flirted with girls, got sweaty at recess, and did his homework at night with Joel. He, too, was nicely balancing school with tennis and hockey. His teacher, Deb Young, shared with me that she and the whole class had fallen in love with his giggle.

I always got anxious at the beginning of a new school year but I was beginning to relax, too. I wanted the new teachers to do well. I wanted every child to love coming to school. I always tried to learn the names of all the students and wanted to know the parents' names, as well. That year I asked the students to bring in a picture of their whole family. We posted the pictures on a bulletin board in the front hallway, and captured the whole school community.

I could just tell, it was going to be a great year.

*   *   *

Hi!

It's early morning, Wednesday, 1:30 a.m. I sure miss you a lot! On the way home from Aspen I had a lot of time to think about you and about us. What I'm trying to say is that in the everyday hustle and bustle of kids and work and all that I think is so important, I'm not so sure I've told you how wonderful you are. I really love you and the thought of spending my entire life with someone as wonderful as you makes me tingle all the time. I love you and I'm sorry I don't tell you all the time. Don't go away again for a while.

Love,
Joel

(Note from Joel. We had all been in Aspen, then he and the boys had returned home and I had stayed to attend a workshop there.)

CHAPTER 14

JUST THE WAY YOU ARE

WHEN SUMMER ENDED and school started, Joel's business would slow down just enough for him to be able to monitor homework and play more squash and tennis. He was always on hand for the boys' fall and winter hockey tryouts.

Family was Joel's first love; tennis was a close second. He especially loved to watch professional tennis on TV or live. Joel and I saw John McEnroe play Bjorn Borg in Denver in 1984. The first time we left the kids alone overnight was to attend the U.S. Open in 1990. The boys stayed with Joel's parents and according to Adam, their grandfather Harvey made them eat horrible vegetables. They requested that next time, they be able to stay with someone less concerned about their diet. With that in mind we took them with us when we went to other Davis Cup tournaments in San Diego and Minneapolis.

In August, Joel's friend Homer Osborne stopped in at Total Tennis and suggested that they go to Las Vegas to watch the Davis Cup tournament in September. Joel thought it was a great idea. He asked me to join them but I said it would be hard to get away from school in September.

Joel got tickets for himself and the boys as well as Homer and his wife Linda. Homer rented a plane. Although I'd said I couldn't go, when I realized Seth would turn eleven during the trip I changed my mind. But there were only four seats on the plane, and Seth was going to have to ride in Joel's lap. I bought a ticket for a commercial flight so I would at least be on hand for Seth's birthday.

The week before the trip to Las Vegas was busy. We were not using a babysitter regularly because the boys had convinced us that they could get home safely from school. On Wednesday, things had not gone as usual, and Adam was stranded at the junior high when school got out. Seth and I jumped in my car as soon as the bell at Broadmoor rang and made the five-minute drive to pick Adam up. I hadn't eaten all day and Adam and Seth were famished as well. We headed to one of our favorite places, Classic Hamburgers. The sauce on their burgers was the kind you wake up in the night craving. I took my first bite and sighed audibly, as my taste buds did a little dance.

"Mmmmmmm."

I took another bite.

"Mmmm. Mmm. Mmm."

My burger was half gone, as was I, in total rapture.

Adam gave me one of his coy looks and said straight-faced, "Mom, you know what? That sounds like you and Dad in the bedroom on Sunday mornings."

He was in seventh grade, alright.

*   *   *

Thursday, September 21, the day that Joel and the kids were supposed to leave for Vegas, the weather was too bad for them to take off. The next morning I dropped them at the Colorado Springs airport, but Joel left a message saying they'd again had a weather delay. By the time I got the message, the weather had cleared, and they'd taken off. I worked a full day at school, then headed to the airport for my commercial flight.

As I flew into Las Vegas, I could see the famous Strip lit up like a Christmas tree against the dark of night. I was excited to be with my family for the weekend. As I walked into the hotel lobby the three of them burst through the crowd to hug me.

Both boys were talking at the same time.

"We just saw a pirate ship and watched a pirate fight!"

"You have to see it!"

"They have another show at 10:30 p.m. . . . "

" . . . so if we hurry we can go see it again!"

Joel gave me a long hug and kiss. He took my suitcase. We rode the elevator to our room, dropped off my luggage, and walked through the casino. We found the pirate ship and the boys laughed and talked through the whole performance. They knew exactly what was going to happen and were constantly directing me, "Watch over there!"

The next day we woke up and sang "Happy Birthday" to Seth in bed. He opened birthday cards and quickly stashed the cash found inside. Joel brought him some shirts from Total Tennis. We went out for brunch then walked to Caesar's Palace, where the matches were being played. Since I didn't have a ticket to the tennis matches, I found a lounge chair by the pool and set up camp for a quiet afternoon in the sun.

The tennis started at noon and by about 2 p.m. Seth was done, even if the matches weren't. Joel and Adam brought him to me at the pool and he snuggled with me for a minute then was off for the water.

After the matches ended, Joel and Adam rejoined us by the pool. They were filling us in on the day's play when none other than Andre Agassi walked by our chairs. The boys didn't miss a beat, running after him and asking him for his autograph. He agreeably signed a paper fan and Seth's hat. When they turned around, there was Pete Sampras! They got his autograph, too. Both players were very gracious and open to talking with Adam and Seth. We were all starstruck. In a state of euphoria, we walked back to our hotel.

It was time for Seth's birthday "party" of dinner and Cirque du Soleil *Mystère*. As we were getting dressed, I started to put on my bra with the prosthesis, but Joel came over to me and asked me not to wear it.

"I think you look beautiful just the way you are."

He took me in his arms. Although I was self-conscious about not wearing my bra, when I was dressed he told me again how beautiful I looked.

On our way to the evening's adventures, we ran into a friend from Colorado Springs. She had won $11,000 in the slot machines that night and was ecstatic. We felt just as rich with our tennis celebrity signatures.

The four of us ate dinner and celebrated Seth. At one point he got up and came over to sit on my lap. Seth had been a snuggler since he was little, which I loved. But the thought ran through my head that now that he was eleven, maybe he was getting a little old for sitting on Mom's lap. I didn't want to smother him. I wanted to help him ease into adolescence. How many times since then have I wished I'd held him on my lap all night, never letting go.

Cirque du Soleil was far beyond anything we had imagined. We were amazed at the jaw-dropping strength and the gymnastic skills of the performers. The boys were convinced that their dad could do the same tricks. Joel flexed his biceps, much to our amusement.

It was a gorgeous night. There were thousands of people walking along the Strip. Joel and I held hands and the boys talked to each other and stayed close. We got back to the hotel and climbed into our beds. The boys fell fast asleep and Joel made love to me.

For the last time.

* * *

September 24, 1995

Today I saw the finals of the Davis Cup. Todd Martin vs Tomos Enquist. Todd Martin beat Tomos 7-5, 7-5, 7-6. Yesterday I went to Cirque Du Solee. It is the French circus. It has all kinds of weird stuff in it.

For my birthday I got $45 and a few shirts. I went in to the arcade and won a football and a tiger.

I had a great time on my trip. Except the plane ride. [sic]

(Last entry from Seth's fifth grade journal, recovered from crash)

* * *

The first time I read that last sentence, penciled in Seth's scribbly fifth-grade hand, I fell to the floor, screaming. Sobbing. Inconsolable. Had he written it on the plane, before the crash, as the weather made the flight increasingly frightening? Worse still, had he had some kind of ghastly foresight?

As I've thought about his words, though, I've come to believe they were nothing more than an offhand, albeit haunting, remark about the Friday flight from Colorado Springs to Las Vegas. Seth told me he'd had to "hold it" the entire trip, because there was no onboard restroom. He missed the free drinks and snacks he looked forward to on commercial flights. For Seth, those small differences between a private plane and the flights he was used to would easily have made the plane ride an exception to a great time.

Nonetheless, the crushing poignancy still gives me goose bumps.

PART 2

CHAPTER 15

AFTERMATH

September 27, 1995

Dear Dr. Saltzman,
  We invite you to come live with us for awhile.

Your friends,
Sammie, Jared, and Maggi Johnson

(Two Broadmoor students and their mother)

* * *

I finished the phone call that effectively ended life as I knew it, and collapsed on the tile steps outside the laundry room. I wailed, sobbed, cried, and wailed again. Donna held me and sobbed along with me. After several minutes I realized I had to do something besides cry. I'd been raised to deal with adversity by focusing on whatever would move me forward.

There are things that need to be done.

I had to tell my family and Joel's family. School would start on time in a few hours and I had to let Dr. Else, my superintendent, know. With something to do, I would be able to get through the seconds and minutes that were looming ahead of me.

I called my parents and gave them the devastating news. I had to pause to cry between statements.

"The plane crashed south of Pueblo."

"It was very bad weather."

"Yes, they were almost home."

"Everyone died. The pilot and his wife, too."

My parents cried silently into the phone between questions.

"We will be on a plane in the morning. We will call Linda, Rob, and Andy."

Next I called Harvey and Sarah Herzog. Our conversation was similar and they said that they would drive from Pueblo the next day to be with me. They called Tracy, Michael, Lee, and Margaret.

I hung up and looked at Donna. We hugged and shed some more tears. The phone rang. It was my brother Rob. Although he had heard the details from my parents he needed to hear them again from me. I told him all that I knew. We cried. He told me that he would be in Colorado the next day.

Before the phone could ring again I called Dr. Else. He offered to take care of everything at school. He would call the school counselor, Scott Stanec, and then the other principals. He would write a letter for parents that would be distributed at school in the morning. He would notify the teachers.

I'm surprised I didn't say I would call all the teachers myself. Not because it made any sense, but because I so desperately wanted to do anything that would allow me to *not think* about life without Joel, Adam, and Seth, *not think* about what actually happened when the plane crashed, *not think* about the giant hole that had been ripped in my world. I wanted to *do something*. And so I just kept answering the phone and retelling the story, first to my sister Linda, then to Joel's brother Lee, then to my brother Andy.

One of the people I called asked, "Are you kidding?" when I shared the news. As sick as this kind of joke would have been, I so wish I'd been able to say, "Yes, I'm kidding . . . now go back to sleep." At the time I thought asking "Are you kidding?" was a curious thing to say, but now, after many years of hearing bad news myself, I understand this response. It is exactly what I have wanted to say when hearing horrible news, maybe because we so want the news to not be real, and our first reflex is to hope what's being said is some kind of awful prank.

In between my calls, Donna phoned Gary and told him that she was going to stay with me. When the phone stopped ringing and there was no one else to call, Donna and I crawled into my bed and I took a mild analgesic. Just as I was about to fall asleep, I heard Donna's voice.

"Just think. Your family has died in a plane crash, and now everyone you love is getting on a plane to come here."

It was true. But I was too thankful they were all going to be with me to worry about the morbid irony.

I fell asleep hoping that somehow, when I woke up, my family would be home and alive. But the problem with sleeping in the middle of a horrific reality is that it all comes crashing back over you when you wake, making you relive the first gut-twisting moments of realization once again. After a troubled three hours of half-sleep, I came to, and there it all was, patiently waiting for me: my family was dead.

Donna had not slept, and we got up. It was 5:30 a.m.

The doorbell rang a few minutes later. Larry Wellman and Barbara Martin, friends I had met through Joel, were standing on my doorstep. Larry was a psychologist and Barb, a social worker. They wanted to offer whatever help they could.

I don't remember it, but Larry told me I said, "I've lost my whole family. Do you think I'm in shock?"

"Yes," he said.

"Oh," came my reply. Donna, Barb, Larry, and I hugged and cried. Larry and Barb talked to me about Adam and Seth's friends and how they would first hear about the crash. They suggested that the parents of the boys' closest friends be notified before school, so they could be with their kids when the children learned the news. It would be hard for students to hear of the tragedy at school, but much tougher for the boys' best friends. This made absolute sense to me and would give me something to do. I reached for the phone. Barb tried to dissuade me and said they would be happy to make the calls (they wanted something to do as well), but I needed to be in action. If I called the parents of Adam and Seth's favorite people, they would have to believe me.

I got on the phone. "I'm sorry to call so early. I need to let you know some terrible news. Joel, Adam, and Seth died in a small plane crash on their way back from Las Vegas last night."

It was as if my phone was the conduit of a massive shockwave, first slamming into me, then continuing its destructive journey as those we knew and loved answered my calls. And with each call, the effect of the blast: stunned disbelief, then sadness and sympathy.

I accepted the expressions of love and care, and they gave me energy to handle the decisions ahead. I was in shock, but I was aware of what was happening. I had lost my family. My husband. My sons. I couldn't bear that they were gone, but I also couldn't bear someone else dealing with the consequences of their death, decisions that needed to be true to Joel, Adam, and Seth. I kept thinking, "What would Joel do? What would he want? How would he handle this if he were here to help me?" With Joel's voice in my head, I knew I could take care of things. For anything I could not do, my family and friends would give me the support I needed.

*   *   *

More people showed up at the house. I don't remember everyone who came by, but I specifically remember that many of my colleagues made the difficult visit before 8 a.m. These educators understood the effect this tragedy would have on my school and on the community. Mike Galvin, Dave Fussel, Linda Macy, and Rob Danin—my Principals at Lunch (PALS) group—showed up together. Lee Vaughn, a friend and principal from Colorado Springs District 11, came by with a hug for me and condolences from his staff. His wife later left homemade soup on my doorstep in a beautiful handmade pottery bowl. Dave Dilley, who had been one of the first administrators I worked with in Cheyenne Mountain, was also there early in the morning. After giving me a hug and telling me a few anecdotes about Adam and Seth from a time when the four of us played golf, he went to Broadmoor Elementary and provided the teachers with words of encouragement. I knew if I could not be with the staff, Dave would know what to say.

* * *

Dear Broadmoor Staff,

I just got back into my office after visiting your school on this morning that brought such dreadful news to us all. I just had to write you to tell you how very touched I was to watch you working with your kids with such courage and love. I cannot fathom the loss your school has just felt and yet your spirit was one of such nurturing for each other and the kids. God bless you all.

Dave Dilley

(An administrator and friend who helped out at Broadmoor the first morning after the crash)

* * *

Gary and Aaron, Donna's husband and son, stopped by the house. A continual stream of people came and left all day. Some of the time I stayed in my bedroom and people came to see me in there. Some of the time I made it out into the living room where there were people standing around, sitting, and talking.

I do remember one person coming by the house that I did not want to see. She was one of the moms from Broadmoor, someone for whom rules never seemed to apply, as I had witnessed at school in matters regarding her or her children. I was barely acquainted with her, but knew of her need to be in the middle of everything—even when it was inappropriate. As soon as I heard her voice, I made a beeline for the bedroom. I sent Donna out to tell whoever was greeting people at the door that I was unavailable. She was persistent.

"I want to see Nancy."

"Nancy is in her bedroom and needs some private time."

"Well, I need to see her today and I want to give her this food."

I wanted to yell from the bedroom, "I AM NOT EATING!"

"Please feel free to leave the food with me. I will let Nancy know that you stopped by."

Not to be deterred, she pressed, "I am going out of town later today and I have to see her before I leave or I won't get to see her until I come back." An unfortunate scheduling conflict—and without question, the very last concern on my mind.

Thank goodness whoever the watchdog was at the time did not buckle and let her back to see me. I wasn't trying to be mean. I just didn't have the mental capacity to deal with busybodies. Her antics did inject some unintentional humor into the grimness, however.

* * *

The phone rang often but someone else usually answered it or let it go to voicemail. When a local reporter called, Donna told him that I was not available. I could tell she was trying to shake him.

"Who is it?" I asked.

"Someone from the newspaper."

"Give me the phone." For the next half hour, I talked about Joel, Adam, and Seth at length. In a crazy way, it was a break from all the sadness and grief. Instead of discussing their deaths, I was sharing stories about the essence of their lives.

I received another call early that morning, from authorities in the county where the plane had crashed. Information was needed.

"We would like to know what to do with the bodies. What would you like us to do?"

What would I like you to do with the bodies? They are not bodies. They are Joel, Adam, and Seth, my family, my world. I would like you to bring my family to me alive.

I had no idea.

"Do I need to come get them?"

The caller said they could bring them to Colorado Springs to a funeral home and notify me when they had arrived.

"Yes, fine. When do you think that will be?"

I was told that Joel, Adam, and Seth would be at the funeral home later that day.

Relatives started to arrive. Friends made runs to the airport. Cars clogged the driveway, then the street. By the end of the day, Monday, September 25, everyone on both sides of our immediate families was together in Colorado Springs.

*   *   *

Mary Polaski, the speed skating coach, showed up at the house sometime during the day. She took all the sheets off the beds and washed them so that family members could stay at the house. I was incredibly grateful, but at the same time wished nothing would ever have to change in the boys' rooms, so I could crawl into their beds whenever I wanted and immerse myself in the wonderful smell of them.

Joel's insurance agent came by. He asked me to sit down on the couch to discuss an important matter.

"Joel took out life insurance policies with me, and you need to know you are well taken care of."

My face flushed with anger. Why did he need to tell me this now? My family had been dead less than twenty-four hours, and he was already talking to me about money? It felt incredibly offensive. I remember thinking I didn't even want the money because of the reason I was getting it, and I certainly didn't want to talk to him about it that day. In retrospect, I now realize he was just trying to ease any financial concerns I might have had. In fact, I am eternally grateful to everyone, including Harvey Herzog, who talked Joel into buying life insurance.

That night, my parents slept in the guest bedroom and my sister slept with me. Rob and Ed slept in one of the boy's bedrooms and I think Lee slept in the other. Other relatives and siblings stayed in nearby hotels.

*   *   *

9/26, 10:49 a.m.

Nancy,

Cindy and Karinn came by to give you a hug. They hugged me instead.

Dad

(Handwritten note found on the kitchen counter)

*   *   *

Tuesday started early with another phone call from the authorities.

"Everything that was found in the plane, and on the ground after the plane crash, has been brought to Colorado Springs. It is all at the Osborne house."

I was given the address and told I needed to come identify and pick up Joel's, Adam's, and Seth's belongings. As several of us got into my truck, I noticed the weather. It was a beautiful day with the sun shining and the skies clear.

How could there have been such a severe storm just thirty-six hours earlier?

For many years after the plane crash, I noticed that there would be two or three days of bad weather the third week of September. This weather would be followed by absolutely clear and dry days until December. Every year I had the same thought.

Why was the Davis Cup held the third week of September in 1995?

When we arrived at Homer and Linda's condominium, not too far from the country club where Joel and the boys had played tennis, I saw that everything was on the front lawn, including gym bags, backpacks, and plastic garbage bags. The garbage bags held things that had been strewn on the ground at the crash site. Items were spread out on the ground because Homer's and Linda's families were identifying personal effects as well. It reminded me of a garage sale.

A sickening jolt ricocheted through me. My eyes landed on what was going to be Seth's ticket to riches: his treasured hat, with Agassi's and Sampras's autographs. Another wave of crippling realization.

We made awkward introductions and hugged Homer's and Linda's families. Then we returned to the task of identifying our loved ones' effects.

Joel's tennis bag and the boys' backpacks were among the items laid out. We picked everything up hurriedly and drove home, where it all went into Seth's room. I opened Seth's pack. Dozens of small, playing card-sized playbills greeted me, adorned with pictures of half-dressed women. He had picked them up off the sidewalks in Las Vegas. The corners of my mouth turned up, ever so slightly. I spotted the corner of a notebook: Seth's journal that he had to write in each day. Seeing his handwriting, I started to lose control and put the backpack down. I would have to make time to read the journal when I was by myself and could fall apart.

*   *   *

Joel's and my siblings and I had an impromptu meeting on the back porch at my house. There were many questions to be answered.

"When should we have the service?"

"Where should we have the service?"

"Who will speak at the service?"

"Who will lead the service?"

"Now that the bodies are in Colorado Springs, what should we do with them?"

"Do you want Joel, Adam, and Seth cremated or buried?"

"If they are cremated, where do you want to put the ashes?"

"If they are buried, where do you want to bury them?"

"Did Joel have a will?"

"Did Joel have life insurance?"

It was, of course, overwhelming. But that didn't seem to matter. I was expected to make the decisions. And I wanted to make the decisions. But in the most intense days of my grief I had to make unfathomable choices and do it without Joel.

Two weeks before the crash, Joel and I had been to a memorial service for a friend at the Antlers Hotel in downtown Colorado Springs. We talked about alternatives to a church or temple. We liked the idea of having a memorial in a big room open to the outside. We agreed that we would like to be cremated. It had seemed so sensible and pragmatic talking about it hypothetically. Now that Joel, Adam, and Seth were the people who had died, it seemed surreal.

I suggested that we have a memorial service in a very large room. The only place I could imagine was the same room in which Joel and I had discussed our own funerals—the Antlers Hotel ballroom. Rob volunteered to be the person in charge. Gary, Donna's husband, contacted a rabbi who was willing to lead the service.

We set the time for 6:30 p.m. Wednesday, three days after the crash. We hoped that the date and time would give everyone coming from out of town time to arrive, but also work for those who were already there and couldn't stay long. Plus, I wanted people from the schools to be able to attend without having to miss work.

The Antlers Hotel ballroom was reserved for the service. Michael Herzog started putting together a slide show with pictures and music. I asked several people to speak and they all graciously agreed. I wanted to talk about Joel, Adam, and Seth, too, so I started thinking about what I would say.

*   *   *

We went to a local funeral home where the bodies had been brought from the crash site. I sat in a conference room with several of my family members and the people from the funeral home. Whatever I decided to do with the bodies, they would have to be placed in coffins first.

"Would you like the simple pine boxes? Or the more expensive caskets?"

These questions made no sense to me.

How could I burn Joel, Adam, and Seth? How could I seal them in coffins and put them in the ground?

I did not want to have them cremated or buried; I wanted them alive.

I'll take "C", none of the above.

I think I picked the least expensive options but I honestly do not remember.

I asked where the bodies were and was told that they were downstairs. I asked if I could see them. Lee also wanted to see his brother and his nephews.

"You do not want to see them," I was told by the staff. "We have some experience with this, and we do not recommend it."

I persisted. Finally, we were taken to the funeral home's sanctuary. The bodies had been brought up on what looked like collapsible cots. They were wrapped in white fabric and looked like mummies. The only face visible was Seth's. His eyes and lips were closed. A little blood was at the corner of his mouth. My heart ached looking at his face and those beautiful lashes he'd inherited from his father. I wanted to hear his laugh and see his smile, but instead I saw only a heavily made-up circle of a face with white cloth covering everything else.

Lee and I asked if we could please see Adam's and Joel's faces. We were told that this would not be a good idea. Again we persisted, but we were not allowed to see anything more. We all touched the white-wrapped forms of our sons, our grandsons, our brother, our brother-in-law, our nephews, my husband. We sat in the sanctuary with them for a long time.

I called school and told Deb Young, Seth's teacher, that if she wanted to come by the funeral home, she could see Seth. She made a visit on her way home. I knew how much Mrs. Young had meant to Seth and I think I called her as much for Seth as for her. The bodies were then taken back downstairs.

*   *   *

The moment I saw Mrs. Young's face was the moment it actually seemed real. Seth was dead. A boy in my fifth grade class, Seth Herzog, and his brother, Adam, and father, Joel, had been in an airplane accident the previous night and were all killed.

Mrs. Young's class sat on the floor and passed the tissue box around. My stomach was filled with black butterflies. Many of those around me were trying to be brave. I was one of the few who wasn't crying, but the grief just swelled up inside of me. Until then I hadn't known that death was so close.

The school formed grief groups for our class. We talked about our fears and how we were afraid of more things since Seth had died. Not wanting to get on an airplane because we were afraid we could die was one of the discussions. We were told not to be so afraid because your fears can control your life. We also did an exercise where we traced each other's bodies on a big piece of paper. Using different colors to represent our feelings (happiness, anger, fear, sadness) we colored in the body. We all ended up with a different picture because we felt our emotions in different places. Sometimes we think we are sick, but we may actually be feeling an emotion. We were feeling lots of emotions when Seth died.

For our Back to School Night we had all made a face to resemble ours and dressed a body form to be us. Before Seth died he had made his. We sat his up in his desk and it seemed like he was still with us in our memories of him. He will also be with us when, in the future, other friends die, because we learned so much from his death.

(From an essay written by Kailey Garland, one of Seth's classmates, two years after the crash)

*   *   *

I still couldn't get my head around the thought of cremating my family, but it's what Joel had said he wanted—even if he'd had no idea I would have to implement his wishes only days later. It seemed natural to choose the same for the boys as well. I decided that I wanted to put the ashes in separate marble urns with nameplates on the top of each. We could bury the urns at a cemetery, where friends and family would be able to "visit" them. I also reasoned that if I ever moved from Colorado Springs, I could retrieve them and take them with me.

I knew about an old city cemetery named Fairview on the west side of town and asked my siblings and Joel's if they wanted to visit it. They agreed to go with me. We climbed into two vans that had been lent to us for the week by Bob Penkus, an auto dealer in town. Bob's children had gone to Broadmoor and his generous offer meant we could make many necessary trips as a group, without taking multiple cars. It was just one of many kind gestures from friends and businesses in the community.

On our way to Fairview Cemetery, the talk in the van was not about the burial. We discussed a TV movie about my family. I don't remember who I wanted to play me, but we thought perhaps we could find a young Robert Redford look-alike to play Joel.

We met with the manager at the cemetery, and he showed us some options. I learned that Joel, Adam, and Seth could be buried in the same plot together. This made me feel better about leaving their ashes at Fairview. I knew I could work on the headstones with another Broadmoor family, the Wilhelms, who owned a company that created monuments. We walked around the cemetery and found a spot we all liked.

Returning to the house, we found the refrigerator packed with food from friends and the school community. Sam Merrill, my mentor and friend with whom I had worked at Horizon Middle School, arrived from Phoenix, where he was now a principal. He set up an Italian kitchen in my house and started cooking breakfasts, lunches, and dinners for everyone. These were welcome gifts, because while I knew others needed to be fed, I had no interest in eating.

Uncles and aunts and close friends from California and Minnesota arrived before Wednesday's service. Joel's friends from Guillermo's Squash Club generously paid for all of these people to stay at the Broadmoor Hotel for as many nights as they wanted.

* * *

On Wednesday, the day of the service, we all—families and close friends—drove to the Antlers together in the vans. When we got to the hotel we were ushered into a room near the ballroom. On our way to the private room I could see children from school, former colleagues, tennis and squash players, and what looked to me like the entire Colorado Springs community. In fact, there were over twenty-five hundred people at the memorial service. It felt like a party atmosphere. People who had not seen each other in years greeted each other with hugs, smiles, then tears.

Just before 6:30 p.m. we entered the ballroom. I heard a piano. There were news cameras. A reporter asked Joel's dad to comment. I remember spotting someone I hadn't seen for a long time and spontaneously breaking into a smile, happy to see her. Then, just as quickly, the smile evaporated, the reason for her presence bringing me back to the moment. I was also moved by the faces I didn't recognize. I surmised many were Joel's customers, there to honor the tennis guy who told jokes, always remembered their shoe size, and bragged constantly about his wife and kids. At the front of the room was Adam's hockey team, sitting on the floor, wearing their jerseys. Next to them sat Seth's hockey team in their jerseys. People flowed out the back and into the hallways. I was overcome by the outpouring of love and support.

The music stopped and the rabbi began speaking. He started with a prayer in Hebrew and then introduced each person who spoke: my brother Rob, Harvey Herzog, Toby and Jack Tieman, Lee Herzog, then me. (Eulogies have been provided in the Appendix.)

People have told me they don't know how I was able to do it. That they couldn't imagine getting up in front of so many and talking about their loved ones. The truth is, I was compelled to talk. Overwrought with love and sadness, I gathered strength from the thousands of people who came to mourn and celebrate those three lives with me. I wanted desperately to hold on to the Joel, Adam, and Seth I knew, and believed I could do so by talking about them.

When I was finished speaking, we presented Michael's beautiful slide-show. We announced that our families would stay until we had a chance to greet everyone personally. I remember that the first person to come up and hug me was Lucia Duran, our housekeeper of many years. Lucia had watched Adam and Seth grow up. I don't remember the last person with whom I spoke, but we talked, cried, and laughed with everyone until 10:30 p.m.

*   *   *

Sept. 28, 1995

Dear Nancy,

Our family attended the beautifully moving memorial service last night for Joel, Adam, and Seth. Although all of the speakers were truly so inspirational, I found your eulogy to have been one of the most profoundly heartrending and touching experiences of my life. My limited past interactions with you, as well as what I saw last night, just reaffirm my belief that you have such a tremendous capacity for love, compassion, and understanding of others.

You, Nancy, are a gift in this world to children that is so special . . . I truly hope and pray that this will help to sustain you as time goes on, both in your personal and professional lives.

We as a family feel so very privileged to have you as our school principal, and look forward to being as supportive and comforting as we are possibly capable of, as time goes on.

Fondly,
Ginny Bullen

(Mother of a Broadmoor student)

* * *

Thursday morning I, my parents, Joel's parents, our siblings, and Donna and Gary met the rabbi at the cemetery to bury the urns. We placed each one in the ground. On top of the boys' urns we placed a few of their prized possessions—stuffed animals, hockey paraphernalia. As part of Jewish tradition, we each shoveled dirt on top of the urns. A prayer was said.

On Friday, two days after the memorial for Joel, Adam, and Seth, there was a service for Homer and Linda at the Broadmoor Community Church. The celebration of their lives was beautiful and a great tribute to the love that Homer and Linda shared. Although I had not known them well, I wanted to be part of the celebration of their lives.

Later that day, Rob, Ed, and I met with Scott Blackmun and John Cook, Joel's friends and attorneys. They had offered to help me figure out what I needed to do with my assets and the store. The life insurance policies would allow me to stay in the house, and I was now able to feel the relief Joel's agent had hoped to provide on Monday. I could not imagine having to move.

There was also word from the National Transportation Safety Board (NTSB) that there would be an investigation into the cause of the crash.

This was standard procedure, but it was also reassuring. Even in my grief, I, and many others, wanted to know what had happened.

By the end of the week there was nothing left to plan, and many people had gone back to their homes. We decided to have a get-together Friday night at the house with friends and the people who were still in town. We had so much food that there was no need to plan. Toby Tieman and I sat on the stairs to the boys' bedrooms. I tried to get drunk on whiskey but was not particularly successful; I really didn't like the taste of alcohol, and hard liquor was the worst.

I was of two minds emotionally. I liked people taking care of me and keeping me company—but didn't like them fawning over me. I wanted my family to stay—and wanted them to go home. Being in a crisis mode only put off starting the true grieving process, and although I dreaded the dark passage ahead, I knew the only way out was through it. Normal wasn't remotely possible, but I needed to find whatever the new version of it was.

*   *   *

Saturday morning my sister Linda and I drove to see Deb Calegar. I had met Deb in 1986 when she put a full set of acrylic nails on my finger-nails to thwart my lifelong habit of nail biting. The compulsion had plagued me since childhood, but when I was an assistant principal at Timberview Middle School, the counselor there had told me about Deb. I started having acrylic nails applied and getting them "filled" every two weeks. To my amazement, it had worked, and for the first time in my adult life, I had been able to have fingernails that weren't chewed to the quick.

Deb and I became good friends. The Saturday after the crash, three days after we had the memorial service for my family, I had a previously scheduled nail appointment. When Linda and I walked into the salon, everyone stopped talking. Deb got up from her table and walked toward me. She burst into tears. She had met Joel and the boys many times over the years; on busy Saturdays they would come with me for my appointment. Deb enveloped me in her zaftig, five-foot, ten-inch frame. I comforted her and told her that I was doing okay.

As Deb did my nails, she told me that everyone in the salon bet that I wouldn't show up for my appointment. Deb was sure I would. She knew I would want to talk to her *and* get my nails done. Our friendship grew stronger after the crash.

Later, during our appointments, I would ask Deb about being single. She was married once for six months, dated infrequently, and seemed to have a full life. When I started dating, she wanted to meet my dates and give me her thoughts about them. Several years into our relationship, Deb left her job as a nail technician and became a paralegal. She continued doing my nails and being my friend, confidant, and dog-walking companion. Tragically—and still hard for me to believe—Deb died in 2009 on a cross-country auto trip with her nephew, mother, and father.

*   *   *

October 1, 1995

Dear Nancy,

Seeing you yesterday left me with feelings of joy as well as sorrow. Sorrow for your loss and deep sadness, joy for your incredible strength: the ability to still see humor and the positive in the tragedy of death is remarkable.

If there is ever a time you need a friend, I am always here—you need only call. It is somewhat of a selfish offer, as I gain such a sense of well-being around you. My thoughts are with you almost constantly—I somehow have a changed attitude about life (a good change). I only hope to have a tenth of the kindness and strength you possess!

I love you!

Deb

(Deb Calegar, my close friend)

CHAPTER 16

IN COMES LOVE, OUT GOES SADNIS

I STARTED TO feel like I was living a separate reality from the rest of the world. The dire, all-hands-on-deck phase was over, family members were returning to their homes. I was emerging from my shock-induced cloud and moving directly to all-encompassing sadness. The full measure of what had happened was taking shape, and it seemed to look at lot like hell. But for all of its pain, this was the beginning of the unavoidable process that would hopefully someday, somehow, result in a state slightly less unbearable than the one I was in now. I believed that the sooner I got started, the sooner I would find myself on the other side—whatever that meant.

I decided I needed to be at work. It would be difficult, surely, but the passion for my job that had sometimes caused guilt and stress now felt like a lifeline. Alone as never before, I needed the bustling noises of children around me, the support of my colleagues, the purpose that I felt so ardently in leading a school. I also felt a keen responsibility to the kids, to model an approach of continuing to move forward, even when terrible things happen, even when it's not easy. It wasn't about stuffing feelings and pretending that everything was okay. It was about acknowledging that loss was a part of life—then showing up and facing the day on the day's terms. I was professional, but wasn't afraid of others seeing me shed an occasional tear as I moved through this challenge.

My sister Linda was still with me. I overheard her talking to the school office, telling them I would return on Monday, a week after the crash. They discussed doing something with stuffed bears because we were the Broadmoor Bears. I pictured myself walking into school with them all watching, then everyone lining up to give me a bear. The idea terrified me; I was sure I'd fall apart. I made wild motions to her while she was talking and tried to get her to say, "NO." Linda finished the conversation.

"You can relax. What they are planning is very sweet and supportive."

The actual plan was for the kids to bring bears to school, but I would be able to go around to classrooms, at my own pace, to greet the students. I should have known my staff would come up with an idea that would allow the students to be involved, but also give me space to connect with them in my own way and time. It was brilliant.

All of my family had gone back to their own homes by Sunday night. For the first time since the crash I went to bed by myself. I took some acetaminophen and crawled into bed on Joel's side. I imagined him lying next to me and turned on the TV. I cried and waited for sleep to overtake me.

* * *

I got ready for school on Monday, trying to guess which shoes Seth would have picked out for me. I looked in the mirror and heard Joel whispering, "You look beautiful." Adam's voice yelled in my mind, "Hurry up Mom, we're going to be late."

I arrived at school after everyone was in the building. I did not want to be there when the students were getting out of their cars, and I didn't want to wave at everyone and act as if everything was fine. I was functioning, but light years from fine.

I walked up the sidewalk and into my office. Everything looked exactly the same as I had left it but of course seemed completely different. I knew that this dual existence was going to be my life for a long time.

I saw a yellow, two-by-two-inch sticky note on my desk.

"In comes love, out goes sadnis. Rebecca."

Rebecca was a first grader. I sat in my chair and let the tears flow.

* * *

As I slowly made my way around to the classrooms, bears and hugs and bear hugs met me everywhere I went. When I got overwhelmed, I had my office to retreat to and the sticky note to read.

I stayed for a few hours that day and left before school got out. Over the next few days, I was able to stay longer. Sometimes I made it through the whole day; others I left early or during lunch to meet with the lawyers, Fran at the Bank of Broadmoor, or Peggy, Joel's accountant. Most days I went back to school after the students were gone, to do whatever I could to stay caught up.

I knew I was lucky to have a job that I felt made a difference. I took strength from the students seeing me *choose* to keep going in the face of a very big challenge. It was, and still is, one of my core beliefs, and it sustained me in those first awful days after the crash.

*   *   *

As I settled back into work, I heard how my school community had responded to the news initially and during the week I'd been gone. The staff had been notified at about 5:30 a.m. Monday, the day after the crash. By the time the news reached the last few people, it was like a game of "telephone" and facts had fallen by the wayside. Some heard Seth had survived. Linda Shea, the band teacher, rehearsed what she was going to say to Seth, only to learn that he too had perished in the crash. Some thought I had also died.

Every staff member showed up early to school for a meeting with Dr. Else and our school counselor, Scott Stanec. Principals and school counselors from other schools in the district arrived to help hand out letters to parents and be available for students. When the bell rang at the beginning of the day, all teachers met their students at their classroom doors. They explained what had happened at an age-appropriate level. They answered questions. Then they made the day as normal as possible for the kids.

I spoke with Dianne Allen, a Broadmoor parent who found out about the crash when she dropped her children off at school. She had been approached by Debbie Pierre, the principal at Cheyenne Elementary School, who walked up to Dianne's car. Dianne rolled the window down. Debbie said, "I have the most terrible news to give you." Dianne was handed a letter from Dr. Else saying that Joel, Adam, and Seth Herzog had died in a small plane crash. Dianne got out of her car to find other parents. She thought it might be a Dianne hoax. But other parents confirmed the news, and together they tried to make sense out of senselessness.

The principals and school counselors from other schools stayed for part of the day. Dr. Else and Caryl Thomason, the assistant superintendent, remained at school for the entire day. Parents made themselves available to take over a class for a few minutes or to hand out hugs that day and for the rest of the week. Scott Stanec played a key role in our recovery. Scott had been one of my fifth grade students in 1976, and we had reconnected when he got a job teaching at Cheyenne Mountain Junior High. I had hired him just a month before school started to be our counselor. Now he had been suddenly thrown into a leadership role at Broadmoor. He kept an eye on Seth's friends, me, and others who might need extra support.

*   *   *

September 8, 1995

Free day: write at least 1/2 page on whatever you wish.

I'm writing about what I wish for. I wish I found my folder. I wish I had a lot of money. I wish I never had any more homework. I wish Mrs. Young was my teacher for the rest of my life.

(From Seth's fifth grade journal)

*   *   *

Several weeks after the crash, Rita Cook joined the efforts to support our school community. Rita was a social worker who was part of a program sponsored by Junior League through Pikes Peak Hospice. She had extensive experience working with children who had suffered significant loss. We decided that Rita would meet with two groups of students each week for the remainder of the school year. One group was Seth's close friends. The other group was students whom the staff thought could use some support. Rita also met with the staff to talk about their feelings and about how to interact with me.

Adam's junior high school was a bit of a different story. The first day after the crash, it was announced over the loudspeaker that students who were upset and needed support should report to the library. Parents who heard the news and went to the junior high to check on their children were discouraged from interrupting the school day. One parent was told, "We have dealt with at least one death a year here. We know how to handle the situation."

I got a call from the school the week after the crash.

"What would you like us to do with the things from Adam's locker? Would you like to pick them up or have us drop them off?"

I was rocked back on my heels.

"I don't know."

The caller repeated the question.

"Umm," I mumbled, "could you drop them off at my office?"

I imagined another black garbage bag of Adam's belongings.

When the items were delivered by a staff member from the junior high,

I heard that the school had never had so many students react so strongly to a classmate's death. I got the impression they were baffled by this. The staff person also seemed completely unaware of who I was, as if sharing this odd phenomenon with someone not related to the situation. I remember saying that Adam was a very special young man. I held his things close as I walked to my car.

Seth's desk remained in his classroom for a few weeks at the request of the students. They had covered it in remembrances. On the back of his chair was the "Seth" he had made out of a nylon, a stretched hanger, and construction paper for Back to School Night.

Rita had started working with Seth's close friends and asked if I would be willing to answer some questions from the group. She warned me that they wanted to ask about the crash. I told her that would be fine.

"Did Adam and Seth know that they were going to crash?"

"Did Adam and Seth know that they were going to die?"

"Do you think it hurt when they crashed?"

"Are they in Heaven?"

These were the questions that everyone wondered, including me, but only the children were guileless enough to voice. I answered as honestly as I could.

"I don't think they knew what was going to happen."

"They couldn't see a thing. It was dark and foggy. Have you ever been on a plane when it's inside a cloud? That's how it was."

"They died instantly. I don't think it hurt."

"I think that they are all together, wherever they are."

The kids were very supportive and reassuring. They shared their own stories of loss. Some had lost grandparents and pets. One student's rat had died.

The junior high counselors called and said they had been working with a group of kids who were good friends of Adam. They asked if they could bring the group over to see Adam's room. This was a tough call. I knew that seeing Adam's friends would be hard for me but I wanted to be with them anyway. I also knew that kids—especially adolescents—deal with grief in different ways than adults, and I was supportive of anything they might find helpful. I consented to the visit. Eight students and the counselors came over. They sat on Adam's bed or stood against the wall and like Seth's friends, they asked questions. I let them choose some things to take with them. After twenty minutes, the counselors said they had to go and asked if I would mind taking home the kids who weren't ready to leave.

Instead of saying, "Sorry, I need to go crawl into bed and sob for a while," which was how I felt, I agreed. It was a double-edged sword, this "showing up during hard times" example I was trying to set. Continuing in my job as I grieved, and believing that growth, learning, and healing could come from it for all of us, provided the meaning I needed to get up in the morning. But it could also give the impression that I was handling it all just fine, resulting in careless presumptions. The counselors left and some students stayed longer. I drove them home, and after dropping off the last student, burst into tears. I was glad that they had made the visit, but once home, I did crawl into bed, sobbing.

* * *

Dear Nancy,

Thank you for opening your heart and sharing yourself during the hardest time of your life. I think of you, Joel, Adam, and Seth often. My heart pains and my soul agonizes, wishing they were still alive.

When I saw you on the Monday that the Junior High learned of the death, I wasn't able to tell you how much the students grieved and showed their love. Many of Adam's good friends such as Matt Rogers, James Kovacevek, Kolsie M. and Graham S., plus other kids who knew him in some way (most of the school), spent the day in the library (which we took over). Sharing their grief, speaking fondly of your family, and wanting them back.

I know you are a strong lady. Continue to know that many will support and comfort you. If there is anything I can do, no matter what, let me know. Please?

Love,
Steve

(Steve Hickory, one of the Cheyenne Mountain Junior High school counselors, former counselor at Broadmoor)

* * *

A few weeks after the crash, I realized that Adam's school picture had been taken right before he left for Las Vegas. I called the junior high and identified myself, asking if it would be possible to get Adam Herzog's pictures.

The person who answered replied, "Alex?"

I said, "*Adam. Adam Herzog.*"

She said, "Let me get you the principal." I was put on hold. I hung up.

I asked my secretary, Lois, to see if she could get the pictures for me, which she did.

* * *

Waking up was a difficult time, as reality would reestablish itself every morning. If waking up was hard, getting up was even harder. Luckily, Shoshi and Squeak, the boys' dogs, would usually overrule my inertia. Joel had tried, with mixed results, to ban the dogs from our bedroom. Now they were not only allowed, but welcomed. If I could, I would get them to sleep with me. They were comforting, but they also forced me out of bed; a dog's needs make no exceptions for grief. Once up, I would usually take them for a run before getting ready for school.

Lois and the staff kept the school going when I was there, and when I wasn't. I did lunch duty, attended meetings, talked to parents and students. Our school was to be renovated; I had to put together a team of teachers and parents to work on plans for the remodel. I had not been back to a leadership meeting with the other principals so I talked to Dr. Else about when I should join the other administrators again.

"Some of the people on the leadership team aren't sure how to talk to you. Do you have any ideas?" he asked.

I had my hands full dealing with my own grief, let alone coming up with tips for others. I suggested that having a grief counselor come to the next leadership team meeting, without me there, might be a good idea. Dr. Else arranged the session with a counselor from the Employees Assistance Program. I don't know what the counselor said, but at the next leadership meeting, my colleagues warmly welcomed me back.

*　*　*

Several weeks after the crash, I met with my attorneys, Scott Blackmun and John Cook, to talk about the results of the NTSB investigation. According to witnesses at the site of the crash in Westcliffe, Colorado, the plane struck the mountainside around 7:15 p.m. Rebecca Sewell was milking goats in her barn when a plane "flying very low" seemed to go directly over her house.

"But the fog is deceptive," she said, "and it was *very* foggy. Just a few moments later, I heard a loud report, very like a high-powered rifle, followed by several lesser 'bangs.' Then all was quiet." Sewell sprinted to the house and called 911. It took rescuers four-plus hours to reach the site of the crash due to the brutal weather conditions. The final report included transmissions between Homer and the tower. Homer had been informed that there was bad weather in Colorado and had responded, "It looks broken up in front of us. We'll let you know later on." It was ultimately determined that the crash was due to pilot error.

*　*　*

Work helped, but my life felt empty and desolate. The initial numbness had given way to relentless waves of comprehension, as my brain struggled to process the facts. I would think I had incorporated the new reality—that Joel, Adam, and Seth were gone, dead, and not coming back—but then it would hit me again in a new way, as if I were hearing it for the first time. It was like one of those dreams within a dream, where you know you're in a dream, and you think you wake up, only to find you're still asleep, just in a different dream. Life seemed one-dimensional, and I was a flat illustration in a book.

I knew I needed to talk to someone besides my friends, a professional who could help me come to grips with it all. I made an appointment to see Dr. Bermudez, the psychologist who had helped me through my chemo-therapy treatments. I told him I didn't want to miss school to meet with him. He asked if I thought it was important for me to talk to him. I told him it was but I didn't want to miss work. He convinced me otherwise.

Dr. Bermudez knew about the plane crash but let me do the talking.

"I want to know how long I'm going to feel this bad. I can't stand it."

My stomach hurt. I didn't want to eat. I pretended that I had energy, but I had none. I weighed less than a hundred pounds.

"Most people who have tragic loss like this start to feel a little better after about four months. For some it's three, others five, but the average is about four months."

I couldn't believe it would be that soon, but I wanted to. Although I'd asked the question, I worried that I might remain in this state for the rest of my life. Did he think I should take an antidepressant? He answered that he wouldn't recommend it at that time, that working with me before had given him a good sense of how I handled traumatic events, and he believed that I would be able to navigate this loss, despite its magnitude, without pharmaceutical aids. I was glad to hear this, because I worried that taking antidepressants might slow my recovery. I was a mess, but still believed it was important to feel my feelings of despair and sadness, while learning constructive, healthy ways to face the future. Dr. Bermudez explained that if my depression did not lift over time that we might consider meds. I wasn't against them if he felt they were needed; as with everything on my journey of grieving, I made no judgments of whether specific coping methods were "good" or "bad." I know many in grief are greatly helped by medications. For me, however, it felt important to try and develop my own set of coping tools.

*   *   *

Dearest Nancy,

I've tried to think of what to say to you. I've finally come to the conclusion that I can't say anything except that I'm ANGRY. I am angry at fate, at life, at clouds and hills and bad weather, at airplanes and those who fly them. I'm angry at loneliness, at loss of love, companionship, friendship, at emptiness.

I'm angry it has happened to you.

I'm angry that I don't know what to say. By being angry, though, I feel that I am losing some of life, its preciousness, its frailty, its beauty, its awesome singleness.

I hope to overcome this anger with time, to get on with living. I—we—will always be angry, there will always be a hole left empty within us. We don't know how to be human when inhumane things happen.

But we will survive, we will grow in our respect for life, day by day.

We want to hold you, comfort you, but we—I—am still angry.

I love you, friend,
Tom

(Tom Mahony, friend of ours and customer of Joel's)

* * *

As time went on, my emotional journey was not a nice, steady course of improvement. I reached a point where the pain seemed endless, and I realized I no longer had any real will to live. I told Donna I didn't care if I died, and stopped wearing my seat belt. It wasn't that I had a plan to kill myself, just that I wasn't going to go out of my way to protect myself from life's perils.

Our conversation went something like this.

Me: I'm so tired of living this way. I'm the only one who has to get up every day and face this reality.

Donna: I would miss you and I know Rob would, too.

Me (petulantly): Fine. I'll wear my seat belt.

I put it on and wore it whenever I was in the car with Donna.

I told Dr. Bermudez how I was feeling, that I was tired of the pain of living without my family. Everyone else could be sad about losing Joel, Adam, and Seth, but I was the only one who had to wake up in an empty house, make it through the day, then go to bed in an empty house. Dr. Bermudez was very specific about what I should do if I ever thought seriously about harming myself.

"You have to get out of your head. You have to call someone. Think of what you would do if you were drowning. If someone threw you a life preserver what would you do?"

"Reach up and grab it."

"Yes. You need to reach up and grab the life preserver. You have to call someone and get out of your head."

This advice had a profound impact on me. Although I couldn't imagine ever feeling happy again, I realized this was a time when I couldn't trust my emotions, especially when I was at my lowest. I needed to be willing to ask for, and accept, help from others.

I was still in a deep abyss, but my desire to be alive was deeper. I had loved being part of a family with Joel, Adam, and Seth. I still loved my parents and siblings, Joel's family, my friends, and didn't want to hurt them. I loved the students and teachers at my school, and felt responsible for them. They had all pulled together to be there for the kids and me. I didn't want to let them down.

Even in—especially in—my darkest moments, I had to keep reaching up and grabbing the life preserver.

*   *   *

Rob and Donna called me every day. My sister and parents called almost as often. Friends took me out and tried to get me to eat. Donna and Gary picked me up one evening for a family dinner at a restaurant. It sounded low-key enough, but when we got to the restaurant there was a forty-five minute wait to be seated. A woman who had children at Broadmoor saw me and came over to tell me how sorry she was.

Then she said, "God took your children for a reason."

Blindsided. I could not think of one good reason why God would take my children. I wanted to say that if she believed this, I thought it would be fine for God to take her children. I wanted my children back. But I said nothing and let my mind wander so I wouldn't have to respond. I wanted to curl up in a ball and cry right then, but managed to wait until dinner was over and we were back in the car.

Valuable lesson for the newly grieving: always take your own car, so you can leave when you need to.

I received letters and notes in the mail every day. Going to the mailbox was something I looked forward to. I worried about the day I would look in the mailbox and it would be empty, but this didn't happen for many months. The letters I received were amazing. They were full of stories about Joel, Adam, Seth, and our family. Some people sent pictures. Most of the letters were from people I knew. Some were not.

There were letters from people who had survived a loss and wanted to share. There were letters from people who said that they could not survive such a loss. There were letters from men who had seen my picture in the paper and wanted to meet me.

I received two books in the mail. One, entitled *A Grace Disguised*, came from Art Daly. His story of loss was as heartbreaking as mine. He was driving over Independence Pass when a boulder fell on his car. His wife and two sons were killed. *A Grace Disguised* was written by Jerry Sittser, who lost his mother, wife, and daughter when they were hit by a drunk driver. The other book, *Companion Through the Darkness*, was sent to me by a woman whose husband died in a small-plane crash. The author, Stephanie Ericsson, lost her husband to a heart attack.

I was enormously touched by these gestures from people who were total strangers, yet took the time to reach out to me. I read both books and gleaned insights from each. My favorite chapter in Ericsson's book is titled, "How Are You?" She writes, "This is the question a grieving person hates. If you ask us, we hate you. If you don't ask us, we hate you." I was indeed sick of people asking me how I was. If I said I was okay (because I was feeling that way at that moment), they would think I was either lying or coldhearted. If I said, "I'm miserable and don't want to take another breath," they would give me advice or be overcome with emotion. If they said, "I know how you feel," my guess was that they didn't, really.

One letter I received was from a man I had known as a teenager. He told me that he had thought about me often, and felt that he had missed his chance for us to be together. He sent me pictures of his two sons who were about Adam's and Seth's ages. A relationship was the last thing on my mind, but I was certainly flattered.

There were always phone messages at home. Most people left messages just to let me know that they were thinking of me. One message was from a representative from the Widow's Association of Colorado Springs.

"Hello. This is Mabel. We get together the third Tuesday of every month. We meet at the Polka Club . . . but we don't do the polka. We would love to have you join us." Pause. "My husband died ten years ago and . . . " Long pause. "I need to tell you that it NEVER gets any better. Please call us at . . . "

I decided the Widow's Association was probably not for me.

* * *

Waking up was hard, but evenings and bedtime were perhaps even more difficult. When the boys were alive, there was so much going on— rushed dinners, often fast food, on the way to or from hockey practices. But we were together. Now, instead of crazy, overlapping schedules, the only things crazy and overlapping were my crying jags and abject misery. Unless I went out or invited someone over, I ate alone. When I did go out with others, I often felt like a fifth wheel. I would have been welcome at hockey practices for Adam's and Seth's teams but I couldn't watch other people's children play hockey. The same was true of tennis. I often stayed at school well into the evening, but eventually I had to go home to take care of the dogs. Sometimes I went to Barnes and Noble or Target, because they were the only stores that stayed open late.

One evening when I was having a particularly hard time, I called an old friend, Tom Cone. Tom had dated one of my roommates at Colorado College and we had run into each other after my divorce from Mike. We became friends and would meet for lunch or drinks and talk about old times. When I met Joel in the summer of 1979, Tom was one of the first people I told that I was in love. Now he lived about five minutes from me. I asked if I could come over to see him. I brought the dogs, and he suggested that we take my dogs and his for a walk. It was 9:30 at night and pitch black out, but I didn't care. We walked and talked. I cried, wailed, talked, and cried some more. I remember wishing that a coyote would eat me. Tom just listened. We walked back to his house, he gave me a big hug, and I went home. Tom let me repeat this drill many times for months after the crash. I have since repaid him for his kindness by encouraging him to go out with a friend. They are now happily married.

At school, if I had to cry, I would go into my office and shut the door. If I needed a break, I got in my car and drove somewhere, crying the whole time. I didn't mind the staff or even the students catching me in a vulnerable moment, seeing evidence of my grieving process—in fact, I thought it was healthy—but I was careful to make sure the major crying jags happened in private. Every so often, I would see the back of a child who looked like Adam or Seth. My heart would jump and adrenalin would course through my veins for several minutes.

When I was alone, I talked to Joel, Adam, and Seth, usually in my head, sometimes out loud. I told them how much I missed them. A few times, I wrote them letters about what was going on in their absence.

I started asking people to tell me things they remembered about my family. A soothing calm would come over me while I listened.

* * *

Dear Ms. Saltzman,

I'm sure you have received notes and cards from many caring people—some you know and some you don't.

I am Joann Geffre, and I share your loss. My husband George and 14-year-old daughter Gina were in a small plane crash on Memorial Day near Last Chance, Colorado. Also on the plane were my sister-in-law and my six-year-old nephew. All four died instantly in the weather-related accident. They were all dearly loved and are greatly missed.

I want to reach out to you and let you know how sorry I am for your tragic loss. And I want to let you know that if you ever feel like talking, please do not hesitate to call, whether it is tomorrow, next week, next month, or a year from now.

Sincerely,
Joann Geffre

(From one of several "radical survivors" who wrote to me of their similar tragedies. It was actually seventeen years before we spoke, but no less meaningful.)

* * *

I had to decide what to do with Total Tennis. When Toby and Jack Tieman came by the house immediately after the crash, I told them they could have the store, but they knew it was the impulsive rashness of a woman not thinking clearly. My attorney Scott advised that the store should be sold, and it should go to someone who loved tennis and people. I knew that Joel thought that Total Tennis was worth a million dollars. I also realized it wasn't worth a million dollars without Joel in the store. Although it was still fall, we needed a buyer who could complete the spring orders. Connie Frazee, who had worked for Joel previously, kindly stepped in to help. She opened the store so people could pick up their racquets or buy something from "Joel's store" one last time. Numerous flower arrangements, left on the sidewalk outside the store, were reminders of how many customers, fellow businesspeople, and members of the tennis community felt the loss.

We put Total Tennis on the market. Offers came in quickly, and we accepted one from a local tennis and squash player.

* * *

I started worrying about the holidays when I saw turkeys advertised in the paper. Taking a short break, I flew to Indiana to be with my parents. They took me out to dinner and got me massages. My mother and I ate lunch with her girlfriends. I was held in the cocoon of their love for four days, and returned in a better frame of mind.

For Thanksgiving, I joined Rob and Ed in Los Angeles. Andy's family flew from Indiana to be with us as well. I especially enjoyed being with Andy, his wife Mary, my niece Rachel, and my nephew Michael, whom I rarely had a chance to see. I was getting used to having two emotions at the same time: my new, anemic version of happiness (which was really just a notch above miserable) and overwhelming anguish. I didn't want to miss going to Disneyland with Andy's family but when I was there, I was overcome by memories of our trips there with the boys. I managed to keep my feelings just under the surface until I was alone. Then they sprung out of me, like a dam giving way.

A couple of months after the crash, I thought it was important for my staff to have time to connect as a group, a sort-of thank-you for their unflagging support. We put together what turned out to be a very powerful retreat at the first of December.

The next week, Rob had a conference in Puerto Rico. I got permission to go with him for five days. I spent most of my time there in the hotel room writing thank-you notes to people who had donated to the Adam and Seth Herzog Memorial Tennis Fund for Colorado. I had "created" this fund as I wrote Joel's, Adam's, and Seth's obituaries. I knew I would be flooded with flowers if I didn't ask for a different kind of gesture, and I wanted people's expressions of sympathy to make a difference. Ultimately, generous donations to the fund totaled more than $35,000, which has been used to support tennis programs for children in rural communities.

I had always been a note writer. It made me feel good to send a card or letter to my friends, teachers, and students. For their birthdays, students at school received a picture of the dogs and me, with good wishes. Now that I was writing notes to people thanking them for their contributions, I realized it was part of my healing. Connecting with people in this way—without the demands of in-person interaction—was good for me. I spent time every day sending notes. When I could focus on others, it made things slightly easier.

After Puerto Rico, there were three weeks until Christmas. I planned a trip to California to be with Rob, Ed, and my parents. Lee Herzog was there, and I would get to see him, as well. I was dreading the holidays but could look forward to being with people I loved.

We had our annual holiday program at school, one during the day, and another performance that night. I was grateful for the proximity of the faculty bathroom so I could duck out for a few minutes, cry in private, dry my tears, and return to watch my students perform.

* * *

Dear Nancy,

I don't know what to say except I love you. There is nothing I can do to make things better or to ease your pain. I feel helpless.

I want to tell you I will hold you and cry with you. I will share my memories of the special things I remember about Seth, Adam, and Joel whenever you want that. I will rail at God, the universe, or the jerks who have been and will be insensitive and outrageous. And, someday, I will laugh with you at the unimportance of things that others and we try to push into some sort of importance.

I feel selfish, too, Nancy, because I don't want anything to happen to you. You have been such a gift in my life—personally as well as professionally. You recognized my passion for teaching and gave me the strength to do what I know is best for kids.

My method of coping has always been to withdraw from people or to fight, in anger, at the injustice of a situation. I am paralyzed, as neither works for me now. I know it must be so much worse for you because the strength you have always used and projected means that others expect you to be strong. There must be a part of you that sometimes screams, "No more! I can't do it anymore!" I believe that strength is an integral part of you and it has allowed you to ask for what you need. Only now, what you need is what no one can give.

All I can give is love, and it is unconditional.

Love,
Vicki

(Vicki Anderson, a Broadmoor teacher and friend)

Remains of the plane in Westcliffe, Colorado, taken September 25, 1995. "There were no survivors."

Harvey and Sarah Herzog with me at Fairview Cemetery, Colorado Springs, September 28, 1995.

Lee Herzog and me touching the urns to be buried with Joel's, Adam's, and Seth's ashes.

The headstone at Fairview. Visitors observe the Jewish tradition of placing small stones on the marker.

Shoshi and Squeak, my constant companions after the crash.

The school community remembers my family one year after the crash, by releasing balloons into the sky. Love notes were attached.

Mother's Day, 1996. My students cheering me on as I carry the Olympic torch in the Garden of the Gods.

Donna Sheldon and me. My best friend forever.

My first (and last) motorcycle purchase.

The second anniversary of the plane crash, September 24, 1997. My parents at the bench made by Dennis Phillips and given to me by my "Breast Friends."

Joe Lychner, who lost his wife and two daughters in the TWA crash of July 1996, made a surprise visit to the dedication of the memorial amphitheater, also September 24, 1997.

Rita Cook, grief counselor who worked with students at Broadmoor throughout the '95-'96 school year, attended the amphitheater dedication.

My family's memorial amphitheater, on the playground at Broadmoor Elementary School.

A favorite picture: recess duty at Broadmoor.

Dr. Else, the superintendent of schools, surprises me (and the entire student body) with the Milken Family Foundation Educator Award and a check for $25,000.

Receiving the National Distinguished Principal Award in Washington D.C.

"Keep your eye on the ball." Accepting the American Cancer Society's Sword of Hope Award. Dr. Terry O'Rourke, my surgeon, in the background.

This sign appeared on my lawn the day Seth would have graduated from high school. So thoughtful; much appreciated.

Me, Mom, and Linda.

Linda and her boyfriend, Charlie Weeks, 2005.

With Charlie (my surrogate sibling) and brothers Andy and Rob at my niece's wedding, August 2011.

Happy in Colorado Springs with Greg's son Jordan, Macy, me, Nacho, and my fiancé, Greg.

On Adam's bench in front of Cheyenne Mountain Junior High.

Life is good.

CHAPTER 17

THE GOOD, THE BAD,
AND THE BIKER PRINCIPAL

DR. BERMUDEZ ENCOURAGED me to take little breaks from grieving called "brief relief." I understood this to mean that I needed to give
myself permission to laugh and try to find some ever-so-small pleasures. I
did take time each day for these escapes.

Our staff had its annual Christmas party and exchanged white elephant
gifts. I remember laughing and having a not-terrible time. I was still a bas-
ket case, too thin, and not eating much, but I was having moments of brief
relief.

My friend from our teenage years contacted me again. We talked on
the phone. He was in New York City and wanted me to join him there for
New Year's Eve. I told him it was too soon. He pressed, and asked me to
consider it. Then he called and said he'd made reservations for us at a big
party on December 31. I was still against it, but told him I'd think about it.

I flew to Los Angeles for the holidays and had a chance to see Lee Herzog. It was good to spend time with him and commiserate with perhaps the
one other person, besides his parents, who loved Joel as much as I and the
boys had. We talked about the crash. Lee was angry that Joel had flown on
a private plane.

"I told him not to fly on a little plane and he did it anyway. I should
have been more adamant." Lee and I both knew that Joel wanted to take
the boys on an adventure. We could not have talked him out of it.

Lee voiced an opinion that others had also shared with me.

"What was Homer doing? Aren't you mad at Homer?" While I understood the rage that many felt—and shared their fury at the sheer senselessness of it all—I was not mad at Homer. When the plane crashed, Homer and Linda died, too. I figured Homer had made what he thought was a good decision at the time. I was sure his family missed him as much as I missed mine and didn't think that being angry at him would help me feel any better.

Lee and I spent time sharing stories and memories with Rob, Ed, and my mom and dad. We were apprehensive about Christmas Day, which may have led to a bad decision on Christmas Eve. In Los Angeles, a thousand or so Jewish men and women go to a singles event called the Matzo Ball on December 24. It is a festival of bands, dancing, and pick-up lines. Lee and I decided that it might be fun, or at least a distraction. My cousin Peter Coleman joined us, with some of Lee's friends.

Upon arriving at the venue, Lee and Peter quickly disappeared. I wandered around by myself, talked to one guy, then hid in a corner. What had seemed like a good suggestion an hour earlier was now exposing itself as the incredibly stupid idea it really was. I wanted to stop people and say, "Hi, I'm Nancy. My husband and two sons were killed in a plane crash three months ago. Can you tell me what on earth I'm doing here?" It took me an hour to find Lee and Peter and ask if we could please leave. I collapsed into bed and realized I had just attended my first official singles event. Woohoo.

Christmas Day was not as bad as I had feared. We opened presents. We had dinner with a large group of friends at the home of Rich Llewellyn and Chris Caldwell. They had two children, Robbie and Rosie, who had gotten to know Adam and Seth on our trips to California. Rich and Chris had come to the memorial service. Their home was warm and welcoming.

The day after Christmas, we all went to Jerry's Famous Delicatessen for lunch. I couldn't believe it when the one guy I had talked to at the Matzo Ball was there, too. We pretended not to recognize each other.

The calls from my friend in New York City started again; now he was phoning my brother's house.

"Please come to New York City for New Year's Eve. It'll be fun." He wanted to send me a plane ticket.

When I told him that I had thought about it but just didn't feel comfortable making the trip, he informed me that I had ruined his New Year's Eve because now he would be "all alone." Once again, I was dumbstruck by what came out of people's mouths.

HE would be all alone? He still had two sons. His spouse and two children had not died three months earlier. If he wanted to know about "all alone," he should come spend a little time at my house. Wait. No, bad idea.

I immediately knew that I had made the right decision.

*   *   *

I was learning that along with the thousands of thoughtful, heartfelt, eloquent sentiments I was receiving—expressions that wrapped me in love, made me smile, buoyed my spirit—there were also those few who, either through discomfort or ignorance, just couldn't get it right. I don't believe that any of them were being intentionally insensitive. And some of it was me. If they'd said those same things to someone else in my situation, it might well have been received differently. Nearly all the instances of what I considered to be bad sympathy manners came in face-to-face or phone interactions. I think the rawness of a close encounter with a grieving person can be so unsettling that some people just want to get it over with. They blurt out whatever pops into their head, so they can make their exit as quickly as possible. This often comes across as blunt or unkind.

I was once again reminded of the "people handle things differently" adage, and decided to give these clueless individuals the benefit of the doubt. I believe they were very upset by what had happened to me. I believe they may have had issues of their own, which made it hard for them to consider how what they were saying, or asking, or doing, might feel from my perspective.

But it didn't make me feel any less crappy when it happened.

*   *   *

Nights continued to be miserable for me, especially sleeping. It was lonely going to bed. I was sleeping on Joel's side of the bed but that didn't make it any easier to fall asleep. I would stay up late, putter around the house, look at things on the computer, then get in bed with the TV on and, hopefully, the dogs snuggled next to me. Eventually, I could not keep my eyes open any longer and would drift off. I wanted to dream about Joel and the boys, but when I did, I got discombobulated. The dreams made no sense. I would wake up throughout the night, disoriented.

I decided to meet with Ruth Adele, a naturopath. When I called her to schedule an appointment, she had no openings for a month. I made an appointment. The next day she called me back. She had found an opening and got me in much sooner. After meeting her, I realized she had created the opening for me because she knew my story. She listened with the sensitivity of a therapist, and after looking over my blood work and health history, gave me some suggestions. I appreciated talking to Ruth because of her knowledge and her gentle nature. She loved dogs, too. The strategies and foods she recommended seemed to help.

*   *   *

Dear Nancy,

I've thought for so long about what I could say in words that would begin to express my sympathy for your great loss. There are no words, only more tears and prayers. Although we may not share a common faith, I pray for your strength and personal peace every day. As one mother and wife to another, I can do nothing else.

I'll never forget the day I met you at Broadmoor Elementary—I felt David was about to enter the most exciting time of his life. Today, two years later, you have become his mentor, his heroine, and one of his "moms away from home." You are an important part of his life and therefore, an important part of mine, also.

As so many close to you care so deeply about you, even in Minnesota many hearts have been saddened by your loss and have upheld you in prayer.

Fondly,
Kathy Peak

(Mother of David Peak, a teacher at Broadmoor)

*   *   *

Just as in the first days after the crash, I found that talking about my family was still a great comfort. It helped to share who they were with others.

So when my friend, Laura Muir, suggested that we give a sportsmanship trophy in honor of my family at the President's Day Hockey Tournament the February after the crash, I readily agreed. I would have a chance to talk when we explained the trophy at opening ceremonies. The speech would be given to several thousand people—hockey players and their families—in the World Arena. I would have less than five minutes to tell my story. It would be nerve-wracking and difficult, but I wanted to do it.

To give me support, Rob, Ed, and Donna sat with me before and after the speech. I was introduced by the president of the hockey association, Tim McConnell. Tim's three sons were Broadmoor students. I heard, "Please give a warm welcome to Dr. Nancy Saltzman," and walked to the middle of the ice on a long strip of carpet.

I began by telling everyone that hockey had played a big part in my life. That the previous year, I had been sitting in the stands just as they were, as a nervous parent. I talked about Adam and Seth's passion for hockey, how their father and I loved watching them play. Then I shared that the boys and their father had died in a small plane crash the previous September, and we would be honoring my family by giving one team the Herzog Memorial Sportsmanship Trophy. I asked that parents please take the time during the tournament to hold a hand, tape a stick, and to tell their children that they loved them. It was a very emotional speech, but I made it through and apparently made an impression—the crowd rose in a standing ovation. When we walked out of the arena, several parents stopped me. They thanked me for speaking and each gave me a hug.

For the next fifteen years, I made a similar speech and gave the trophy to one special team each year at the annual tournament. Mike Bertsch, my first husband, told me that one year he was sitting in the stands with his team while I was giving the speech. His assistant coach turned to him and said, "I need to go to the doctor more often!" Mike turned to him and said, "That's my ex-wife." His assistant replied, "You wish buddy, you wish." Mike said, "No, really," but his assistant remained skeptical. The story made me laugh out loud.

*   *   *

During a meeting with friend and attorney John Cook, he told me he had received pictures of the crash site. I asked if he had pictures of Joel, Adam, and Seth. He said that he did, but he didn't think I should see them. I insisted. Because I had not gotten to really see them at the funeral home, I wanted to view the photos, thinking it might help my brain come to grips with the fact that they were truly gone. John handed them to me in a large white envelope.

I took the pictures home and opened the envelope. I saw the plane. It was broken into pieces that were spread across a grassy field. The picture of Joel was next. He was lying on the ground, on his back. You could tell that he had been moved to this place. His leg was severed below the knee and had been placed to the left of his body. I couldn't see Joel's face because

John had covered it with a sticky note. I didn't remove it; John had emphatically directed me not to look at Joel's face. Seth and Adam were lying in the grass. They looked asleep, though their bodies were not in natural positions. Adam was twisted in the shape of a "C." The pictures shocked me, but I didn't regret looking at them. Someone else in my situation might not have wanted to see the pictures, but I did.

Needless to say, though I knew I needed to view the photos, now they were all I could see in my mind's eye. I spoke to Dr. Bermudez about this. We did some specialized work that helps people deal with trauma. It helped me be able to think about the pictures without becoming overwhelmed. I still have the photographs, but have not looked at them since that day.

*   *   *

I survived Valentine's Day by giving everyone I knew a card and celebrating with the kids in the classrooms. For my March birthday, Jackie Kirk, the owner of a women's clothing store in Colorado Springs, gave me an outfit that she thought Joel would have bought for me.

Mother's Day was one of those "dueling emotions" times. Not surprisingly, I woke up feeling extremely lonely and sad. I had been a mother for nearly thirteen years, and even though my children were gone, it seems once a mother, always a mother. But there would be no hand-made cards. No specially chosen, poorly wrapped, off-the-wall gifts.

However, there was an upside to the day. I still had my own mother to celebrate. And I had been chosen to carry the Olympic torch as it made its way through Colorado Springs, after my wonderful school secretary and friend Lois had nominated me. Rob flew out from L.A., and half of the student body from Broadmoor showed up with signs to cheer me on. Filled with emotion, I took my torch, received the flame from the runner before me, and ran through the Garden of the Gods. As I started my run, I caught myself looking for Joel, Adam, and Seth. It sounds clichéd, but I truly felt them in my heart. Spectators cheered. I didn't have far to go and was happy to get the flame to the next runner without any mishaps. There were lots of hugs. In the end, it was an incredibly exhilarating and sad day all rolled into one.

I went out for a few lunches and dinners with men I knew in Colorado Springs. Some were brave souls who had been friends of Joel. A few were friends of mine. I enjoyed sharing a meal with them but being around men other than Joel seemed to make me miss him more, if that was possible.

The school year ended in the usual way. We had sixth grade graduation. We worked on class lists for the next year. On the last day of school, teachers hugged students and sent them off for summer vacation. Rita Cook, the social worker who had met with Seth's friends every week, held a special celebration for her groups. They had all gotten through the year. By allowing the students to talk, read, draw, and write about the loss of their friend, Rita had made a huge difference.

I anticipated the months off with great anxiety. In the past, I would have been in constant motion with tennis, hockey, and plenty of family fun in the sun. This year, there would be new teachers to hire in June, but the rest of the summer lay wide open before me, empty and scary.

*   *   *

Dear Nancy,

Thank you for allowing me to work with the fifth graders this school year. I've learned so much as I've journeyed through their grief with them and with you. Those of us who have been touched by you and your tragedy have been blessed with the gift you give—we will be forever changed. I hope you find some comfort from knowing that in the short time Joel, Adam, and Seth had on this earth, they touched many lives and made a difference by their very presence. That is, without a doubt, the greatest gift we give while here.

Your men will live on in the memories of others for many years to come.

In peace and love,
Rita

(Rita Cook, the grief counselor who worked with our school)

*   *   *

Lee Vaughn, one of my principal friends—and a principle friend—had a motorcycle. Though I had never ridden a motorcycle in my life, in fact was scared to death of them, he somehow convinced me that I would enjoy the freedom a "bike" would give me. I signed up for a Motorcycling 101 class.

When I talked to my parents the week of the class, they were not happy.

"Don't do this. We don't want anything to happen to you."

I assured them I would be safe. I didn't know if I would be safe but I wanted to take a risk.

The first class was held on a Friday night. We had to learn all about motorcycles before we rode them. There was a written test at the end of the evening, which I passed with a ninety-six percent. I was on my way.

The next morning we were "given" a Honda Nighthawk 250. We had to push it up a big hill, sit on it, and ride it down the hill—all without turning on the engine. By the time I pushed the motorcycle up the hill I was having second thoughts.

What was I thinking? The only risk here is having this thing fall over on top of me.

I got on the bike and rode it down the hill. I did not kill myself. But I did have to push it back up the hill again. By now, a woman I knew who was also an educator had dropped out.

After passing the push-the-motorcycle-up-a-hill test, we learned how to start the motorcycle. We drove into the parking lot at Pikes Peak Community College. We practiced driving around in circles all day Saturday. By the end of the day, I knew how to ride a motorcycle. I was not very good at driving a motorcycle, but I had not fallen off or hit anything.

To receive our license, we had to practice more riding on Sunday morning, then take a driving test. If we passed, we would be issued a driver's license that had an "M" stamped on it for "Motorcycle License."

Have I mentioned that my hands are very small? The brake and the gas are both controlled by your right hand. When you twist the right handle, the motorcycle speeds up. When you squeeze the brake with your hand, you slow down. Somehow I managed to do both at the same time. I would accelerate, accidentally brake, and slow down. It was funny, but not that funny. No matter what I did, I was jerking forward and backward.

By lunch on Sunday I had decided I was not meant to be a biker chick. At lunch break my classmates and I went to McDonald's nearby, in our cars. I said I wasn't going back to take the test.

"I'll be a danger to myself and others if I'm ever allowed on the road."

A Harley-Davidson owner who was taking the class to support his girlfriend, a fellow "newbie," knew I was a school principal.

"You're going to quit? What are you going to tell the kids at your school? That you're a quitter?"

I had to think about that. Unfortunately, I had told people at school that I was taking the class. What would I say if I quit? I decided I had to at least try to pass the test.

When we got back from lunch, the instructors explained the driving assessment. We'd get points for things we did incorrectly. Any score less than twenty-one would pass.

We got on our bikes and waited in line. We had to drive in a circle, then straight toward the instructor. When we got close to him he would point left or right. We had to react correctly and turn. We were not supposed to hit the instructor with our motorcycles.

I watched my classmates perform the test with ease. I put on my helmet. I drove toward the instructor, then screamed and turned right when he pointed to the right. I was thrilled I didn't hit him.

I got twenty points. I told the instructors I knew the only reason I passed was that they liked me.

"We would lose our licenses if we passed someone who should have flunked," was their response.

After class, I went to the motorcycle store, picked out a used Honda Nighthawk 250, and bought it. Unwilling to place any of my fellow street-using citizens in peril, I had Lee, the motorcycle-riding friend who had instigated this whole crazy idea, drive it home for me. Once home, I drove it around the block and into the garage, right where Joel used to park the Total Tennis Jeep. The next time I rode the motorcycle was for the school's Fourth of July parade. I put on a red and white shirt, blue jeans, and my helmet, and rode my red motorcycle two blocks. Then I parked the bike in the garage again. Soon thereafter, I gave it to Will Vasquez, the school's building manager. I figured he had saved my life—and possibly others— by taking it off my hands and that seemed like payment enough, but he also painted my house. I have not ridden a motorcycle since, although I still have a license stamped with a big, fat "M."

* * *

After the motorcycle class, I visited my parents in Indiana on my way to a principals' conference in Nashville. My parents drove me to the Indianapolis airport to catch my flight. When I made the reservation, I specifically asked what type of plane I'd be on. I had been assured it would be a jet. I had flown many times on jets since the crash, and always felt fine. I loved flying and looking out the window.

The plane I saw had propellers.

I burst into tears.

"What's wrong? What's the matter?" my parents asked.

I could hardly get the words out.

"I can't go on a propeller plane . . . I can't go on a propeller plane . . ."

They assured me we could figure something out, that they'd be happy to take me home if I didn't feel safe.

"It's not that I'm afraid," I sobbed.

"I don't want to feel what it was like for Adam, Seth, or Joel before their plane crashed. It was a propeller plane, too."

My parents repeated that we could just go home. They held me for a few minutes. I calmed down. I *really* didn't want to get on that plane, but I decided that I needed to do this. I boarded, curled up next to the window, and cried all the way to Nashville. It was the last time I took anything other than a jet for a long time.

* * *

Dear Nancy,

There is no reason you should particularly remember me, we've met a few times at your folks' old house—usually on occasions when Saltzman children were home and people were invited who had children who'd know them.

Like many people in Bloomington we were shocked and deeply distressed by your tragedy. Two weeks ago your mother gave us a copy of the program for the memorial ceremony . . . it made me think of our daughter's death; I guess I was in an optimal (in some sense) mood of readiness when I read the celebration text; I wept as I haven't for years.

Even as I wept, however, I found myself thinking how wonderful an experience the four of you had together—an experience that can't be taken away however abrupt its ending and however sharp the before and after differences. There is lots of evidence in the celebration document about legacies left by your three to many, many people.

We think of you often. Nothing can fully restore your life, there are mitigations in memories, the support of friends and family, work.

Love and PEACE!
Allen

P.S. Please don't feel compelled to acknowledge this note. Go to a movie instead!

(Allen Grimshaw, a good friend of my parents)

CHAPTER 18

EMERGENCE

THAT SAME SUMMER of 1996, Harvey Herzog, Joel's father, turned seventy-five. Joel's mom Sarah, his siblings, and their spouses met in Aspen to celebrate the special day. They invited me to join them and I asked Donna to come, too. We hiked, ate, and shared stories.

Spending time with Joel's family was wonderful. It was also very hard. Being with them was like having him close but just out of sight or reach. I was reminded of everything about him. Having Donna there helped me stay focused on the reason we were all together. Although the family was in Aspen for a week, Donna and I only stayed two days, which helped me balance my emotions.

On July 17, Harvey's birthday, we were in Harvey and Sarah's hotel room when reports of a plane crash came on the TV. Everything in the room stopped. A TWA jet had taken off from New York and crashed into the ocean. We watched in silence as parts of the plane bobbed in the water. I had flashbacks to the night of the crash. After a few minutes, I had to leave the room.

The last week of my summer vacation was spent with Andy and his family on Nantucket, and my parents, sister, and her boyfriend Charlie on Cape Cod. It was good to see everybody and be on the Cape, but it was lonely to be by myself. Several times I watched small, single engine planes fly overhead. It was so unsettling I had to look away from the sky and cover my ears.

What if one crashed as I watched?

I was ready to return to school and was happy when August came, and I could be back in my office. There was lots to do and I stayed busy. But by the end of August, I was nervously anticipating the upcoming anniversary of the crash. I felt nauseated most of the time. At night, I talked on the phone with my family and Joel's until I could fall asleep. Our fifteenth wedding anniversary would have been August 22. Luckily, that was a school day, which meant I was too busy to focus on anything other than work.

* * *

It was during August that I got a curious phone message. It was from a woman named Joy, who identified herself as the sister of Joe Lychner. In her message she said that Joe had lost his wife and two daughters in the TWA crash we had heard about on Harvey Herzog's birthday. Joy lived in Colorado Springs and knew my story. I called her and she asked if I would be willing to call Joe, in Houston, to give him some support. I phoned him and left a message explaining who I was and why I was calling. He didn't return my call. Joy contacted me again several weeks later and asked me to try again. I left another message and this time Joe called back while I was out.

His message broke my heart. Not because of what he said, but how he said it. There was no life in his voice, just a flat, "Hi. This is Joe Lychner." Pause. "My sister told me to call you." Pause. "I'm in Houston." Then he stated his phone number.

I phoned again, and this time we connected. We talked for over an hour. Joe told me all about his family and what had happened. After the plane crashed, the survivors flew to New York to find out if their loved ones' bodies had been recovered. Many of the families stayed in the city until positive identifications had been made. The relatives also were given recovered items from the flight that were found in the water.

"I hate coming home at night," Joe confessed. "I see the lights on in my house and I forget for just a split second that Pam and the girls aren't there. I think I see Pam in the kitchen, at the window." I knew exactly what he was talking about. I had the same experience at my house.

Joe and I talked almost every evening for several months.

One thing we discussed, which I could not fathom, was that he would likely not get the bodies of his wife and daughters returned to him. They would identify the remains using DNA samples. I felt grateful that I did not have to rely on forensics to confirm that Joel, Adam, and Seth had perished.

I told Dr. Bermudez about Joe. He was interested to hear about the conversations and how Joe was doing. Dr. Bermudez also explained that some of the strategies that had helped me make it through each day might or might not help Joe. I realized that I shouldn't expect Joe—or anyone else—to grieve exactly the same way I did.

* * *

Dear Nancy,

What happened to you is a tragedy beyond my comprehension.

I didn't know Seth and Adam well but I will never forget their big eyes and their big, happy, kid-like smiles. They were truly beautiful children and their smiles certainly could brighten anyone's day. Their legacy will always live on with me, as I will always see their faces in your face, their smiles in your smile. You know better than anyone that Joel was a wonderful person and I truly believe God took one of life's finer people too early. He will never be forgotten by anyone who knew him.

You are a special, special person who was an integral part of your family. Now that your family is gone in body you must remember you are still that very special individual. You have been blessed with many gifts—especially working with, helping, and caring for kids. Please never lose sight of this truth.

May all the tender, wonderful, intimate, funny, crazy, loving, hard, and unique moments and memories you shared with Joel and the boys be tucked away in the innermost chambers of your heart—to be drawn on the rest of your days, and may that light never die. Our prayers remain with you.

(From a parent of students at Broadmoor)

* * *

The anniversary of the crash and Seth's birthday were quickly approaching. I had more problems sleeping. I started taking a mild over-the-counter sleep aid and it helped a little. I obsessively thought about everything I did the week before the crash, reliving each moment when I was alone. I cried. I didn't want to eat. My parents flew out to Colorado to be with me. We "celebrated" Seth's birthday, the day before the anniversary of the crash, by going out to dinner and having a birthday cake.

The next day, my mom, dad, and I had been invited to Cheyenne Mountain Junior High at lunchtime. The PTO, led by Marilyn Newell, had organized a brief ceremony to celebrate Adam. When we arrived, there were about a hundred students standing by the flagpole, wearing purple ribbons in honor of Adam. Behind the students was a new stone bench. "In Memory of Adam Herzog" was chiseled on the front of the seat. On the legs of the bench were his birth year and the year he died. The bench was placed where someone driving by the school could read Adam's name. It was a touching surprise, and I was deeply moved. Tears ran down my cheeks as I thanked the students and parents. I still drive by the junior high about once a week, just to see the bench.

My staff had asked what I wanted to do for the anniversary of the crash at our school. I thought that having a balloon release after school would be a positive way to mark the day. I wrote a column for the school newsletter and let parents know that no one was required but everyone was invited to come launch a balloon on September 24.

When the last bell of the day rang, we started handing out balloons. Friends from around the city joined us. My Breast Friends arrived with a second poignant surprise: another beautiful bench, crafted by my friend Dennis Phillips, and dedicated to my family. Dennis and I had worked together at Timberview Middle School. Once again, I tried to convey my gratitude, though my efforts fell far short of the depth of love I felt for my friends and colleagues.

I told the students I was going to write notes to my family on my balloons. They could write anything they wanted on theirs—it didn't have to be to Joel, Adam, or Seth.

We found every Magic Marker or Sharpie in the school. Parents and staff members helped students, then wrote their own messages. Just before the balloon release, a parent asked to meet with me. He was not happy.

"Why are you doing this? My son just got over losing Seth. This is just reminding him of his grief."

I thought about what to say and my commitment to giving everyone the benefit of the doubt.

I'm sorry. I wish the plane hadn't crashed. I wish Seth was still here to be my son as well as your son's friend. I didn't intend this event to open wounds, but to allow the children and adults who are still grieving to express their feelings, and to create something beautiful out of sadness.

I thanked him for letting me know how he felt.

As the balloons were released, it took my breath away. The clear blue sky provided a perfect backdrop for the ascending rainbow.

*   *   *

Eleven days after the anniversary of the crash was Adam's birthday, October 5. Joel's birthday was October 17. I honored both days with friends by going out to dinner and singing "Happy Birthday."

For Thanksgiving, I made plans to be in Indiana. It turned out Joe Lychner was coming to Colorado Springs to spend Thanksgiving with his sister and her husband. I would be able to meet him the day before I left.

I called Donna and told her Joe was coming to Colorado Springs. She had been with me in Aspen when we first saw the plane crash and knew that I had been talking to him daily. I was very excited. I had enjoyed getting to know Joe over the phone but wanted to see and talk with him in person. When I got to his sister's house and met him officially for the first time, we hugged for a long time.

I had seen pictures of Joe in *Time* magazine and *The New York Times*, because he had become one of the spokespeople for the families of those killed in the TWA crash. The pictures had not done him justice. He was tall and well-built, with a winning smile. When I told people that I was talking to Joe, a man who had also lost his family in a plane crash, they had imagined us falling in love and living happily ever after. Seeing him in person actually made me consider it for a moment.

He understands the pain. He's a very nice man. He's great looking.

But I also knew these thoughts were just that . . . thoughts. Joe and I had a special bond that connected us—just not in a romantic way.

We picked up Donna and made our way to Jose Muldoon's. When we dropped Joe off at his sister's house after midnight, I suspected he might have a hangover the next morning—I had imbibed, myself; I remember having a bit of a hangover, too. It had been wonderful to meet Joe in person and to spend time with someone who was surviving the same thing I was. Although we don't talk every day like we did then, we stay in touch. He is happily remarried and has two children.

I left the next day for my trip to Bloomington.

*   *   *

Dear Nancy,

While in morning prayers you came through loud and clear—I knew I had to write you.

From the horror you've been through you have witnessed the other side of the coin, too—the amazing outpouring of human caring . . . which in itself gives a new light of insight . . . wordless . . . and I guess it has to be . . . because we humans can be troublingly awkward at times, regarding the very things which matter most.

I just had to write you.

Love,

Norma

(Norma Beversdorf, both a close friend of my mother's and the mother of a friend from high school)

*   *   *

When Joe was in Colorado Springs, he had asked why I still wore my wedding ring. After all, I was no longer married. I loved my ring. Inside the band Joel had inscribed our wedding date and "Love, Joel." It had a blue sapphire, placed horizontally between two little diamonds. Looking at the ring made me think of Joel in the middle and the boys on each side.

After Joel's wedding band was returned to me, I put it on my finger. It was much too big, but it kind of fit behind my own wedding ring. The band had belonged to my great grandfather and was engraved with Joel's and my great grandmother's initials. I wore it on my hand for about a week, then worried that I might lose it so I put it on a chain that Joel had given me and wore it around my neck. Several months passed before I stopped wearing Joel's band and kept it in a special ring box where I could see it daily.

Now it had been over a year since Joel died; I was not married. Joe had a good point. When I went to the doctor's office, I checked "widow" instead of "married" on medical forms.

I took off my ring and put it in the box, touching Joel's ring.

I was preparing . . . to get ready . . . to maybe think about . . . dipping my toe in the dating waters.

I talked to Dr. Bermudez about it, asked for suggestions on how to meet people, and discussed his opinion of online dating. His belief was that relationships have the best chance of success when the people have several things in common. We talked about all that Joel and I had shared.

A brave friend of Joel's, someone he knew through the shop, asked me out for breakfast on a Sunday. We had a relaxing time and talked about Joel quite a bit. It was a good training run.

At a January 1997 education conference in Denver I met a very interesting man who rode motorcycles. He came into the meeting wearing leathers. I told him that I had a motorcycle license and entertained him with tales from my class. We had a lot in common and went to lunch. I told him about my family. He seemed sensitive and caring. We were attracted to each other. He was interested in seeing me again. I thought about it, but decided that I still wasn't quite ready.

At the President's Day Hockey Tournament in February, I ran into an acquaintance. She asked if I had started dating. I told her that I was working up to it.

"Why?" I asked.

"Well, I know that you and Joel had a very good sex life so I was wondering if you'd talked to Joel's friends at the squash club about, you know, helping you out?"

Joel had never been shy about our love—or our love life—so it was no surprise that people were aware of some of the more intimate aspects of our marriage. But I'm pretty sure I did a double take at her suggestion. I imagined a sign-up sheet like they used for squash court times, with a "Taking Care of Nancy" schedule. I answered that it had not crossed my mind.

* * *

Dear Mrs. Saltzman:

I'm a member of the International Polka Club (card enclosed) in Colorado Springs. We've never met.

If you like to dance, consider this an invitation to attend our dances every Saturday night. It is a great way to unwind on a weekend as well as a good health practice.

Although these are polka dances, other types of music are also included, e.g. waltz, disco, country western, etc.

I read with sorrow of the tragedy in your family. My heartfelt condolences. If this is too soon for you to be dancing and socializing following the tragedy, please disregard this letter. Otherwise, I'd like to see you at our dances. I know what you look like and would be looking for you to come and sit at one of our singles tables.

"An Interested Party"

* * *

One memorable pseudo-date was with an officer of the law. I met him through a friend. He was about my age, greying, handsome. We drove to a local restaurant to eat dinner and talk. I enjoyed our conversation very much. It was stimulating and interesting. When he took me back to my house, he walked me to my door.

"Can I kiss you goodnight?" he asked.

I nodded.

He reached out to hold me then gave me a kiss. He stepped back.

"Did you feel my gun?"

A "loaded" question if ever there was one! I gave him a sweet smile, trying to figure out how to respond. All I could come up with was, "Thanks for dinner." We talked on the phone after that but never went out again. I'm not sure why and am still curious as to whether he asks all of his dates that question.

Some girlfriends invited me to Cowboys nightclub. It's a local country bar with a huge dance floor. I danced with several men, trying to ignore how strange it felt to be contact-dancing with someone other than Joel.

Then a good-looking man wearing tight jeans asked me to dance. We had a great time and he didn't mind that I wasn't an expert at the two-step. He patiently led me around the floor until I could do it without stepping on his feet. We introduced ourselves; his name was Mark. He was similar in build to Joel, but taller. When I was ready to leave, Mark gave me his phone number. I put it in my wallet, thought about calling him, but never did. He was cute, funny, a good dancer, and about ten years younger than I was. I went to Cowboys a few more times, but didn't run into him.

I waded in a little deeper and told my friends and some of the moms at school that I was beginning to date. Several gave me the names of single men they knew. Instead of the elaborate subterfuge I had used to meet Joel, the older and wiser Nancy decided the best route was just to call these men and ask them out. Once they got over the shock, most agreed to meet me for a drink or coffee. All were interesting—none "clicked" with me.

* * *

I was asked to speak at the National Association of Elementary School Principals conference in San Antonio, Texas. I put together a session titled "Good Grief." I shared with the participants strategies for helping a school community survive the loss of a student. I needed someone to introduce me, so I asked Donna to join me. An added benefit was that Joe Lychner was only a couple of hours away, and he would come to San Antonio to see us.

My session was packed. I shared the journey of my career, including the fun stories I had told in other presentations. Then I explained how my life had been abruptly and tragically turned upside down. I had to stop to breathe, but made it to the end. Afterwards, a line formed so that the participants could talk to me. Although the session had been very emotional, I believed it had made a positive impact on everyone present.

That night Joe arrived. We went out for dinner, drinks, and a night on the town. We danced and laughed. Although the trip was stressful and emotional, it was good for me. I was making a difference for others.

I was healing.

* * *

Dear Dr. Saltzman,

I know I haven't been at Broadmoor for a long time, but one of my good friends recommended a book she had read, called Chicken Soup for the Soul.

At first I thought it would be boring, but as I continued, all I could think about was your story and how it affected me. I'm sure many people have already told you this, but your strength and reassurance helped me get over the same big loss you suffered, and many others that have followed. I know that I'll probably never get a chance to change someone's life as much as you've changed mine, but I'll try. Thanks to you, I've been able to deal with family and school better, and I've helped many, including myself, because of it. I just wanted to thank you for everything and tell you I will always remember what you did for me.

Sincerely,
Pamela Mauer

P.S. I'm in seventh grade now, and I really miss Broadmoor and the rest of Colorado Springs.

(A former Broadmoor student)

* * *

For Mother's Day 1997, my mother and I met in New York City. We shopped and saw several shows. I also remembered that my friend who had wanted me to visit him for New Year's worked in the city. I was still wary of him, but as long as we were in his backyard, it seemed silly to not make contact. We spoke and he was happy to hear from me. He suggested meeting in a bar near our hotel. My mother and I walked around several times before I spotted the person I thought was my friend. I said his name, and he smiled and greeted us. I introduced my mother. We sat down and ordered drinks.

The first tip that it was going to be an interesting evening came when I glanced at his hands. He was sporting silver acrylic nails that were longer than mine. After some small talk, my mother, having noted his fashion statement, suddenly felt "tired" and politely retreated to our hotel room.

My friend and I chatted for a while about the usual updates and news.

"I still work in finance," he noted.

I couldn't stand it any longer.

"So, what's up with the fingernails?"

"Well, I want to talk to you about that."

He nonchalantly explained that he had come to the realization he was really a woman inside, and was in the midst of a sex change. He was taking female hormones and would need several operations. One would surgically move his waist up. Then he would have breast implants. He would also be castrated. "Ouch," I said. "No kidding," he replied. He said he had thought about meeting me dressed as a woman, but decided against it when he heard I would be with my mother.

I was surprised and curious. He was the first transsexual person I knew.

"How do your sons feel about this?" He had two sons a little younger than Adam and Seth would have been.

"My family is dealing with it."

"Will you be attracted to men or women after the sex change?"

"Both."

"Are the surgeries painful?"

"Hell, yes. But worth it."

"Will you keep your same job when you're through with the transition?"

"Yes, they can't discriminate based on gender."

We took the subway to another bar. At one point he said, "When you wouldn't come visit me for New Year's Eve, I decided to go ahead with the operations." I just looked at him. I assumed and hoped he was kidding.

When I got back to the hotel, my mom was eager to talk.

"That seemed odd. Was he wearing fingernails?" I told her the story. It had been for different reasons, but my decision to not join him for New Year's in 1995 was looking downright visionary.

It was while I was in New York City that I learned I had been chosen as Colorado's National Distinguished Principal of the Year. It was a wonderful Mother's Day present. Because I was with my mother, it was very special. She and I celebrated at the airport before we left on our respective flights. I arrived back in Colorado Springs early on Sunday evening. As we landed, the flight attendant announced that Colorado's National Distinguished Principal of the Year was on board. I was embarrassed, but also very proud. When I got off the plane, I saw parents and students holding signs that read "Congratulations, Dr. Saltzman!" Tom Duchen, the dad of one of Seth's best friends, had organized the celebration.

It reminded me of what Joel would have done for me if he'd been alive.

CHAPTER 19

FRIENDS: TWO-LEGGED, FOUR-LEGGED, AND MORE-THAN

I WENT TO Cowboys with friends again. This time I spotted Mark, the man I had previously hit it off with, across the dance floor. I sidled up next to him. "Sidled"—that's how you talk at Cowboys.

"Hi, there. Remember me?"

"I do. Why didn't you ever call me?"

"Why didn't you call me?" I had saved the number but had convinced myself he was too young for me.

He asked me to dance. In between dances, we interviewed each other. Mark worked in the computer business and was a program manager. He liked to hunt with his dog. It sounded like he had many of the trophy animals he had bagged mounted in his house. I wasn't sure that we had a lot in common, but we had a good time dancing. At the end of the evening, Mark walked me out to my Toyota 4-Runner.

"Are you religious?" he asked matter-of-factly as we got to my truck.

"No. Why?"

"Seems like most of the women I meet are very religious. I'm agnostic."

Well, there was something we had common. We liked to dance; that made two. We liked dogs; that was three. Neither one of us drank—four. Another plus? There was a definite spark between us.

I leaned forward to kiss Mark goodnight before I got in my truck.

As I moved forward, he pulled back.

"I don't kiss on the first date."

I thought he was joking and tried to kiss him again, but he meant it. I laughed and got into my truck with a smile on my face, intrigued.

On our second date we did kiss. We went out for dinner and talked all the way through the meal. I found myself enjoying his company very much. It was a little strange for me, but nice. Mark wasn't shy about his plans: he wanted to get married and have children. He had a niece and nephew and enjoyed spending time with them.

"I'm not sure I want to get married again. I can't have children because I had a hysterectomy." It was noted, but he didn't get up and walk out.

We started spending weekends together. Sometimes Mark would come to my house, but most of the time we stayed at his house. I met Mark's mom and his siblings. We took some trips together to California. He met Rob and Ed.

Mark met my friends, but we spent most of our time just with each other. I enjoyed learning about computer programmers and libertarians. We disagreed on most political issues but had spirited conversations. I even went bird hunting at 5 a.m. with Mark and the dogs.

Mark and I dated for almost two years. We talked about getting married but I think we both knew it wouldn't have worked. Mark was ready to get married; I was not. He wanted children; I couldn't have them. Mark looked into surrogacy and I considered it, but my heart wasn't in it. Although it seemed that our days as a couple were numbered, Mark agreed to be my date when I went to Washington, D.C., to get my award as a Nationally Distinguished Principal. It was hard to say goodbye to him when we finally broke up, but we remained friends. He did get married and has a daughter and two stepchildren.

*   *   *

Broadmoor and its PTO wanted to do something permanent to honor my family. Once again, I felt the seemingly boundless love of my school family and the community, and their determination to not forget. It was decided that an amphitheater dedicated to Joel, Adam, and Seth would be built at the front of the school. Sharon Enoch, the PTO president, put together a committee and spearheaded an effort that brought together many to make the landmark a reality. Services and materials were donated and the amphitheater was dedicated on September 24, 1997. Linda Shea, Broadmoor's band teacher, wrote a special piece of music for the students to perform. Deb Young wrote a beautiful dedication.

My family, Joel's parents, Lee Herzog, Mark and his mother, and many people from the community came to the dedication. Joe Lychner flew in from Houston to surprise me. Many of Joel's friends from Denver and Pueblo joined us. My brother Rob and Joel's brother Lee spoke. The ceremony was perfect. And I once again had a chance to express my gratitude for another lovingly crafted, lasting tribute to my family, as well as for the immense support I had received in the two years since the crash.

The idea of an amphitheater could not have been more inspired. It is frequently used for classes and by the community.

* * *

Two years—
Slow moving clouds of memories linger
Tornadoes of anger moving through me
Moments of tremendous sadness

Images of the three boys,
Scattered throughout my mind
Hopes and dreams, shattered.
Loss imposing on us.

Subtle life changes crystallizing.
More self-acceptance abounds
Implications of the loss
As the lava slowly moves.

A new shape is forming inside,
Blessings handed to us
Choosing which lens to see through
New paths to experience.

It's about appreciating this moment
Knowing this is it
Just being—
For it all can disappear at any moment.

— Lee Herzog

* * *

After Mark and I broke up, I tried a bit of computer dating, keeping in mind what Dr. Bermudez and I had discussed. I sent e-mails to two men.

They both responded and when I wrote back, I told them about losing my family. I never heard back from one. The other wrote right away, saying how sorry he was for my loss. We exchanged e-mails occasionally, but never met. A friend met a Jewish guy on a dating site and thought I might like him. He and I went out to lunch—a very long, painful lunch. I had to chuckle at her presumption that just because we were both Jewish, we would automatically hit it off.

I wasn't having much luck meeting someone, but I was okay with that. I had started making friends with more single women. I had an occasional date. Sharing my dating adventures made for good storytelling in the teacher's lounge or with my friends.

A Broadmoor mom told me that she had met a man she thought I would like. Everyone thought they knew the kind of man that I would be attracted to. She said that he was a "Joel clone": shorter than six feet, athletic build, and sandy brown hair. His name was John and she had met him through a friend. She knew nothing about him except that he was good looking, my "type," and seemed genuine. I gave her my contact information.

She didn't give it to John for a year.

* * *

I was dating but I was mostly focused on my work at school. Our counselor, Scott Stanec, and the librarian, Susan Brock, attended a workshop that was taught by Denny McLoughlin. They returned brimming with excitement.

"Nancy, you will love it!" exclaimed Susan.

Scott chimed in. "We're already doing similar things at Broadmoor and it would be great for our staff."

I couldn't imagine what could be so great about something called "ARFF," but I had faith in Scott and Susan's recommendation. I registered for the workshop.

From the first moment, I was captivated. Denny's enthusiasm was infectious. His philosophy of how to work with children and adults was very similar to what we were implementing at Broadmoor, only better. He demonstrated how teaching children to think and be responsible, while establishing mutual trust, could maximize their learning. His model was based on sound educational theory that he had broken down into concrete skills that children and teachers could learn.

When the workshop ended I convinced Denny that I could get enough people to attend a class at Broadmoor. We found a Thursday through Sunday that would work. I took all of my staff development money and gave it to the teachers to enroll in the workshop. Scott, Susan, and I talked almost everyone we knew into participating. Including our staff, we recruited fifty people.

Denny began by telling participants about our four basic needs as humans: achievement, respect and love, fun, and freedom—ARFF for short. We need all four; just like a car needs four tires. If you are missing one of your ARFF needs, it's like having a flat tire. You have to fill it up to run smoothly.

We met as a faculty and developed a plan to introduce ARFF to our students. We made posters of a big dog saying "ARFF." We asked the students about their ARFF. If a student was having trouble we asked him or her, "Which part of your ARFF is missing? What do you need to do to fill your ARFF?"

The kids weren't the only ones helped by the ARFF model. When I struggled with deep sadness—which was an ongoing challenge—I thought about what I was missing from my ARFF and what I could do about it. I thought that finding the love and respect that I had with Joel and the boys would likely be impossible. Sometimes, getting more of achievement, fun, and freedom helped mitigate my sadness. Many times I had to remember the love and respect that I had with my family, and let the memory prop me up.

* * *

I also continued my search for someone with whom I could fall in love. A woman I met in a class introduced me to Tom. He had gone to Colorado College and was thirteen years younger than I was. Tom was, and still is, the founder and principal of a leadership development firm.

Besides our age difference, there were a number of reasons Tom and I never got very serious—he wanted marriage and kids, for which I wasn't the best prospect. Our life stages and goals were different, too. Tom was also torn about making a life with me. But I looked forward to my talks with him very much. He had a great sense of humor and was very bright. He told me repeatedly that he had never dated anyone with whom he could communicate as easily. We enjoyed hiking, and he introduced me to some beautiful places in the foothills near Colorado Springs. He liked my dogs and we would take them on our hikes. Tom also loved hanging out with my friends, "learning what middle-aged women talk about." It was slightly unsettling to learn that I was now considered middle-aged, but I liked that he appreciated my friends.

While dating Tom, I learned that the American Cancer Society had chosen me to receive its Sword of Hope Award, the association's highest honor. Dr. Terry O'Rourke, my fantastic surgeon, was to present me with the award at a black tie dinner. When I told my mom about it, her response was, "The Sort-of Hope Award?" I laughed—there had been many times during both cancer and grief recovery when "sort-of hope" was exactly what I'd felt.

I asked Tom to be my date, though we were on the downhill side of our "run" and would soon part amicably. He was an especially good sport when I received the award. I spoke about being a cancer survivor and Joel's dedication to focusing on what was important in life, adding that in Joel's vocabulary, that meant "keeping our eyes on the ball." I pulled a tennis ball out of the right top of my evening gown and threw it into the crowd. "Keep your eye on the ball!" Then, I pulled a second tennis ball out of the left side and threw that one. My friend Larry Wellman caught one, I'm not sure who caught the other.

*   *   *

September 23, 1999

Dear Nancy,

I am sad this week and a little perturbed. I figure that, when I have these feelings, even a bit, you must have similar ones, only stronger. So, I will say a few things to you:

I miss your family. I miss talking to you and laughing with Joel. I miss seeing your wonderful boys grow. It hurts me that we move on and they are not with us, not in the tangible way I want them to be.

I speak with you often—silently in my mind. I have done this off and on for the past four years. I just say, keep going forward. I tell you how important you are to all of us. I hope you hear me now and again.

Sally and I love you very much. We are your friends, always.

Yours,
Randy

(Randy and Sally Wagner, good friends and parents of Broadmoor students)

*   *   *

When Tom made his comment about middle-aged women, one of the women he was referring to was my friend Deb Riekeman. Deb was also a widow; her husband Bill had been flying an ultralight plane with a photographer aboard when it crashed. She, too, had been deeply in love with her husband, and we shared many cry-fests. Deb had two daughters from her first marriage; Bill was her second husband. We would often meet at her house, where she would cook wonderful meals, or at local restaurants. Our first "dates" out were at Walter's Bistro. Eventually we added The Blue Star to our favorite places. Owner Joe Coleman heard our stories, was touched, and took on the role of big brother. He also offered dating advice, which I enjoyed immensely.

During one visit to The Blue Star, Deb and I were in the ladies room. We were in the stalls and I started talking about a date I'd had with a lawyer in town. One of the parents at my school had set me up with him.

"The conversation was interesting, and he's nice enough, but I don't think I'll see him again. He's newly divorced and I just don't think we're a match."

Deb asked who he was. I said his name. I came out of the stall and started to wash my hands. One of the other stall doors slammed open and a woman I didn't know walked out and approached me. She announced who she was. It was the same last name as the attorney I'd gone out with. She asked if I'd just mentioned him.

"Yes . . . " I answered cautiously.

"He's my husband."

Deb slipped silently out the bathroom door.

"I thought he was divorced."

"Well, yes, we are. Are you going out with him again?"

"No, I'm not planning on it."

"Well, I know who you are and it's okay with me. I do want to tell you something, though. I think getting divorced is harder than being widowed. At least your husband isn't around for you to have to deal with."

Another zinger out of left field, to which I had no ready response. And, another valuable lesson learned: Don't talk about people in bathroom stalls unless you know everyone in the stalls.

*   *   *

About a year after Deb and I had met, she called me at school. It was noon and she was crying.

"Alexis got sick in California. I went to get her this weekend. She's in the operating room right now and I think she might die." Alexis was Deb's twenty-year-old daughter.

I could not believe what I was hearing.

"Deb, she can't die. That doesn't make any sense. We can't have another bad thing happen to us."

"I know."

At 3 p.m., I was putting on my orange vest to do my parking lot duty. I looked up and saw Katie Flesia, a good friend of Deb's.

The look on Katie's face told me the worst had happened.

"No! Get out of my office. I do not want to talk to you. Get out of my office."

Katie walked toward me and took me in her arms. I burst into tears. Katie held me for a long time. When we stopped crying, we drove over to Deb's house. Other friends had gathered in her living room. Deb was there when we walked in. I held her and cried, as many people had already done that day. We stayed all afternoon in Deb's living room and people told stories about Alexis. I had never met her but I learned about Deb's talented, sweet, gorgeous daughter. It reminded me of the morning after the crash.

While we were sitting in Deb's living room, a fawn came up to the window and looked in at us. It stayed for several minutes. Deb said that it was a sign from Alexis.

* * *

Another death laid me low in 2000. My dad had been diagnosed with and treated for prostate cancer in 1975, and while it had been in remission, it came back in 1995. As his condition worsened over the next few years, my siblings and I made trips to Bloomington to be with him as much as possible. With the help of hospice, he was able to stay home until the end. I saw him two weeks before he passed away and, although in pain, he still had his great sense of humor.

Dad: You keep saying, "I love you."

Nancy: I do love you!

Dad: Everyone says it so much now that I think we should rename ourselves the Lovely family.

He died surrounded by his lifelong friends and my mother. I lost the man I admired most in my life and my mother lost her best friend. I still miss hearing my dad tell me how much he loved me. It was no less painful or sad, no easier, no quicker than any other mourning I'd done. But I did know the territory, and had some hard-earned tools for coping.

* * *

Dearest Nancy,

Once again thanks for your sharing time here. I love seeing you and always enjoy having you around. I think everyone who knows you feels the same way.

You and I do share the bond of having those we loved most snatched away. But as great as my loss is, it can't compare with yours. And though I too miss Joel and the boys, I can't even imagine how you have managed to deal with your loss, and create a life for yourself that has so much meaning and gives so much to others. Of course Irv was the core of my life but I was fortunate to be able to share it with him for almost 52 years. And regardless of how lonely I may feel at times, I always have those years to look back on.

Thanks for your caring, awareness, and sensitivity.

Much love,
Mom

* * *

When Joel was alive he constantly told me that he loved my body just the way it was. I thought my body was okay, but I did only have one, very small breast. When I had my mastectomy and radiation in 1992, the doctor said I couldn't have reconstruction because of the radiation. But it had been eight years—maybe things had changed. At Deb's suggestion, I got some names of plastic surgeons and interviewed them. I looked at pictures. After meeting one particular surgeon, I got excited. He convinced me that I could have successful reconstruction. It would be almost a year-long process, and would involve stretching the skin where my breast had been. My biggest concern was work. He assured me that I could keep working as my chest "grew." I scheduled the first surgery for Adam's birthday, October 5, 2000.

My boss, Dr. Else, called me in the middle of September to tell me that a representative from the Colorado Department of Education (CDE) would be coming to Broadmoor on October 5, to give our school an award. I told him I had plans to take that day off. After everything he'd been through with me, I wasn't surprised at his response.

"Nancy . . . is everything okay?"

"Well, yes. I'm having some minor surgery. I'm taking that Thursday and Friday off."

With my health history, I knew he would worry. I had to tell him the truth.

"I am having breast reconstruction."

Silence. Then, "I think we can reschedule the visit."

I wasn't especially excited about the CDE award because we were being honored for our test scores. Good test scores were fine, but I thought our school was about so much more. I reluctantly organized an all-school assembly. With the student body gathered, I announced that we had some very special guests visiting to celebrate our achievements. Dr. Else congratulated the students and teachers for their hard work and introduced the representative from CDE.

I realized the assembly was taking an unusual turn. It was announced that a very large monetary award was about to be presented. I wondered when they had started rewarding good test scores with cash. The guest from CDE teased the kids and made them guess how much money the award was for. When they heard that the amount was $25,000, there was a collective gasp—they could hardly contain their excitement.

Then I heard the words.

"It gives me great pleasure to announce that your principal, Dr. Nancy Saltzman, has been awarded the Milken Family Education Award, along with a prize of $25,000."

Dr. Else hugged me, gave me a wink, and said, "GOTCHA!"

I felt like I'd just been given the best surprise party ever.

I was very happy that CDE had been able to reschedule the assembly. It was a wonderful honor, and I was thrilled to share it with the students and staff at Broadmoor. The only thing that could have made it better would've been to have Joel, Adam, and Seth there to see the look of surprise and wonder on my face as I held a three-by-five-foot check.

*   *   *

Dear Nancy,

Running into you this afternoon at the hockey game reminded me how often I think about you. I've started a dozen notes, but I never know what to say. (Religion is not one of my strengths so I don't have any standard comforting statements.)

I can't imagine a greater sense of grief than to have to bury <u>one</u> of my children—so to comprehend what you've experienced is beyond me. I hope that the passage of time is working its course. I would hope that in time some of the pain would ease but I don't know that anything could lessen the tremendous sense of loss.

I admire your strength and stamina.

Fondly,
Barb Jones

(A friend)

*   *   *

My friend posse expanded. Besides Donna, Deb, the teachers and staff at school, and an eclectic group of acquaintances, I also met Laura Kadlecek around that time. Laura was a divorced high school teacher. We hit it off immediately and compared notes on dating, discovering that we had even dated some of the same men! She was a wonderful, supportive influence, and we enjoyed dinners, hikes, biking, and generally hanging out together. We became extremely close, and I was welcomed into Laura's equally exceptional circle of women friends. Several of us also traveled together, taking cruises to Hawaii and the Yucatan peninsula.

Laura was a terrific hostess and on Sunday nights, friends would gather at her house to eat dinner and watch *Sex in the City*. The show always prompted sharing our own tales from the dating trenches, along with much laughter.

I still see women from that remarkable group, as part of a book club and to celebrate our birthdays.

* * *

In November of 2000, I heard from John, the man my friend had thought I should go out with a year earlier. We laughed about how long it had taken for us to connect. During our conversation I realized that he was thirteen years younger than I was. Another young pup! I told him that I thought our age difference was too great, although I appreciated his call and our conversation. He convinced me that we should at least meet. We set a date.

John showed up at my house, bearing a rose. We went to a CC hockey game. Walking around the arena, I showed him a picture of Mike that was prominently displayed with some other hockey players from CC. That gave us a good laugh. Nothing like showing a guy a larger-than-life photo of your ex-husband on the first date.

After the game we went out for dessert. When I reached across the table to hold his hand there was instant chemistry. So much for the age difference.

I told John that I'd had a mastectomy in 1990, and was in the middle of breast reconstruction. He was curious and asked a few questions, but didn't seem overly concerned.

We started seeing each other regularly. When I talked about school, John listened with real interest. He too was in a leadership position. He worked at Memorial Hospital in Colorado Springs, had served in the Air Force, was a serious runner and weight lifter, and loved conversation. John had a lot of friends. His colleagues liked working with him. He went with me to hear Denny talk about ARFF. He met my single girlfriends, and they invited him to join us when we all went out. He liked my dogs and even took Squeak running with him. We talked a lot and I loved our discussions.

We had a lot in common—and we had some significant differences. There was the age difference. He had two young children who were in elementary school. The children had a mother, John's ex-wife, with whom he shared custody. I wasn't sure how I felt about dating someone with young children, but I imagined we would figure it out if we got serious.

Religion was an important part of John's life. He was a practicing Lutheran and attended church with his children every Sunday. His children were enrolled in a private religious elementary school.

We decided that what we enjoyed about each other outweighed our differences. I eventually met John's children. Being with them was wonderful and hard for me. I wanted to get close to them but was afraid to get too close. It was confusing.

I had not seen Dr. Bermudez in a couple of years but made an appointment to discuss my concerns. We talked about the challenges I faced establishing a relationship with someone else's children. I talked about the comparisons I made between Joel, Adam, and Seth and John and his children. John's kids were great; they just weren't Adam and Seth. John was a great dad; he just didn't parent the same way Joel did. I now had more insight into what life was like for parents at my school who were in blended families. If John and I got married, we would have to work all of this out. For the time being, Dr. Bermudez advised that I needed to relax and not overthink the situation.

John and I saw each other on the evenings he didn't have his kids. On Sundays, after they all went to church, the four of us would go out for Indian food. Then we would do something fun together at my house or in the mountains. During the summer of 2001, John, his children, and I went to his brother's wedding in Ft. Wayne, Indiana.

I fell in love with John, which brought me hope that I could be truly happy in a relationship again. There was even a possibility that I could be close to children other than those I knew at school. But despite all the positive aspects, down deep I just didn't believe John and I were right for each other. I loved him, but I had learned long before that love wasn't always enough.

When we had been dating for six months, John asked me to go to Easter services with him.

I laughed. "Isn't Easter about the resurrection of Jesus?" Since the Jewish religion doesn't recognize Jesus as a messiah, I thought John would see the irony. He wanted me to go anyway. I got dressed in my Easter best and joined John and his children at the Lutheran Easter services. I went for John, but religion was not going to play a major part in my life.

I also worried about being so much older.

"What will it be like when I'm seventy and you're fifty-seven?"

"You look young. Men tend to age less gracefully so it won't be that big of a deal." I wasn't so sure. I knew what my mom looked like at seventy. She looked great, but she didn't look fifty-seven.

In the end, after much soul-searching, I told John I thought he should find someone else to date.

"I think you should be with someone who is Christian. And divorced or widowed, with children." He didn't agree but knew that neither of us was going to change. We loved each other but once again, it wasn't enough. I shed many tears and got reacquainted with my old friend sadness, but believed it was the best decision for me. Within a year John had met a divorced woman with children of her own who was a Christian. They fell in love and married.

Right before John and I stopped seeing each other, I got a puppy. Shoshi, Adam and Seth's dog that had seen me so valiantly through the roughest days of my grief, had passed away during the summer. Squeak and I missed her. I looked in the paper for golden retriever puppies and found one in a nearby neighborhood. The puppy was born on the Fourth of July. Squeak was initially wary of her but they quickly bonded. I looked through lists of names and when I saw the name Macy I knew it was right. I had just lost my good friend Linda Macy, one of my PALS colleagues, to leukemia. Plus I knew I would spend as much on this puppy as I would if I went shopping at Macy's.

* * *

Dear Adam and Seth,

I want you to know that Shoshi passed away on Saturday, June 28. She died in her sleep, probably of old age. But then, maybe you already know that. Maybe she's with you.

She had been having a hard time getting around because of her arthritis but she still wanted to go for walks in the park, so I would lift her into the truck and help her out. Her favorite thing was sitting in the stream.

The last week of her life she couldn't really get up and down so I sat on the floor and fed her, gave her water, held her, and talked to her. It reminded me of the times that you, Adam, would get mad about something and lie on the floor and talk to her. She always listened intently.

I cried on her a lot, too—I wanted you guys to be here just to let her know how much she was loved. I did talk to her about you and your dad and, to tell the truth, I told her that if she wanted to, she could join you. I don't really have any idea what happens when you die, but I said, "You can go be with Joel, Adam, and Seth if you want to."

Seth, you wrote in your journal just a few days before the crash,

> *"The happiest day in my life was when I got Shoshi.*
> *She was hardly opening her eyes. Her fur was bright*
> *white. Shoshi was my very first dog. She sat in my lap*
> *and whined. Shoshi was born on Valentine's Day. Her*
> *mom's name is Lacy. There were eight in the litter. I*
> *love Shoshi."*

I remember that day, too. Your dad told us that Mary Polaski's dog Lacy had had puppies. He said that we could go look at the puppies but we couldn't get one. I told him if we went to look at the puppies, we'd be coming home with one—I mean, who can look at a golden retriever puppy and not get one? You guys picked her out of the litter and when your dad took one look at Shoshi, it was all over—she was ours. I don't remember who ended up training her but I think she pretty much trained herself. She was smart enough. We mostly just held her and petted her and took her for walks. She figured everything else out on her own.

The day after you died Shoshi lay down on the floor and would not get up. I called Dr. Ireland. He came to the house and took her to the dog hospital. She had three infections! She sensed that things weren't right. When she came home from the hospital she just wandered around the house, looking for all of you.

Shoshi and Squeak saved my life those first few months after you died. I missed you with every inch of my body but I was never alone. I would lie on the floor with them next to me, licking the tears off my face. Now it's just Squeak and me and he has to try and lick my tears away all by himself. He was really sad for a few days when Shoshi died. He took naps in Shoshi's favorite spot.

I think I may get a new puppy. I don't think it will be the happiest day of my life like it was for you, Seth, but I think it will still be a happy day.

Love,
Mom

CHAPTER 20

A NEW CHAPTER, A TALL TALE

IN THE FALL of 2003, I agreed to co-teach a class with a friend and mentor, Dale Gasser.

I talked to the class participants, all of them teachers or administrators in Colorado, about how much I enjoyed being a principal. Then I spoke more at length about the challenges I had faced. I described what had happened to my family and how the school and community had responded to the tragedy.

During a break from class, Tammy Clementi, one of the students, asked me if I was dating.

"I have a neighbor," she said, "a retired Air Force colonel, who just lost his wife to breast cancer. I thought he was an arrogant jerk until I heard him speak at his wife's service. He seems like a very caring, loving, and sweet man. I wondered if you would be interested in meeting him."

I said I would, but it seemed a bit too soon; his wife had died in August and this was September. I told her I'd write him a note in a month or two. She gave me his address.

In November, Tammy asked me if I had contacted her neighbor yet. I hadn't, but with her prompting, I sent him a note introducing myself and explaining how I'd heard about him. I put my business card in the envelope and mailed it.

*   *   *

Dear Greg,

I met Tammy Clementi in a class that I'm co-teaching this fall. As part of the class, I talk to the students about dealing with tragic loss and working with children. My husband and two sons died in a small plane crash in September of 1995, and both of my sons had been students at my school. Tammy told me about you and your wife. It was clear to me that you dealt with an impossible and devastating tragedy in the best way possible—with love and care. Tammy thought that you might enjoy talking with me and I told her that I would love to meet you, but we could let you decide if it was something you wanted to do. Coffee? Chai tea? A beer? Feel free to give me a call at home or work if you want to get together, but please don't feel obligated.

Love and hugs,
Nancy

*   *   *

Five days later, at 8 a.m. on a Sunday morning, my phone rang. It was Tammy. The widower, Greg, had gotten my note.

"Would you like to come to dinner at my house tonight? It will be me and my husband, my neighbors, my sister, and Greg."

First I had plans and couldn't go. Then Greg had plans and couldn't go. Then Greg's plans changed and he could go. And I changed my plans and could go. The blind date was on.

When I walked into Tammy's house I could hear laughter coming from another room. Shoes had been placed neatly next to a railing. I removed my shoes and put them next to a giant pair of men's shoes—I imagined they must be Greg's because Tammy had said he was tall. I could easily have put my shoes inside his.

I followed the voices into the kitchen. Pots and pans were hanging over the granite island. I saw a very tall, dark-haired man duck under one of the pots as he walked toward me to introduce himself. His blue eyes reminded me of my father's.

Placing my hand in his made me think of my first teaching job interview with Mr. Millar in the Widefield School District. He had been six foot five, and his hand had engulfed mine. Greg's did, too, but in a kind, protective way. Like when Gulliver discovers the little people. A smile broke out on his face as he introduced himself.

"I'm Greg. It's nice to meet you. Would you like something to drink?"

Maybe a shot of tequila?

I was nervous enough to consider enlisting the help of alcohol.

"I would love some water, thank you."

Greg's neighbors Teny and Gary Nudson, Tammy and her husband, and Tammy's sister were sitting at the dining room table drinking beers out of the bottles. I guessed from the volume of the conversation that I was several drinks behind.

Introductions were made and Gary told me that he and Teny had known Joel. They had taken tennis lessons from him at the Colorado Springs Racquet Club. Gary remembered him well. "What a great guy. He was a terrific tennis teacher. We lived right by the racquet club so we saw him quite a bit. And the jokes he used to tell! I miss him." A lull fell over the group.

Great way to start a blind date—reminiscing about my dead husband.

But Greg listened and seemed to take it in stride. The conversation moved on to neighborhood pranks.

"Remember when we took an arrow and stuck it through the Christmas deer decoration in Greg's yard last year? Fake blood all over the place?" Gary started the story. Teny continued. "The best part was that Greg would pull into his driveway every night and not do a thing about it. Gary would stand at the window watching as Greg walked out to get his mail and did nothing. It drove Gary nuts! To really bug him, Gary took the deer from Greg's yard and put it in our yard. Still—no reaction!" Everyone was laughing—including Greg.

"I knew I could make Gary crazier if I didn't do a thing," Greg explained.

I enjoyed the dinner but didn't add much to the conversation. As everyone began leaving, I asked Greg to walk me to my truck. When we got there, he gave me a hug. We said goodbye. I drove home thinking about whether I wanted to see him again. I had felt like a fish out of water at dinner. I wasn't sure if Greg liked me, and I didn't know if I was attracted to him. He was six feet, four inches tall and nothing like anyone I had ever dated. He certainly was not my physical "type." He had a ten-year-old son from his first marriage and shared custody with his ex-wife. As Tammy had told me, his second wife had passed away from breast cancer.

When I got home I called his phone number and got the recorder. I left a message thanking him for including me in the dinner.

Greg called the next day and said he would like to take me out for a relaxed dinner, just the two of us. I was leaving on Tuesday to go to Indiana for Thanksgiving and wouldn't be back until Saturday after the holiday. He said he would call me when I got back, and that we would go out for dinner on Sunday, a week away. I left for my trip not sure if I would actually hear from him again.

True to his word, Greg called when I got home. He picked me up on Sunday to take me out for dinner. He wanted to go someplace where I had never been, but my attitude toward cooking was quickly revealed— I'd been to virtually every restaurant in town. We ended up at The Blue Star because it was close. Joe Coleman, the owner, saw me and bellowed, "Saltzman!" He came over to our table and asked how I was, warning Greg to be nice to me.

Greg and I talked our way through a delicious dinner and when he dropped me off at my house, gave me a very sweet kiss goodnight. When I shut the door my phone rang. It was Greg. He wanted to tell me how wonderful it was to have met me. He said he was looking forward to seeing me again.

This time I had really enjoyed being with Greg. While he wasn't my usual type, he was tall, dark, and handsome and fascinating to talk to. His background was very different from mine. He was born in Philadelphia, went to elementary school in Colorado Springs, high school in Vicenza, Italy, and college at the Air Force Academy. His dad had also served in the armed forces and his mother was from Belgium. He had twin brothers who were nine years younger.

Greg had spent twenty-three years in Air Force intelligence. He had lived in Greece, Korea, Germany, Panama, Japan, and Washington, D.C. He retired as a colonel in 2002 when he learned that his second wife, Pat Flannery, had cancer. He chose to stay in Colorado Springs to be close to his son Jordan. That told me a lot about him and his commitment as a father.

We didn't have tons in common but we shared the loss of a spouse, which was an important touchpoint. We talked about Joel and Pat. Greg told me that when Pat was dying she told him that she didn't really want him to fall in love again. But, she knew he would. She had raised two boys as a single parent while becoming a colonel in the Air Force. She wanted Greg to find a woman who needed him—maybe someone who had children, so he could be their father figure. I didn't really fit the bill in that respect but it was true that I wanted someone wonderful to love me.

*   *   *

Greg and I started seeing each other every evening. When I told him that I was going to Mexico for Christmas with friends, we agreed we would get together for New Year's. Much to my surprise, Greg figured out a way to get to Mexico, even though he didn't know if there would be a place for him to stay when he arrived.

When everyone met him, they liked him immediately. We relaxed, played cards, swam, ate, and drank. Greg was able to get a room for every night except the last one. It didn't seem to bother him when he had to sleep on the deck of one of our rooms on a baby crib mattress. He especially enjoyed sneaking onto the tour bus back to the airport, using the skills he had learned as an intelligence officer.

Greg and I continued to see each other almost every day. For Valentine's Day he had a barbershop quartet surprise me at school. It was very romantic, although the kids were the ones who really enjoyed it. I was kind of embarrassed. One of the sixth graders gave Greg a big thumbs up.

We spent more time together and as we fell in love, the relationship became more serious. I discovered he was as kind as Tammy thought when she first told me about him, but also much more. He was devoted, but not smothering. Supportive and engaged, but also had his own goals and interests. Those were very important attributes to me. He also generously embraced my family—including the furry ones—with open arms.

I met his son and his ex-wife. Greg traveled with me to Bloomington to have Thanksgiving with my mom, her friends, my sister and Charlie. For Mother's Day, we had a brunch at Greg's house with my mother, Joel's father, Greg's parents, and Donna's mother. Talk about blending families.

For the 2005 holiday, we made the trip to Bloomington to be with my mother. We flew in on December 19. But as we drove into town, Greg veered from the usual route to my mother's house.

"Where are you going?" I asked, slightly irritated.

"Relax. I know what I'm doing."

"This isn't the right way."

"I know! I have an important question to ask you. I want to go to your dad's bench and tree."

That got my attention.

I fell silent. I didn't know what Greg had in mind but I didn't want to make the same mistake I had in 1981 when Joel had wanted to ask me "a question."

Greg parked the car behind the psychology building. We got out of the car and walked to my dad's bench. Greg took my hand.

When we got to the bench he asked me to sit down. Then, sure enough, he got down on one knee.

"I love you, Nancy. Will you marry me?"

Tears stung my eyes as I managed an emotional "Yes."

We kissed . . . for a long time. Then we sat down on the bench. On my right hand I was wearing my maternal grandmother's diamond ring. I moved it to my left hand. Greg then gave me a pair of sparkling diamond stud earrings that he'd picked out, knowing I already had a ring.

I put them on, and realized I felt both happy and lucky—two things I could never have imagined ever feeling again, ten years, two months, and twenty-five days earlier.

*   *   *

When Greg and I got engaged, some saw it as me finally being "back." I had at long last gotten over my losses and found happiness; I was once again the Nancy they had known before the crash. I understood the sentiment, but it couldn't have been further from the truth.

First of all, I never left. I was always me, just a me that had to walk a long, unimaginably difficult path that only I could travel. Just like my Olympic torch run, I had lots of support, people cheering me on and pulling for me—but it could only be me putting one foot in front of the other. Second, I was never going to stay the exact person I was on September 23, 1995, anyway. Even if the crash hadn't happened, I would have lived, grown, learned, matured, and evolved into a more seasoned version of myself. A version that, happily, continues to grow and evolve.

I have also tried concertedly to not let the crash define me. In some ways, that attitude has been forced on me by the blunt reality that just because one horrific thing happens to you doesn't give you a "Get Out of Bad Things Free" card. Yes, I got cancer. Then my husband and sons died. Awful, terrible things. Then I lost a close friend. And another. And a good friend's daughter. And my dad died of cancer. More terrible things.

There is no tragedy quota. No immunity.

Each time something bad happens, I call on the tools I was born and raised with, and the lessons I've learned, to help get me through.

But most important, because I now have some experience with bad things happening, I try to share what I've learned with others going through their own trials.

My tools may not suit others. My lessons may be different. But here's the secret: The simple act of reaching out and holding a broken heart with care and love is the most powerful help and comfort anyone can ever offer.

And that's something every single one of us can do.

CHAPTER 21

PERSPECTIVE

IT HAS BEEN seventeen years since the plane crash. A lot has happened during that time—good and bad. As I've stated, life doesn't keep track of your adversity score, and it certainly doesn't offer exclusions from further grief and sadness. Besides the misfortunes of friends and family that I mentioned earlier, there have been other losses. In 2005, my sister Linda died in her sleep of sudden cardiac arrest. Sarah Herzog, Joel's mother, died of complications from diabetes. My mother started having memory problems and was diagnosed with Alzheimer's disease. After driving her car through the garage into the dining room in her home, my brothers and I took her car away. She told Rob, "I don't mind that you drove my car through the garage wall, I just wish you wouldn't lie about it." She had a series of caretakers, whom she generally disliked, and was able to stay in the home she loved until right before she died of pneumonia. Greg and I were able to be with her for her last few days before she passed away in 2008.

* * *

In 2006, I left my job at Broadmoor Elementary School. I had thirty-two years in public education and qualified for early retirement. I loved the teachers, students, and families at Broadmoor, but was ready for some new adventures. My first semester after leaving Broadmoor, I taught Educational Psychology one day a week at the University of Colorado at Colorado Springs (UCCS). It was intellectually stimulating to work with young adults who were thinking about becoming teachers or school counselors.

A good friend of my mother's, Saul Rockman, the principal at a research company, asked me to do some work for him. I observed and recorded data in five after-school programs in the Denver Public Schools. I worked with a dynamic investigator to summarize the data and present it to the program director. It was all new learning for me and I found it extremely stimulating. Of course, the best part was being around kids again.

I continued my work with Kidpower as the president of the board. I volunteered at Memorial Hospital through the American Cancer Society until my mother's condition started requiring frequent trips to Indiana. Through my hospital work I made a wonderful new friend, Debra Plotkin.

Greg and I sold both of our houses and bought a new one in December of 2006. Jordan, Greg's son, moved in with us his freshman year of high school so he could go to Cheyenne Mountain High School (CMHS). The looks I got from former Broadmoor parents when they saw me at CMHS Back to School Nights was very amusing. I joked that I just couldn't stay away, then explained why I was there and introduced them to Greg and Leslie, Jordan's mother.

As I learned previously while dating John, finding an appropriate role with a partner's child is tricky business. I didn't always agree with Greg on how to raise Jordan. It was especially challenging when Jordan pushed the limits of what I thought was reasonable behavior in our home. We all survived, and I love the remarkable young man Jordan has become. I also love being part of this family of three (five counting the dogs). Greg and I are now empty-nesters, since Jordan went to college in the fall of 2011.

In 2008, Rob and Ed got married in Los Angeles. Greg and I attended the ceremony along with their close friends. I was Rob's Best Woman.

I see Joel's dad a couple of times a month. Greg and I meet him at the Pueblo Nature Center, eat lunch, and visit the large boulders that are engraved with the names of Joel, Adam, Seth, and Sarah Herzog. In July of 2011, Harvey celebrated his ninetieth birthday with his family and over a hundred friends. He continues to play tennis three times a week and is looking for love. He prefers a woman with no grey hair.

Lee Herzog lives in Los Angeles with his wife and two children, Sofia and Samuel. Samuel was born on Seth's birthday in 2003. Sofia is eleven. Lee is the counselor at Brentwood Middle School, and a psychological analyst with his own private practice. His wife, Jessica Anderren Herzog is also an analyst. They are both Dr. Herzog. My brother and Ed see them socially on a regular basis. When Greg and I are in LA, we see them too.

Greg still works in the field of intelligence as a defense contractor. He also owns Rhino's, a sports bar, on the east side of Colorado Springs, which he opened with some friends in 2007. He plans to retire in a few years. We bought a vacation home outside of Palm Springs. The house is close to the clay courts on which Joel and Lee beat the professionals at La Quinta Resort. When I walk by, I can see Joel hitting an ace.

I love my life. I love Greg. I see my future with Greg until "death us do part," although it is not important to me to get married again. Right now I am Greg's fiancée and Joel's widow. They coexist in my life.

* * *

"How did you do it? I could not have endured the loss of my family."

I have heard this so many times since 1995. My answer is always the same.

"What choice did I have?"

I could end my life or I could choose to live. I made a conscious decision to live.

I grew up in a loving family with high expectations. I always had their love, but to gain the respect of my parents I had to do well and develop an inner strength. They taught me to believe that when I faced adversity, I could overcome it. When Joel and the boys died, both of our families were profoundly affected. I was held by them in a caring, supportive safety net, despite the geographical distance between us. They continue to sustain me. Rob has been, and will always be, my touchstone.

Meeting Joel after being divorced from Mike taught me that I could love again after a relationship ends. Being separated from Joel when I was in Virginia showed me that I could be alone—although that was perhaps the most agonizing aspect of my grief.

I like immediate gratification as much as the next person, but I developed patience. Working with children requires a serious commitment of time. Children do not learn in a split second. They don't change overnight. To be an educator means to be patient. Teach, reteach, teach, reteach, teach, reteach. Celebrate. Love.

During my cancer treatment I learned to take one day at a time. I could not speed up the process. If my white blood cell count didn't bounce back each month, I had to wait an additional week or two before having chemo again. Before I could begin radiation, I had to wait for my white cell count to rise. When the treatments ended, it was almost a year before my hair was long enough to go without a wig.

I waited ten years to have breast reconstruction. Every two weeks I had to drive to Denver to have saline injected into a pouch under my skin. When I was ready for the permanent implant, I had surgery and waited to heal. The whole process took almost a year.

Being diagnosed twice with breast cancer forced me to deal with my own mortality. Joel and I had discussed what he would do if I lost my life to cancer. He knew that I wanted him to remarry and be happy again. I believed that if he could have told me what to do after he died, he would have encouraged me to fall in love again.

I asked people to talk to me about Joel, Adam, and Seth. I talked about them frequently.

I stayed committed to my job at Broadmoor Elementary. My sense of purpose there fueled me, even when my tank was below empty. The teachers and staff, all of whom were there for each other and the students after the crash, were a constant in my life. They were so much more than colleagues; I'm honored to call them my friends.

I took one minute, five minutes, one hour, one day at a time. But I was also conscious of the hundreds of small eyes on me, and I recognized both my responsibility and opportunity to model behavior few young people ever have a chance to see: self-affirming ways to approach and move through hard—even catastrophic—times.

Because I am not particularly religious, I believe that we have to make a positive difference while we are alive. If this translates into going to Heaven or some other great place when I die, all the better. If it doesn't, I know that I had an impact while I lived.

I also let people give me love and support. In the first days after the crash, I accepted food that I knew I would never eat. As a Broadmoor parent explained to me, "We can't make *you* feel better, but at least *we* feel like we're doing something if you let us bring food." Dianne Allen, one of my writing buddies and a parent of students at Broadmoor, told me, "During the weeks and months after the crash we watched the person who was grieving the most show everyone else how to handle their grief with courage. We couldn't have done it without you."

*   *   *

My friends have always been there for me. Donna was with me the night of the crash and continued to be my anchor for the endless days and nights that followed. I still consider her my "BFF." All my friends showed me such kindness and taught me that after so much crying, I hadn't forgotten how to laugh. These caregivers—in the truest sense of the word—listened to me, held me, cried with me, laughed with me, sent me notes, took me out, and were lifelines for me over and over again. I owe my life to them, and am forever grateful.

I received thousands of letters after the plane crash. I still have them. They are kind, thoughtful, humorous, and loving. Many spoke of a renewed appreciation for loved ones in the wake of what happened, and that warms my heart. I'm so happy to be able to share in this book some of the wisdom and compassion they expressed.

Occasionally, I'll see a parent of a child who went to school with Seth or Adam, or someone who either didn't know or has forgotten what happened. They'll ask me how one or both of the boys are, and I'll tell them as gently as I can. I feel worse for them than for me; it's not as if they're reminding me of something that isn't with me all the time.

In reference to losses, I would like to add that people tell me, "Losing a child is the worst thing that can happen to you." I agree that losing a child is unspeakable. But losing a sister prematurely is also terrible. Having a close friend die in a car crash is awful. Watching your brilliant mother go through the ravages of Alzheimer's and your father die of cancer are extremely painful. It makes no sense to me to try to put these things on a relative scale. I would not want to have to choose one over another. On the tragedy scale, I don't think there are gradations. In February of 2001, one of my PALS, Linda Macy passed away from leukemia. During one of my visits with her, I told her that I was so sorry that she was going through such a challenging time. She looked at me and said, "I don't consider this challenging at all compared to what you had to endure." I smiled. I didn't want to think about having leukemia; she didn't want to imagine losing her family.

I try to keep things in perspective. I have always appreciated small things: that froggy green of new spring leaves, the bottomless sympathy in a devoted dog's eyes. Now I take pleasure in life's tiny gifts even more.

*　*　*

I've heard people talk about catastrophic events they've experienced as being a good thing—that they're better people for having lived through the hard times. I do have a wonderful life today, but it's definitely in spite of my losses, not because of them.

I will never "get over" losing Joel, Adam, and Seth. I miss them too much. I read a quote that said, "Grief is love that will not go away." What has changed is the intensity of the pain I feel when I think about people I have lost from my life. It has decreased over time. I think of something every day that reminds me of my family, and the other people I have lost. Not all day like I did when they first died, but intermittently. My thoughts usually make me smile, although sometimes I still cry uncontrollably, just like in the first days, weeks, and months. When I am alone on a beautiful day walking the dogs, on Joel's, Adam's, or Seth's birthdays, or when there is bad weather in September, I am overwhelmed with grief.

I wish I could have been Seth and Adam's mom as they went through junior high, high school, and college. I wonder if Adam got his first kiss before he died. I asked Katherine Hess, the girl he was in love with when he died, if he had kissed her. She told me, "No," but added, "I wish he had." I love her for saying that. Seth, ever the shaker and mover, might very well have stolen a kiss from someone.

I wonder if the boys would have played hockey and tennis in high school. Would they have gone to college, and if so, where? Would they have stayed in Colorado or gone someplace warm that their father would have liked? Would they be stringing racquets at Total Tennis, working for their dad . . . or working in education like me . . . or following some other calling?

I imagine that they would be, or would have been by now, in at least one serious relationship—maybe even be married. I wish I could be a grand-mother. I think my grandbabies would have huge eyes and long lashes.

CHAPTER 22

RADICAL SURVIVORS

IN 1998, I FLEW TO Houston to be with Joe Lychner as his wife and two daughters were memorialized at the dedication of "Love's Embrace," a bronze statue created in his family's honor. I sat in the crowd listening to Joe speak about his loved ones. He became emotional and paused to gather himself. I felt his vulnerability and got up from my seat to stand near him, just for a minute, to provide him with some comfort and support. So much of moving through grief is done by oneself, but I didn't think he needed to be alone in that moment.

I learned about Pam Bull through Lisa Davis, a friend from college. Pam's husband was sailing with their two daughters in Lake Michigan and did not return home. The three drowned. Pam had stayed home for the day with her infant son. I called Pam. We spoke on the phone several times in 1999. I told her about Joe.

In November 2006, Ann Vessels, a good friend who had moved to Denver, called me. I had an eerie feeling why she was calling. I had just seen the news and a man named Frank Bingham, his wife, and two young children had been struck by a drunk driver. Frank survived but his family had not. By coincidence, Ann lived next door to the Binghams. She gave me his contact information. Frank and I met at a Starbucks in Denver. I knew what he looked like from the news reports. When I came through the door and saw Frank sitting by himself at a table for two, I hesitated for a moment.

What do you say to someone who has lost his whole family?

I had spoken on the phone with others who had lost multiple loved ones in a single accident—Joe, Pam—but this was the first time I'd met someone in person so soon after their tragedy. I think for the first time I realized how strange it must have been for people to see me after the crash. Undoubtedly, my friends and family had also wondered, *What do you say to someone who has lost her whole family?*

Frank stood up and we hugged. I told him how sorry I was. He told me what he remembered about the accident. I told him about what had happened to me. I discovered that Frank had been a principal and was presently working with principals while going to law school. We had a lot in common and spent a couple of hours together. Since that time we have gotten together for dinner and coffee, and Frank graduated from DU Law School.

Bonnie Blair Cruikshank, the Olympic gold medalist in speed skating, called me in July of 2011. I know Bonnie through her sister, Mary Polaski, the friend who changed the sheets in my house after the crash. Bonnie knew of the Buerkett family. Mr. and Mrs. Buerkett, their daughter Morgan, and their two dogs died in a small plane crash on takeoff outside of Chicago. Their other daughter, Ashley, was not on the plane. Bonnie asked if I could contact her. I sent her an e-mail and she responded immediately. We have corresponded through e-mail and Facebook. I hope to meet her in person someday.

Sometimes, when I tell people my story of loss, they have to ask me to repeat myself. They can't get their heads around what they heard. Some say, "I am so sorry," with tears in their eyes. Others have no idea what to say, and so say nothing. I understand that people like Joe, Pam, Frank, Ashley and me—and so many others, with their own stories of radical survival—are part of a strange, small, unlikely club. But we who have lived through extreme loss have a shared experience that will forever connect us.

In October of 2011, I received a message from a young woman, a stranger, on Facebook. She said that when she was seventeen she went through a very difficult time. She was sexually assaulted, placed in foster care, and lost two very dear friends; one in an auto accident and the other from suicide. She wrote,

> *I decided I didn't want to live anymore. I didn't feel like I had much of a reason to live, but most of all I was tired of opening my eyes in the morning and trying to make it through another day. My friend who killed himself is buried next to your family. I was sitting at his grave one day and couldn't help but notice the names on the headstone next to his. At that*

time their pictures weren't on the headstone, but someone had placed a picture there. I looked at the photo. I don't remember the details but it was a photo of all of you. It was then that I noticed that the only name that wasn't on the headstone was yours. I didn't know at that time what had happened to your family. I could only imagine how it felt for you to open your eyes when you woke up, only to remember that they were gone. That moment changed my life forever. I felt like if you were out there somewhere . . . alive . . . making it through each day, that maybe it was possible for me to make it through another day, too. From that day forward, every time I felt like giving up, I would remember that picture of your beautiful family. I would remember that I wasn't the only person who had suffered loss and experienced pain. Even though I don't know anything about you, I felt your strength, and it has inspired me to keep living. I have kept you in my thoughts and prayers . . . and I think of you every time I visit my friend's grave. I'm so sorry for your loss, and so grateful for your life.

Me, too.

ACKNOWLEDGMENTS

I owe gratitude to at least a thousand people and apologize for not being able to list every individual here.

Thank you:

To Shoshi, Squeak, Macy, and Nacho.

To everyone who sent me a note or card or left me a message right after the crash and many times since 1995. I know they were hard to compose. Even though you often said words could not express your feelings, they did, and they helped me "reach up and grab the live preserver."

To everyone who asked for my nonexistent book, which encouraged me to write it.

To the Colorado Springs and Pueblo tennis, squash, and hockey players, and their families.

To the Colorado Springs *Gazette*, for remembering; especially Anslee Wolfe and Barbara Cotter.

To my brother Rob's friends, who became my second family.

To Paul Saltzman, my favorite cousin, for taking over the job of family historian.

To Lee Carmen for harassing me until the book was completed.

To Dan Cook for asking me, "Can I read your book?" when it was still five poorly written chapters, and Kathleen Krushas for your designer's eye and talented hand. This book would not exist without the love you two poured into the project.

To Tom and Priscilla Turner for providing me a home away from home to edit my book.

To my Breast Friends.

To all my girlfriends. You know who you are, and you know what you have meant and will always mean to me.

To Sarah Michel for mentoring me when I was a principal, speaker, and now author.

To Bonnie Blair Cruikshank for writing a beautiful foreword.

To Tom Cone for always being there to walk with me while I cried and yelled.

To Drs. O'Rourke, Sayre, and Bermudez for ensuring the "survivor" part of "Radical Survivor."

To Lighthouse Writers.

To Gus Lee and my first writing group. Who knew that your feedback and enthusiasm would lead to a real, live book?

To Ceil Malek, Linda Thompson, June Loterbauer, Vicki McNeil, and Margie Arnold, my current writing group. Will you each publish a book this year, please?

To Richard Skorman and the staff at Poor Richard's for letting me write in the bookstore week after week and month after month.

To Liz Stedem for being my friend, writing coach, and cheerleader.

To Julie Talbot. Now I know why everyone says, "I could not have done this without my editor." I don't want to write another book but I might have to just so I can continue to work with you.

To my family at Broadmoor Elementary School: the teachers and staff who did what needed to be done for the students and me after the crash even though they were in shock, too; the parents who were present day after day to give hugs and bring food; the students who kept me focused on what is important. To Rebecca for the sticky note that was on my desk the day I went back to work. To Linda Shea for writing music that captured the essence of my family, for telling me things I didn't know about Adam and Seth, and for going to Mexico with me so we could try to fill the holes in our hearts with warmth. To Debbi Young for being Seth's teacher in 1995. To Scott Stanec for helping us navigate the grief process. To Rita Cook for putting her arms around the students and me for a whole year.

To the Herzog family for always holding me close. Harvey still introduces me as his daughter-in-law and Lee-Lee's children call me Aunt Nancy.

To Charlie Weeks, my sister's life partner, who is really a Saltzman.

To Linda, who was the best sister and aunt anyone could ask for, because your memories of my family have kept them alive in my heart and head.

To my brother Andy, who was not a tumor at all but my little brother and who put me on a pedestal. And to Mary, Rachel, Michael, Anna, and Caroline.

To my brother Rob, who is my touchstone. You know and understand me so well that I think maybe we were twins separated by two and a half years. Thank you for loving me unconditionally. You and Ed have made your home my home so many times and I love you both.

To Donna Sheldon, who has been my best friend for thirty-six years. We need to stop avoiding mirrors and "feel good about ourselves" anyway! Thank you for helping me remember and celebrate everyone we have lost—your brother Bob, Joel, Adam, Seth, my dad, your dad, Linda, your mom, and my mom.

To Jordan Roman. What a privilege it has been for me to watch you grow up.

To "my lover" Greg Roman for reading every draft and telling me you were deeply touched and inspired at the same time. For loving me constantly and encouraging me to go for my dream and reach for the stars. Do you really say and do all the right things because "foreplay is a twenty-four-hour-a-day job"?

To my mom and dad for raising me in a family full of fun, laughter, smarts, high expectations, and love, which allowed me to go to the edge and not fall off. Without your love and guidance I would not have made it.

To Joel, Adam, and Seth. The original "Lovely family" my father talked about right before he passed away. Few families have it better than we did. Writing about you made it possible for me to spend time with my memories and let love and joy wash over me. It was a gift.

And finally, to all the radical survivors out there, taking one minute, one hour, one day at a time and slowly but surely finding your own path.

APPENDIX

Transcriptions of eulogies and memories shared at the Memorial Service for Joel, Adam, and Seth Herzog, September 27, 1995.

ROB SALTZMAN

My name is Rob Saltzman. I am Nancy's brother, and it is my honor to participate in our celebration of the lives of Adam, Seth, and Joel.

To begin, on behalf of everyone in our families, let me thank all of you in this community who have responded so tremendously to help Nancy and all of us get through this disaster. Your outpouring of affection and assistance has been simply overwhelming. And we appreciate you more than we can adequately express.

I have so many wonderful memories of this family. It's hard to know which ones to share. I'll start with one of my memories of Joel. Most of you probably know that Joel liked to wear tennis shorts, regardless of the weather, or the formality of the occasion. In fact, if Joel were here physically in this room tonight, most likely he would be wearing tennis shorts or sweats—or making fun of what he was wearing instead.

Last December, I had a meeting at Colorado College. Unfortunately for me, during the day it snowed a foot and a half. I called Joel at the store to see if he might pick me up, but he had already left downtown to pick up the boys. When I finally reached him at home, he immediately offered to come all the way back downtown to get me.

Two things from that day stick out in my mind. First, only by accident did I learn that it had taken Joel over an hour to get home the FIRST time. Joel didn't tell me THAT, of course. Second, despite the freezing temperature and still-falling snow, Joel walked into the Rastall Center at CC wearing tennis shorts and a tee shirt.

Adam was well on his way to following in Joel's footsteps. He was just as charismatic, and he was devoted to his family and friends. I recall, for example, last Memorial Day when Nancy and Joel and the boys joined Ed and me and our friends for a large gathering in Palm Springs. All told, there were forty-five of us staying there, including twenty-two kids under the age of ten. Adam was the oldest child, and we might have expected him to complain about being bored, since there weren't a lot of other kids there his age. Instead, what we saw was more like "Adam the Pied Piper."

Literally, for hours, over many days, Adam served as camp counselor, babysitter, and punching bag for the younger kids. The image is still vivid in my mind of Adam, giggling and laughing, as at least six younger kids held him down on the ground so that they and their pals could climb all over him. And it sure seemed that Adam was loving it.

During that long weekend, I heard, over and over, more than one toddler ask first thing in the morning (or after a nap), "Where's Adam?" or "Where's my Adam?" At the end of the weekend, one particularly precocious—and, I might add, beautiful—five-year-old girl announced that she and Adam were engaged to be married. Adam heard this news for the first time along with the rest of us, but he accepted graciously and with that wonderful smile of his. He was certainly not going to do anything to embarrass his new friend. He even sat with her for the taking of an engagement photograph.

Adam was, quite simply, an extraordinary child who would have been an extraordinary man. Nancy and Joel did such a marvelous job of raising him together.

And then there was Seth.

For me, one story about Seth is a lesson for all of us. As a five-year-old, Seth was playing on his first hockey team. At the first practice, the coach, Mike Bertsch, lined up the players in full uniform and asked each of them what he would suggest as the team name. Down the row they went: one suggested Tigers, another offered Sharks, and on it went down the line. Little Seth was the last in line and by far the smallest. But he was so proud to be wearing all that equipment—even though the sleeves covered his gloves, the jersey went below his knees, and the pants went over his skates to the ice. When it was Seth's turn to suggest a name for the team, he looked up, his dark eyes so big, and said as loud as he could, "I want us to be the Giants!" In those seven words, Seth said so much.

To me, Adam, Seth, Joel and Nancy ARE giants. Although Adam, Seth, and Joel are no longer with us here, their giant spirit for living remains. I think Seth would tell us that it is up to each of us to be a GIANT in whatever ways that suit us.

Nancy is a giant, as a devoted friend, daughter, sister, wife, and mother. She is also a giant as perhaps the best school principal that a generation of kids, parents, and teachers will ever know.

Nancy will miss Adam, Seth, and Joel terribly. But we all know that to them, she was THEIR loving giant. And boy, did they love her more than anything! Indeed, one of the most moving and visible aspects of Joel's love for Nancy, as was so evident to everyone who ever saw them together—and as you will be able to see again in the slides you view here later tonight—was that after fifteen years of marriage, Joel remained utterly and completely infatuated with Nancy, and considered her to be the most beautiful and wonderful woman in the whole world.

Those of us here tonight, from the youngest to the oldest, are still learning how to be giants. But, since everyone here loved Adam, Seth, and Joel, I hope that we can all honor them by living our lives as the giants that Seth wanted each of us to be. Let's remember them and meet that challenge.

Thank you.

HARVEY HERZOG

My dearest family, dear friends,

What can a father say when he sees his beloved son and grandchildren taken away in the prime of life? Joel was the kind of son any parent would be proud to call their own. He was outgoing in meeting friends and strangers. He showed genuine interest in the concern of others. He was helpful to the needs of all he knew. And he will always be remembered as a first-class tennis player.

In looking back to the very beginning of his life, let me briefly entertain you with the following true story. During the last days before Joel was born, I had been working in Denver, believing that there was ample time to return before his birth. Wrong. On Saturday, October 18, I got a call from St. Mary Corwin Hospital in Pueblo to the effect that Mrs. Herzog had given birth to a boy. This being my first experience and not realizing that the first baby could come any time, I argued with the nurse as to a mistaken identity. She merely confirmed that I was Harvey Herzog and then hung up the phone. I ran to my car and started on a slow journey to Pueblo on the old Highway 85-87 (not a four-lane highway). After three and one half hours I arrived in Pueblo and found out that the nurse was right and I wrong. My dear wife had delivered a wonderful son whom we named Joel. And that I called a wonderful start. The rest of his life you have come to appreciate.

Thank you.

TOBY TIEMAN

Hello,

My name is Toby Tieman. I was a very good friend of Adam and Seth, and also was their babysitter for the past ten years. I was asked by Nancy and the family to share with you today a few things, moments, or stories about the boys. When I was asked, I felt very honored. My first question was how do you put ten years of beautiful relationship into a three to five minute speech? I say relationship, and I don't mean the typical babysitter-to-child one. We had much more than that. It may seem crazy, but two of my best friends were ten and twelve years old. Many times we would tell anyone we met or saw that they were my little brothers. It might even come as a shock to some of you that we weren't really related.

It's very hard to explain what those two boys meant to me. I know some people say I helped raise or mold them into perfect little gentlemen, but really they taught me, and many of you. I think we learned together. One great example of the three of us learning together was the following: I was eleven or twelve and Seth's diaper needed changing. I changed him and not five minutes later, the new diaper fell off. I tried over and over, but it wouldn't stay on. Adam, three or four at the time, told me I was doing it wrong, and he taught me that the straps fastened toward the back of the diaper, not the front. I had it backwards. But of course, even so young, Adam the perfectionist taught me the right way.

I'd like now to share a couple of stories that are kind of funny, so please don't be afraid to laugh. I know they would, and if we all look back, when weren't those two smiling or laughing? When I would put the kids to bed, usually about fifteen minutes late, plus ten extra TV minutes (like any good babysitter), I could tell when they were up to something. Adam, when I asked what was going on, would look at me and say, "We aren't doing anything. I swear!"

That was always my first clue. Then the stern look at Seth, and with his goofy little giggle, big eyes, and beautiful smile, he would start laughing. Then Adam would ask Seth what he was laughing about, and I then would pull the covers off the bed, and lift the pillows, and usually I would find candy, toys, or Joel's newest issue of *Playboy*. And after all of the laughing and begging, and pleading, I would usually give in for a piece of candy or a couple of throws with a ball.

Every Saturday at six for three years, Joel would pick me up, shaving in the car of course, and we would go to the house on Winter Park Lane, and then Espanola, and we would have Domino's there by 6:30, and we would start our TV shows at 7 p.m. We all sang our songs and did our dance in front of the TV to Sidekick and Sledgehammer. During the commercials, the football, basketball and hockey games would commence in the living room. Couches and chairs were moved, tables were dragged out of the way, and Seth and I would always play Adam.

Another funny story. Adam and I would pick on Seth because he knew I would kid him, but not his brother Adam. During this past Christmas break, Adam and Seth and I went to the school to play basketball and floor hockey. Well, basketball was through, and we got out the sticks and pucks and started screwing around. After Adam and Seth took their turns as goalie, I was up. I started floating the pucks off the floor, and fast, at them. Seth warned me that if I did it again, he would take a slapshot at me. Well, sure enough, I did, and he did, and could never have made a better shot if he sat there and aimed. Just over my left shoulder, through the kitchen, and right through the window. We were all three in shock, and Seth got scared to death. I told him, with a wink to Adam, that the only thing we could do, and had to do, was call the police. Just then, the phone rang in the office, and I answered. Someone had the wrong number so I pretended to be talking like the police had called us. I had Adam talk to them to prove it. Adam went along with it and said they wanted to talk to Seth. Well, Seth just broke down in tears, scared he was going to jail for breaking a window, and we had him convinced. I couldn't hold it any longer and neither could Adam. We started laughing hysterically. That made Seth furious.

He was outraged, screaming at us, "You jerks, it's not funny!" Then following it up with, "I'm not really going to jail . . . am I?" Then we all started laughing. We called Nancy and Joel and got it taken care of. Then I took them to McDonald's for some fries.

In closing I would just like to say thank you to Nancy for scheduling all of the unnecessary lunches and dinners and movies so I could take care of the kids. For almost ten years, I gave up one of my weekend nights, college vacations, and any other time I was asked to sit—or I should say, get paid to play and do what I loved, with whom I loved. There's no easier job in the world than playing with the Herzog boys for money. They meant a lot to me, and all of you; that's why we're all here in support.

To Nancy, you can kiss my cheek and say I love you any time you want, even though it used to embarrass the heck out of the boys. I love you and feel for you, Nancy, and all of the rest of the family. Thank you for bringing me in and accepting me as another one of yours. I love you, Adam and Seth.

JACK TIEMAN

I want to make it clear that I am not up here this evening to express my feelings about Joel. I am here in an attempt to express the collective words of those of us Joel touched.

Over the last few days, I have accumulated a list of words that many people have used to describe Joel. I would like to share these words with you.

Competitor: Joel was the ultimate! How often did Scott Blackmun, Ed Biggs, or Bill Palmer hit the shot of their lives in a squash match, only to see Herz run it down and rip it back for a winner?

Role Model: Joel was looked up to by his family and friends as a person to emulate.

Motivated: If you ever purchased a racquet, or played as his partner, you were pumped to be successful. He even won a few tennis matches with Howard Sheldon and Craig Carris.

Rabbit: This nickname was frequently attributed to Joel after he ran down his opponent's difficult shots. I think the rabbit caused back problems for Larry Wellman.

Caring: Joel would always listen and lend his genuine support. He even bought insurance from people like Randy Kilgore and Tom Castle. Now that's caring.

Happy: He was always up and laughing. Remember that little smile after he would hit one of the patented decoy shots? If you don't remember, ask Pam Sattler or Jeanette Paddock.

Late: Was he ever on time? How many times did you hear, "I was there, but you guys must have just left!"

Sponsor: Joel did more than his share of sponsoring tournaments and teams. Many of us benefitted from his generosity. From USTA teams to squash and hockey tournaments, Total Tennis was present with support.

Coach: Joel coached tennis at many levels. His words of wisdom enabled many of us to improve our game. Just look what he did for Tom Peck. The only person Joel wasn't able to coach was his brother Lee. Joel used to confide in me that Lee just didn't get it!

I saved the final three words for last because they are the most descriptive. These words are Friend, Father, and Husband.

Joel was a true friend to most all of us in this room. He was attached to us by feelings of sincere personal regard. He always had time for us.

As a father, the beauty of Seth and Adam speak for themselves! The look in their eyes when Dad would speak was genuine respect and love. With all of his talents, Joel spent his last moments doing what he did best, being Adam and Seth's father.

Finally, as a husband, his devotion and love for Nancy was unsurpassed. This was the tightest unit of a family I have ever seen.

Thank you, Joel, for being with us in life. We will miss you!

LEE HERZOG

This is a celebration of Joel's, Adam's, and Seth's lives. We who have been touched by them in our lives feel very lucky to have had this experience. Mary Polaski shared a story with me from last week. The boys were all sitting around at the hockey rink. Adam was doing his homework and Joel was helping him. Nic Polaski and Dustin Williams were there and a conversation ensued about brothers and how each boy wanted to trade brothers with the other until finally Joel stepped in and said, "Just wait until five or six years from now, guys. Your brother will be your best friend."

Joel was my best friend. We spoke to each other two to three times a week and our discussions usually centered on the boys. Joel was so proud. I listened as he spoke about Adam and Seth's last hockey game . . . how Adam and Seth had both competed and won their respective races in their age divisions . . . how both boys had fared in the Corley Cup tennis tournament . . . how he wished that they could play more tennis. Our phone conversations almost always ended with the new joke of the day which Joel had surely passed on to most all of you.

I had the privilege of getting close to Joel because of our connection as doubles partners on the tennis court. Joel and I loved playing doubles with each other because we played as a team and because of the mutual respect, admiration, and love that we had for one another. Joel took pride in his quickness on the tennis court. I tried and tried but I could never run as fast as him—Tom Peck used to always address Joel as the "older, faster brother." We spoke to each other through tennis—our phone conversations in the past ten years always included insights into the latest tennis event. I think we lived somewhat vicariously through each other's lives . . . Joel as proud of me as I was proud of him and his family. I love Adam and Seth so much . . . I had a unique connection with them because of my connection with their dad. We all felt it.

As the eldest of five siblings, Joel set the standard for my brothers and sisters and me. And it was a tough act to follow. But we all admired him and wanted to get close to him. We all wanted to be like him when we grew up. Surely none of us could ever have been as witty as him . . . although my brother Michael is actively working on his joke collection and presentation abilities . . .

I had a conversation today with Randy Wagner, who shared stories with me of how Joel was the center of a circle of friends. Randy's first comment to me was how Joel was his best friend and that there were probably ninety-nine other people saying the same thing. Joel had the uncanny ability to make people from all walks of life feel comfortable, important, and a part of the community.

The center of Joel's community was Total Tennis. Total Tennis was a place where friends came to visit with Joel while they did business. It was like the local coffee shop where everyone could stop in and express themselves, share the joke of the day, get their racquet strung, talk to Adam or Seth while they tested racquets on the backboard. Total Tennis was the place to come and kibitz.

Joel lived for his family. He spoke of retirement often and how he and Nancy would move to Arizona someday to worship the sun. He saved for his children's college educations and constantly had the future of his family in mind.

I had a wonderful time working and playing with the boys on the tennis court the past few years and especially this summer. Joel asked me if I would come and work on their tennis games at a resort in Arizona in the middle of July. Who else would plan a tennis vacation in Tucson in July? It ended up being a special time for the brothers and their significant others to get together. We bonded with the boys as they frolicked like seals in the pool and then dashed back to the tennis courts in 110 degree temperatures.

We are all very lucky to have been touched by Joel, Adam, Seth, and Nancy in our lives. They provided us with a dreamlike picture of how the "perfect" family should be. Joel was the ideal father and his boys exuded confidence and a joy for living that had been instilled by both parents. We will cherish loving memories of Joel, Adam, and Seth in our hearts, forever. Thank you all for your loving support.

NANCY SALTZMAN

I know that you can't see all of the people who are here from where you are sitting but it is incredible, powerful, and overwhelming. Thank you all for being here.

I saw Joel for the first time in my life in the summer of 1979. He was stringing racquets at Le Bounce on Boulder Street. He didn't see me but it was love at first sight—he was truly gorgeous (or, in Kate Kilgore's terms, "buff"). I asked my best friend, Donna Sheldon, if she knew him. Her father, Howard Sheldon, was the quickest tennis player in Colorado—other than the Herzogs, of course. Howard and his wife Dorothy highly recommended him. Donna and I had the habit of going to Jose Muldoon's "restaurant" every Friday night. Every week we would walk down the street and say to each other, "We'll be the best looking women in the place" and "Just remember, if you're feeling good about yourself, don't look in the mirror!"

However, this Friday night in July was a special night for both of us. Joel and Lee had just played in the Broadmoor Family Tennis tournament. They lost to Hatton and Warren (or was it Snow and Young?) for the first time they could remember. Joel went home to drown his sorrows. Lee was hanging out there, too. A friend came by and dragged them out to Jose Muldoon's—it was a set-up Joel didn't know about. When Joel walked in the door, he was wearing a torn tee shirt with a saying that would be inappropriate for me to share with you today, and thanks to the beers he had before he arrived, there was a slight sway to his walk.

I went up to him and said, "Hi, I'm Nancy." He looked up and said, "Uh, hi. I'm Joel. What do you do?" Lee said, "Great line, Joel, great line." Little did I know that this was the beginning of what turned out to be the most incredible sixteen years of my life.

(Before I forget to mention this, I want to add that Donna met her husband, Gary Nicholson, the same night that I met Joel.) Anyway, the next day I went to the Broadmoor to watch Lee and Joel play tennis. The whole Herzog family was there and we all went to Mr. Steak after the match. I sat next to another incredible Herzog—Harvey, Joel's dad. In true Herzog fashion, he pumped me for my credentials. He asked me how old I was and I told him twenty-seven. He told me that Joel was the same age. It wasn't until about a year later when Joel and I were looking at his college yearbooks that I discovered that Joel was actually two years younger than I was! Thank you, Harvey.

Our courtship was wild. I moved to Virginia to work on my Ph.D. but I missed Joel too much and came back to Colorado. He told me he had claustrophobia and he wanted me to leave. I moved to Denver. He came to Denver to ask me to marry him and I asked him, "Why?" One thing for sure, I made Joel crazy, but lucky for me, he loved me anyway. We got married on August 22nd, 1981 and had the wildest, craziest wedding and reception I have ever attended. We were always glad so many of YOU were there. Amazing to me, I had been accepted into the bigger family of Joel Herzog—his friends.

In case you ARE wondering why we got married, Joel explained to me that this is what two people do who love each other and who want to have children. So, we did! When I went into labor with Adam, Joel was by my side. He helped me every push of the way and when I delivered Adam, he said, "It's a boy! It's a boy! It's a boy!" He could not have been happier. I worked three days a week and Joel took Adam to work with him with bottles, backpack, baby food, toys, and playpen on the days I worked. Two years later, almost to the day, Seth was born and Joel continued the tradition of taking the boys to work with him when I was at work. The day I defended my dissertation in July of 1985, my "boys" waited outside on the hills of the DU campus. Two hours of waiting and then they all hugged me and called me Dr. Saltzman. I never knew how Joel handled all of this, but he was an amazing person—truly unique.

Many of you know that I have had breast cancer twice. I was bald. I was tired. I was sad. My body was mutilated. Joel never saw any of this. He told me every day that I was beautiful, sensual, striking and sexy. Every day of my life I would look at him in the morning and he would say, "You look great. You have too many clothes . . . but you look great." (It wasn't my fault. He was always buying clothes for me.) He loved me like no woman has ever been loved and my heart aches with sorrow for my loss of him.

Adam and Seth. What can I say? They were the nicest, most beautiful children in the world. They looked like their father and they had his sense of humor, intelligence and incredible athletic ability. I loved them. I looked forward to driving Adam to school every day this year. He cared about me and let me in his life—he shared everything with me and let me rub his back every night before he went to sleep. I so wanted to watch him go to college and become an adult.

Seth. Seth was my soul mate. Sam Merrill, my mentor and friend from Horizon Middle School, reminded me of how much Seth and I were alike when he was cleaning my kitchen. When I interviewed to be an assistant principal for Sam I had spaghetti on my blouse. Seth always had food on his clothes. My favorite story about Seth and food was one that Joel told me. Joel bought Seth a meatball sandwich. He said, "Seth, be careful, eat over your plate." Seth took one bite and a meatball rolled down his shirt. Joel made him change his shirt and when Seth took his shirt off he turned to Joel and said, "Hey, it may look bad, but it sure smells good!" I don't know how I'll get off to work any more—Seth always helped me pick out my shoes. All three men in my family told me I was beautiful every single day.

I don't want to stop talking to you because I don't want to start living my life without my family. We spent the most wonderful weekend together in Las Vegas—Seth had the best birthday anyone could ask for. Adam and I shopped and I promised I would buy him Oakley sunglasses. Joel, true to form, jumped my bones three times. I wish I could have been with them on their final journey.

I know that all of you will help me through the rest of my life, and believe me, I am counting on you. I want to especially thank some people who have made me believe that I have to go on.

To Donna Sheldon, for so much I can't tell you—coming over to my house at 11 p.m. Sunday night, and hearing the horrible news first, and for always being there for me. To my parents, whom I called before I knew what was really happening because I knew they would be there for me. To my brother Rob, who you already know is an incredible human being and who has nursed me through EVERY phase of my life. To Ed, my brother's soul mate, and the one who keeps telling me that I'm not responsible for what happened to my family. To my sister, Linda, who is organizing everything to perfection and whose heart is breaking just like everyone else's. To my brother Andy and his wife Mary who brought me letters from Adam and Seth's cousins with the honesty of children, and who we were hoping the boys would get some height from because he's six foot five.

To the whole Herzog family, including their significant others, who Joel and the boys loved deeply. To Mary Polaski, for taking off all of the sheets in my house, washing them, and putting them back on before people started to arrive, and for sharing Ken, Scottie, and Nic with me so that I could hug them relentlessly. To Homer and Linda Osborne who spent a wonderful weekend with my family and me, and who loved tennis and sun as much as Joel. To Caryl Thomason and Harlan Else for their clear-headed thinking and the arrangements they made for today. To the Sheldons for loving Joel and me as their own children. To all of my relatives and friends who have flown in for today. To all of the families and children from my school who have come to help me deal with my grief and sorrow. To my teachers and colleagues, and particularly to Scott Stanec, Sam Merrill, Lee Vaughn, Barbara Martin, Larry Wellman, Jack and Toby Tieman and certainly to all of Joel's squash friends from Guillermo's—you guys will never know how much you meant to him.

I couldn't be standing here today without your love and I won't be standing tomorrow without your continued support. Thank you for loving me and my family.

PHOTO CREDITS

QUESTIONS AND DISCUSSION
TOPICS FOR *RADICAL SURVIVOR*

Invite Nancy to attend your book club in person or on the phone
nancysaltzman@yahoo.com 719-491-9675

1. Nancy survived cancer and the loss of her husband and two sons. Do you think she was able to deal with her losses because of who she was (nature) or how she was raised (nurture)?

2. Did the deep love between Nancy and her husband and sons make losing them easier or more difficult for her? In what ways?

3. The school where Nancy worked was significantly impacted by the plane crash. Do you agree with how the teachers and staff at her school dealt with the tragedy, and how the teachers helped the students deal with their grief? What about the approach taken by her son Adam's school?

4. Do you agree with Nancy returning to work only a week after the crash? How about her decision to allow her students and staff windows into her grief, to share aspects of her process while maintaining her job as school principal?

5. In the chapter titled "Perspective," Nancy says that people frequently asked "How did you do it? I could not have endured the loss of my family." She says "What choice did I have?" Do you think she had a choice? How do you think you would react if you had a significant loss similar to Nancy's?

6. Nancy mentions several incidents in which people said or did things that seemed insensitive after her loss. Do you think these people were aware of how their actions were perceived? What would lead people to behave in such ways?

7. Nancy describes herself as an optimist. Do you agree? Do you think she had the same personality after the crash as before?

8. Nancy is not afraid to use humor to tell her story. Is it appropriate, given the tragic nature of the circumstances? Do you think humor has a place in the face of extreme loss and sadness?

9. Nancy's parents were still living when she started writing this book. Do you think she make a conscious decision to wait to finish the book until after her parents passed away? Do you think the book would have been written differently if her parents were alive?

10. Some people were angry with the pilot for flying into Colorado when he had been told about the bad weather. Nancy says she was not mad at the pilot. How would you feel if you lost loved ones under the same circumstances?

11. The title of Nancy's book is Radical Survivor. She also writes about others she considers radical survivors. Do you think this is an apt description? What specific qualities make Nancy, and the people she describes, radical survivors? Do you know other radical survivors?

12. Has this book changed the way you think about and deal with the tragedies of friends or family? How? How has it impacted the way you deal with your own losses?

13. Nancy started the book with the plane crash. Do you think this was a good way to introduce you to her story? Did the book's style and format enhance or detract from the story? How about the letters and entries from friends, family, Joel, Adam, and Seth?

14. What is the most important thing you learned by reading this memoir? What is/are the key message(s)? Can you apply things you learned in this book to your daily life?